Kipling in India

Kipling in India

LOUIS L. CORNELL

MACMILLAN
London · Melbourne · Toronto

ST MARTIN'S PRESS
New York
1966

MACMILLAN AND COMPANY LIMITED
Little Essex Street London WC 2
also Bombay Calcutta Madras Melbourne

THE MACMILLAN COMPANY OF CANADA LIMITED
70 Bond Street Toronto 2

ST MARTIN'S PRESS INC
175 Fifth Avenue New York NY 10010

Library of Congress catalog card no. 67-10223

PRINTED IN GREAT BRITAIN

FOR

S. D. L.

AND

S. S. M. C.

Contents

Preface

THIS book is about Rudyard Kipling's literary apprenticeship. Because Kipling spent his apprentice years in India, and because he emerged on the literary scene as an Anglo-Indian writer, a principal theme of my study is the relationship between the young author and the Anglo-Indian world in which he grew up.[1] Thus, I have explored some of the ways in which the values, attitudes, and literary conventions of British India in the 1880's helped to shape Kipling's writings, and, at the same time, I have attempted to trace the outline of the vision of India manifested in Kipling's stories, essays, and verse.

But no writer is wholly the product of his environment. Ambitious for literary fame, the young Kipling, like most novice writers, devoted much of his energy to technical experiments with words, styles, and genres. The conditions of his work as a journalist were almost ideal for such experimentation: voracious editors were eager to publish nearly everything he wrote, and he himself was in close day-to-day contact with his readers. These conditions led him to produce verse and prose in extraordinary quantities. About four hundred separate items, many of them never collected, date from the period 1882–8: ranged in chronological sequence, these pieces enable us to trace with unusual clarity and fullness Kipling's development from a raw sub-editor to an acknowledged master of the short story. Accordingly, my emphasis throughout this book has been literary rather than biographical or political; I have treated Kipling less as a

[1] 'Anglo-Indian' is used here and throughout this study in its old sense to mean an Englishman living in India.

personality, less as a social or political commentator, than as an artist.

Ushered in by the appearance of Charles Carrington's splendid biography, the last decade has seen the publication of enough notable books and essays on Kipling to suggest that a full-scale revival is under way. This is as it should be; for three generations Kipling has had too little of the right kind of attention paid him; and yet, for all its recent activity, the present state of Kipling studies leaves much to be desired. Among various deficiencies, I should like to single out one in particular: the fact that students of Kipling live in divided and distinguished worlds, in separate compartments labelled 'biography', 'bibliography', and 'criticism'. We need go no farther than to point out that the three most important recent books on Kipling — the Carrington biography, Dr. Tompkins's fine critical study, and the *Bibliographical Catalogue* of Stewart and Yeats — have little or nothing to do with one another; they emerge as it were from different realms. And even the individual compartments are subdivided into virtually airtight chambers. In Andrew Rutherford's valuable collection of critical essays, for example, nearly all the contributors, whether established critics or newcomers, write about Kipling as if no one had ever read him or written about him before, as if each critic were forced to discover and reconstitute Kipling single-handed.

To a modest degree, the present study tries to break down some of these artificial barriers. I have maintained the chronological form of the traditional literary biography in order to emphasize Kipling's artistic development, but I have made no attempt to rewrite Professor Carrington's book. Thus, the reader who is chiefly interested in Kipling's personality and his growth towards the public stature of his middle years will find that I have disagreed with Carrington in relatively few particulars: instead, I have re-examined in detail only such biographical data as seem to bear directly on Kipling's literary career. At the same time, in so far as this is a critical study of Kipling's early writings, I have tried to take some account of the many critical formulations I have encountered. Almost every one of Kipling's critics has had something to say about the early poems and stories; in some cases I have registered a divergence of opinion, but for the rest I have assumed that the reader will view my theses against the background provided by such critics as J. M. S. Tompkins, C. S. Lewis, W. H. Auden, Edmund Wilson, Lionel Trilling, T. S. Eliot, George Orwell, and Randall Jarrell. I have attempted, in other words, to steer a middle course between the neglect of other views that so often marks Kipling's critics, and the plethora of quarrelsome footnotes that the opposite procedure would have entailed. In all matters pertaining to bibliography, however, I have tried to keep my lines of research as clear and explicit as possible. Most of the Kipling bibliographies are aimed at the collector rather than the literary scholar, so that it is not always easy to find out what the young Kipling wrote, when he wrote it, and where the surviving manuscripts — if any — are to be found. This is one of the plagues of Kipling scholarship that I have tried in some degree to remedy.

Adopting this combination of biographical, critical, and bibliographical techniques, I have written about Kipling as if no revival of his reputation were in fact necessary. Assuming Kipling's stature as a writer, I have attempted to understand rather than re-evaluate him. It may be asked whether there is justification for examining in such detail the work of a writer whose ultimate value is still the subject of dispute. I can only reply that the controversy over Kipling's value — a controversy of some seventy-five years' standing — has been singularly barren of insight into the principles of his artistry. How could it be otherwise, when his supporters have until quite recently praised him for his superficial qualities, and his detractors have scarcely been willing to admit that he possessed any artistry at all? Instead of reviving old battles — aesthetic, moral, and above all political — I have found out all I could about the circumstances of Kipling's literary apprenticeship, for the best defence of an author lies not in polemics but in the informed and sympathetic reading of individual works. And that is what *Kipling in India* sets out to provide.

ACKNOWLEDGEMENTS

MY debt to Kipling bibliographers and collectors is manifested throughout this book. In particular, I wish to call attention to the work of two dedicated amateur scholars, James McGregor Stewart and Admiral Lloyd H. Chandler, who laid the bibliographical foundations upon which my study is based. My many references to Professor Charles Carrington's *Rudyard Kipling* point to the extent of my indebtedness; without the help of his fine biography I would not have known where to begin. It is likewise a pleasure to acknowledge the help I have received from former teachers and present colleagues at Columbia University. I owe special thanks to Jerome H. Buckley, whose lectures first attracted me to the study of Victorian literature, and to Carl Woodring, whose wise counsel improved this book at every stage of its development. The manuscript was read in one form or another by Professors Susanne Howe Nobbe, Frederick Dupee, John Rosenberg, Steven Marcus, Ainslie T. Embree, and Royal Weiler: for their criticisms and suggestions I am most grateful.

This book could not have been written without the aid and hospitality of many librarians. The bulk of my research was carried out amidst the superb facilities of the Yale University Library. I owe the staff particular thanks for their generous decision to allow me privileges to which I had no title. I want also to thank the authorities at the Berg Collection of the New York Public

Library, the Rare Book Room of the Library of Congress, the Houghton Library at Harvard, the Pierpont Morgan Library, and the Libraries of Dartmouth College and Columbia University for permission to consult material in their possession and for their assistance in the use of their facilities.

Finally I am grateful to Mrs. Bambridge, Methuen & Co. Ltd., and Doubleday & Co. Inc., for granting me permission to use various quotations from Rudyard Kipling's works, and to the Editor of *English Literature in Transition*, for allowing me to reprint those portions of my book which first appeared there.

L. L. C.

New York City
June 1965

1. Gigadibs, the Literary Man

I

RUDYARD KIPLING was born in Bombay on 30 December 1865, and spent the first six years of his life in British India. From the beginning, the sights and smells of the Orient thrust themselves upon him; his sensuous education began with an impression, vividly remembered, of 'daybreak, light and colour and golden and purple fruits at the level of my shoulder'. There was no call for the little boy to understand what he saw: the impressions succeeded one another without a hint of paradox or contradiction: in the Hindu temples were 'dimly-seen, friendly Gods', and the vultures from the Parsee Towers of Silence might drop the hand of a dead child into the Kiplings' garden; 'the menacing darkness of tropical eventides' haunted the man for the rest of his life, and in the same breath he asserts: 'I have loved the voices of night-winds through palm or banana leaves, and the song of the tree-frogs.'[1] Thus, India presented herself to the boy as a succession of images, some menacing, some reassuring, and before he had time to put these impressions into a coherent order, he left India for England: the paradoxes remained unresolved; the contradictions, unanalysed. The menace of tropical evenings and the charm of the night-winds remained, for an older Kipling,

[1] Rudyard Kipling, *Something of Myself for My Friends Known and Unknown*, 'Library Edition' (London, 1951), pp. 1–2. Kipling died in 1936 before completing and revising his autobiography; but, although reticent and fragmentary, the book is an important source of information on Kipling's life and opinions. I shall refer to it hereafter as *Something of Myself*.

simultaneous expressions of an India too rich, too complex to be resolved into a set of consistent propositions.

In the India Kipling knew, one of the most important of these paradoxes concerned the relationship between a fundamentally idealistic race of conquerors and a civilized but alien and incomprehensible race of subjects. Kipling was exposed as a child to this enigmatic relationship, but in such a way as to predispose him towards the particular values and attitudes of the Anglo-Indian community. Like nearly all Anglo-Indian children, he grew up amid a retinue of servants, for household labour was cheap and jobs were in great demand. It was a pleasant way of life for a child, and Kipling returned to it nostalgically in several of his stories. His Majesty the King prays for 'his many friends, from the *mehter's* [sweeper's] son to the Commissioner's daughter'.[1] Tods, one of the earliest of Kipling's child heroes, 'was the idol of some eighty *jhampanis* [porters], and half as many *saises* [grooms]. He saluted them all as "O Brother". It never entered his head that any living human being could disobey his orders. . . . The working of that household turned on Tods, who was adored by every one from the *dhobi* [washerman] to the dog-boy.'[2] Children were so constantly in the servants' company that they spoke and thought in Hindi as a matter of course; Kipling remembered being 'sent into the dining-room after we had been dressed, with the caution "Speak English now to Papa and Mamma"'.[3] Or else parents found that their children were beginning to view life in Indian terms: Strickland of the Police, himself an adept at mimicking Indian ways, is embarrassed to find that his little son Adam has

[1] 'His Majesty the King', 5 May 1888. (Throughout this study all of Kipling's writings published between October 1882 and March 1889 will be identified in the notes by date of first publication. The reader can then locate them in Appendix I, 'A Chronological List of Kipling's Writings', where further bibliographical information is supplied.)

[2] 'Tods' Amendment', 16 April 1887.

[3] *Something of Myself*, p. 3.

taken over wholesale the menservants' code of *izzat*, or honour.[1] Thus, the Anglo-Indian child spent his early years as part of a natural and accepted pattern of Indian life. Unconcerned with the implications of their position, the children in Kipling's stories treat their Indian servants as both friends and inferiors, and the Indians respond with a combination of deference and affection. Though many of his Indian tales present the bewildering complexity of the Indo-English relationship, Kipling never fully outgrew the innocence of his first six years: in a sense, the loyal and affectionate servant remained for him the prototype of the admirable Indian native.

To most Anglo-Indian parents, however, this free and natural intercourse between children and servants was not so much an idyll as a path strewn with dangers; responsible fathers and mothers began from their children's birth to look forward unhappily to the day when the family would have to separate and the children return to England for their education. In some degree the dangers these parents responded to were objective. India was hot and unsanitary; cholera, typhoid, and malaria were ever-present threats; and even children who escaped these scourges seemed to droop in the Indian heat. The pale, sickly Anglo-Indian child occurs regularly in the writings of the period: in *Echoes*, for example, Kipling turns the stereotype into a macabre joke.

> Hush-a-by, Baby,
>   In the verandah!
> When the sun drops
>   Baby may wander.
>
> When the hot weather comes
>   Baby will die —
> With a fine *pucca* tomb
>   In the ce-me-te-ry.[2]

[1] 'The Son of His Father', first published in December 1893 and January 1894; collected in *Land and Sea Tales* (1923).

[2] 'Nursery Rhymes for Little Anglo-Indians', in *Echoes* (November 1884). Another good example of the stereotype appears in 'The Mysti-

Indian servants, far from helping to protect children from these objective dangers, were felt to constitute an even more serious threat than climate and disease. Loyal and affectionate though they might be, they were aliens and therefore not to be trusted: it was, for example, a sinister commonplace among mem-sahibs that some ayahs would pacify babies with doses of opium. Similarly, the Anglo-Indians almost universally agreed that native servants spoiled their charges, who repaid their deference by becoming imperious and ill-mannered; continued intercourse with obsequious Indians prevented children from learning English standards of rectitude, self-denial, and honesty.[1]

But all these concerns were symptoms of a thinly disguised fear and hatred of India herself, a dread lest children raised in the country become acclimatized to it and lose their national and racial identity. The following passage from 'The Son of His Father' reveals how this dread could overcome even the unwillingness of parents to send their children so far away, for so long a time:

'It's awful', said Mrs. Strickland, half crying, 'to think of his growing up like a little heathen.' Mrs. Strickland had been born

fication of Santa Claus' (25 December 1886): Santa meets 'a pale little boy about seven years old, with a fretful expression in his face and big dark rings round his eyes.'

[1] This view underlies 'The Mystification', where the little boy mistakes Santa for a pedlar and orders him out of the house. It is supported by an anonymous American article, 'Child-Life by the Ganges', *Atlantic Monthly*, i (1857–8), 629–30. The journalist describes 'the frailness, and premature pensiveness of the little Civil Service', then explains how these children become spoiled and bad-mannered through being allowed to bully the servants. Evidently, Kipling felt this was the reason he had been sent home, for his friend Mrs. Hill wrote to her family in America of 'the bad influence the close contact with the native servant has on the child'. Her remarks take the form of general statements, but they are made in connection with her description of Kipling writing 'Baa Baa, Black Sheep', the story of his own childhood exile from his family. See Edmonia Hill, 'The Young Kipling: Personal Recollections', *Atlantic Monthly*, clvii (1936), 413.

and brought up in England, and did not quite understand Eastern things.

'Let him alone,' said Strickland. 'He'll grow out of it all, or it will only come back to him in dreams.'

'Are you sure?' said his wife.

'Quite. I was sent home when I was seven, and they flicked it out of me with a wet towel at Harrow. Public schools don't encourage anything that isn't quite English.'

Mrs. Strickland shuddered, for she had been trying not to think of the separation that follows motherhood in India. . . .

For the English, we must recall, never considered themselves colonists. To adapt to Indian conditions was to conform to an inferior standard. It was better to be alien and uncomfortable than to incur any suspicion of becoming like the natives of the country. Children were sent home, then, in order to ensure that they learn to be English; and so in April 1871 Rudyard Kipling and his sister Trix left Bombay with their parents for the beginning of the long Anglo-Indian separation.

II

When the time came for Rudyard and Trix to return to England, their parents were faced with a choice between lodging them with strangers or with members of the family. Their mother chose the former course, and the children were left in the care of a couple who were altogether unknown to the Kiplings, mere names discovered in a newspaper advertisement.[1] This solution was not unusual among Anglo-Indian families, but it was known to entail risks: stories of the mistreatment of Anglo-Indian children were commonplace in British India. 'I have heard of some', wrote a missionary some fifteen years later, 'for whose education and comfort large fees have been paid, being half starved, badly taught, and made little better than domestic drudges by those who

[1] Charles Carrington, *Rudyard Kipling: His Life and Work* (London, 1955), p. 14.

ought honestly to have treated them well: and all this time the children were compelled to write to their parents elaborately false statements speaking of the kindness they received, and of the comforts they enjoyed.'[1] But in spite of such warnings, the Kiplings were prepared to take the risk; as a friend of those days remembered: 'Unlike most mothers in India Alice [Kipling] said this was a good arrangement: she had never thought of leaving her children with her own family, it led to complications.'[2] What were the complications that determined John and Alice Kipling to gamble on the suitability of an unknown Mr. and Mrs. Holloway, proprietors of Lorne Lodge, Southsea?

The eldest of five beautiful and talented sisters, Alice Macdonald Kipling had left England in 1865; she and her new husband, John Lockwood Kipling, sailed for India about a month after their wedding, amid the regrets and fears of their relations.[3] The Macdonalds had formed a loving and cohesive group, but for the children life was not always easy: their parents' high standard of obedience and achievement was in some instances more a burden than an inspiration. Harry, Alice's elder brother, struggled along a difficult road of study and scholarships as far as Oxford, where, driven too hard, he underwent a breakdown or collapse of the will from which he never recovered.[4] Alice, the second surviving child, chafed under the restraints of life in a mid-Victorian clerical family. Scolded by her parents for staying out too late, warned by her father against being a flirt, she once showed her resentment by throwing a carefully preserved lock of John Wesley's hair on the fire with the

[1] W. J. Wilkins, *Daily Life and Work in India* (London, 1887), pp. 57–58.

[2] Arthur Windham Baldwin, *The Macdonald Sisters* (London, 1960), p. 115.

[3] 'G. B.-J.' [Georgiana Burne-Jones], *Memorials of Edward Burne-Jones*, 2 vols. (New York, 1904), i. 290.

[4] Baldwin, *The Macdonald Sisters*, p. 27.

words: 'See! A hair of the dog that bit us!' She was a brilliant and perceptive girl, quicker to blame than praise, endowed with a scalding wit, eager to establish and maintain her independence.[1] Before she married John Lockwood Kipling at the relatively late age of twenty-seven she had made and broken at least three engagements.[2] Independent at last, she must have been anxious to remain free of family entanglements.

On one occasion since her marriage she had been given a taste of the complications that result when growing families are reunited. In 1868 Alice had returned to England with her young son in order to give birth there to her second child. She made the voyage home to find the close family circle of the Macdonalds broken up: two of her four sisters, Agnes and Louisa, had married in her absence, and her father, worn out by a life of exacting duty in the Methodist ministry, was an invalid close to death. While Alice spent her confinement with another sister, Georgiana Burne-Jones, Rudyard was left with Louisa and Alfred Baldwin at Bewdley, in Worcestershire, where his young aunt and uncle were raising their own family and caring for the aged Macdonalds.

The two-year-old Rudyard proved a difficult visitor. Although the Baldwins and the Macdonalds occupied separate houses, there was little room to spare; Rudyard had to share a bed with his aunt Edith and pointedly remarked that his grandparents had 'gone and tooken the best rooms for themselves'. Louisa's son Stanley — one day to become Prime Minister — was only a year old, and his mother had begun to suffer from a weak constitution that was to plague her for the rest of her life. Any two-year-old would have been hard to cope with, but the Anglo-Indian child, used to constant attention from native servants, was particularly demanding, and the

[1] Many of her friends and relatives vividly remembered Alice's quick wit; see, for example, the autobiography of her brother, Frederic William Macdonald, *As a Tale That Is Told* (London, 1919), p. 334.

[2] Baldwin, *The Macdonald Sisters*, pp. 32–35.

arrival of Alice with a newborn daughter strained her sister's hospitality to the limit. 'Her children', Louisa wrote, 'turned the house into such a bear-garden, & Ruddy's screaming tempers made Papa so ill, we were thankful to see them on their way. The wretched disturbances one ill-ordered child can make is a lesson for all time to me.'[1] Nor was Louisa the only member of the family to have her patience strained by the visitors. After Alice's second trip to England, old Mrs. Macdonald wrote: 'I feel so thankful that . . . we have never had one misunderstanding nor one sharp word. We met in peace and we parted in peace, for which I say, thanks be to God.'[2] Evidently, there had been sharp words and misunderstandings during that first visit to the overcrowded Baldwin household, and neither Alice nor her mother had forgotten them. Injured pride, perhaps, on Alice's part was sufficient to overcome even the good-natured charity of Alfred Baldwin, who offered, before the children were left at Southsea, to take sole charge of his niece and share the custody of his nephew; the offer was declined, and the children were left in December at Lorne Lodge, the place they would refer to, for the rest of their lives, as the 'House of Desolation'.[3]

III

In 1888, while he was staying with his friends the Hills in Allahabad, Kipling was asked to write a long story for the Christmas Supplement of the *Week's News*. 'R. K. brooded over this awhile', Mrs. Hill wrote; 'the result was "Baa Baa, Black Sheep", which is a true story of his early life. . . . It was pitiful to see Kipling living over the experience, pouring out his soul in the story, as the drab life was worse than he could possibly describe it. . . . When he was writing this he was a sorry guest, as he was in a towering rage at the recollection of those days.'[4]

[1] Baldwin, *The Macdonald Sisters*, p. 114. [2] Ibid., p. 115.
[3] Ibid., p. 193. [4] Hill, 'The Young Kipling', pp. 413–14.

Written in anger, 'Baa Baa, Black Sheep' is not so much a 'true story' of Kipling's early life as an intense and bitter work of art; and yet it remains a document of the greatest importance for understanding some of the early experiences that helped to shape Kipling as an Anglo-Indian author. To be sure, Kipling exaggerated or invented a number of 'Baa Baa, Black Sheep's' details. A loyal and affectionate son, he had no wish to turn the story into an indictment of his parents, so that their fictional counterparts become little more than helpless bystanders, tearful at the beginning of the action and indignant at the end. In fact, although Alice Kipling was distressed by her son's unhappiness, she did return her daughter to the Holloways', where Trix boarded for several years; she evidently did not react against the House of Desolation with as much indignation as her son would have liked.[1] The credibility of the story is further qualified by another version of the same events, the first chapter of *Something of Myself*. Here, Kipling emphasizes childhood pleasures — well-remembered books, holidays in London with his Burne-Jones cousins — and thus drains away much of the bitterness that permeated his earlier reminiscences. Nevertheless, for all these qualifications, 'Baa Baa, Black Sheep' cannot be set aside. Read in conjunction with Kipling's autobiography, it reveals above all what most impressed Kipling himself about the effects of this experience upon his developing mind.

Life at the Holloways' was unlike anything the young boy had yet known. Especially perplexing was his sudden introduction to the darker side of Victorian piety, for his Anglo-Indian background had done nothing to prepare him for Lorne Lodge. The Anglo-Indians were noted for wearing their Christianity lightly, and Lockwood and Alice Kipling, both of whom had abandoned the Methodism of their forebears, allowed their children to pick up from the servants a confused mixture of Hindu and Roman

[1] Carrington, *Rudyard Kipling*, pp. 16–17.

Catholic notions. From Mrs. Holloway's standpoint, the child's ignorance and his propensity for lying marked him as one of the unredeemed. The cure for both sins lay in threats — 'a private sitting at which all the blinding horrors of Hell were revealed to Punch with such store of imagery as Aunty Rosa's narrow mind possessed' — and the relentless questioning that formed so large a part of the spiritual discipline of the evangelicals. The latter task seems to have been the particular delight of Mrs. Holloway's son. 'For an hour and a half [Punch] had to answer that young gentleman's questions as to his motives for telling a lie, and a grievous lie, the precise quantity of punishment inflicted by Aunty Rosa, and had also to profess his deep gratitude for such religious instruction as Harry thought fit to impart.' It was altogether bewildering for the child: 'He learned to know the Lord as the only thing in the world more awful than Aunty Rosa — as a Creature that stood in the background and counted the strokes of the cane.'

But for all their terrors, Mrs. Holloway's pious inquisitions perhaps disturbed the child less than his inexplicable loss of status, a status that all members of his Indian household had recognized: 'As the unquestioned despot of the house at Bombay, Punch could not quite understand how he came to be of no account in this his new life.' Soon even Punch's name is taken from him: the servants are encouraged to call him by his hateful new nickname, 'Black Sheep'. To a caste-conscious Anglo-Indian child this reversal must have been acutely painful; Mrs. Alice Fleming (Trix Kipling) remembered years later that Rudyard had retaliated by branding Mrs. Holloway a '*Kuch-nay*, a Nothing-at-all', 'of such low caste as not to matter'.[1]

This loss of status, however, was merely symptomatic of something larger, for what Punch suffers in 'Baa Baa, Black Sheep', what Kipling suffered in real life, was an

[1] Alice M. Fleming, 'Some Childhood Memories of Rudyard Kipling', *Chambers's Journal*, ser. 8, viii (March 1939), 169.

immense and agonizing dislocation. The Anglo-Indian child was torn not only from his home and family, but from a whole world of 'daybreak, light and colour and golden and purple fruits', of 'far-going Arab dhows on the pearly waters, and gaily dressed Parsees wading out to worship the sunset', a life of gaiety, freedom, and order that had suddenly given way to narrowness, discipline, and hardship: to the life, in short, of many a lower-middle-class English child of the period. At an age when children need constant reassurance that their world is stable and permanent, Rudyard underwent a radical displacement; the bottom of things dropped out, leaving him with a sense of vertigo from which he never fully recovered. In his later life, this seems to have afflicted him as a kind of perpetual homelessness; thrice he committed himself to a new home, in British India, Vermont, and Sussex, and each time his commitment was sudden and in a sense excessive: wholehearted, but with the wholeheartedness of the unbalanced climber snatching at a secure handhold. And his heroes, like their creator, engage in a quest not so much for the inner truth about themselves as for a place in the social or professional world to which their talents ideally suit them. Rarely psychological or metaphysical, their vertigo can be assuaged by the discovery of a firm place to stand.

At least two consequences of the young boy's exile are especially significant. To begin with, 'Baa Baa, Black Sheep' owes part of its vividness to Kipling's having found what he thought was a solid foothold in British India. The child's perspective, which both obscures and exposes the adults' motives, is also the perspective of a wholly naïve Anglo-Indian confronted by the paradoxical queerness of English life. Aunty Rosa must be a white ayah, Punch speculates, but he cannot understand why she doesn't call him Sahib. His Southsea schoolmates are equally baffling: 'Some of them were unclean, some of them talked in dialect, many dropped their h's, and there were two Jews and a negro, or some one quite as dark, in the assembly. "That's a *hubshi*," said Black Sheep to himself. "Even Meeta used to laugh at a *hubshi*. I don't think this is a proper place."' Punch's thoughts are undeniably ugly, but their frank ugliness makes Kipling's point more effectively than would a more palatable tolerance. This is the voice of a young Anglo-Indian, echoing the race and class prejudices not only of his own caste but of his Indian friends and servants as well. Writing for the Anglo-Indian, not the English, reader, Kipling knew that Punch's attitudes and values would place him in that reader's mind and thus turn the story into a confrontation between British India and lower-middle-class England, with the reader's sympathy strongly engaged on the side of the former. From the security of this Anglo-Indian vantage point Kipling could not only re-enact his early displacement but could assert that, in consequence of it, he too was an Anglo-Indian, akin to all the other children who had been taken from their world of daybreak, light, and colour to be left with strangers in an alien country.

The other important consequence of Kipling's Southsea exile was that it laid the foundation for his later choice of the writer's profession. He himself felt this to be the case; comparing himself to Browning's Fra Lippo Lippi, he credited Mrs. Holloway's severity with having sharpened his powers of observation, with having trained him in 'the noting of discrepancies between speech and action; a certain reserve of demeanour; and automatic suspicion of sudden favours'.[1] These suggestions were made in a spirit of irony, but they form part of a larger pattern, for, driven back on his own resources, the child took refuge in the life of the imagination. Once he learned to read, the books he discovered made a profound and lasting impression on him; he devotes as much space to them in his autobiography as to the miseries of the House of Desolation. But one instance of the use he made of his reading is especially significant. Like many imaginative children,

[1] *Something of Myself*, pp. 115–16.

he found *Robinson Crusoe* fascinating and 'set up in business alone as a trader with savages'.

> My apparatus was a coconut shell strung on a red cord, a tin trunk, and a piece of packing-case which kept off any other world. Thus fenced about, everything inside the fence was quite real, but mixed with the smell of damp cupboards. If the bit of board fell, I had to begin the magic all over again. I have learned since from children who play much alone that this rule of 'beginning again in a pretend game' is not uncommon. The magic, you see, lies in the ring or fence that you take refuge in.[1]

Exiled from his own world, the boy made another world with a fence around it, and both the fence and the magic suggest an aspect of Kipling's writings that led W. H. Auden to call him 'the poet of the encirclement' and C. S. Lewis to find the key to his thought in the idea of the 'inner ring'.[2] But if we attach another significance to this passage, we can see that the fence protected the world of literature and the imagination from the inquisitions of Aunty Rosa — that the fence enclosed a world, separate from hers, to which Kipling soon discovered that he had a proprietary and hereditary claim. Instead of being forced to come to terms with Aunty Rosa, he could flee from her into a realm of values where she and her odious pieties counted for nothing. Even before he began to think of himself as an Anglo-Indian, Kipling had decided to be a writer.

By seeking in literature a refuge from piety, Kipling recapitulated the behaviour of his parents' generation. Not only had Lockwood Kipling, the son of a Methodist minister, become a professional artist, but nearly every member of the large Macdonald family wrote and published at one time or another. From the literary games of their childhood the girls went on to write poetry, fiction,

[1] Ibid., pp. 9–10.

[2] Compare W. H. Auden's 'The Poet of the Encirclement', *New Republic*, cix (1943), 579–81; and C. S. Lewis's 'Kipling's World', in his collection *They Asked for a Paper* (London, 1962), pp. 72–92.

and family history; even Frederic, who became a leading Methodist churchman, pursued a simultaneous career in belles-lettres. By marrying Edward Burne-Jones, Georgiana Macdonald gave her family's connection with the arts a substantial and permanent basis; the Macdonald sisters were at home in the circle whose centre was William Morris and whose periphery contained nearly every literary notable of the late Victorian period. Georgiana in particular, and her sisters to a lesser degree, thought of the arts not so much as means of earning a living but as the very embodiment of the ideal. They were too sensible and intelligent, perhaps, to form prototypes for the 'intense' young women of the nineties, but their enthusiasm for the mission of Burne-Jones and his friends was fired by the same zeal that had, in another guise, inspired their Methodist forebears; and it was not unlike the quasi-religious passion for the arts that was to burn, in a later generation, with a hard, gem-like flame.

During his confinement at Southsea, the boy Rudyard was partially aware of his family's involvement with the world of art and letters: he spent a number of holidays — the happiest times of his early childhood — with his Burne-Jones relations, and there he found himself in the midst of painters painting and writers writing. One day the aloof Morris, in default of an adult audience, swung to and fro on a rocking-horse as he told the eight-year-old boy and little Margaret Burne-Jones the story of Burnt Njal — a happy prefiguration of a time many years later when a grown-up Rudyard would entertain Margaret's daughter Angela, herself to become a well-known writer, with his own *Just So Stories*.[1] But these interludes always ended with a return to Lorne Lodge, where, if the boy made up stories or tried his hand at writing, Mrs. Holloway would accuse him of lying or showing off. Aunty Rosa's obsession with lying in 'Baa Baa, Black Sheep' must stem from a Puritanical suspicion of the

[1] *Something of Myself*, pp. 114–15; and Angela Thirkell, *Three Houses* (London, 1931), pp. 87–88.

imagination on Mrs. Holloway's part, and this suspicion, combined with all the other unsympathetic elements in Mrs. Holloway's character, would have helped make the antithesis between her way of life and the artistic way extraordinarily sharp and clear. Everything to which Rudyard was attached — reading, holidays, the free exercise of imagination — had to do with the arts; everything he detested seemed leagued against them. He may have begun to write before he left Southsea: the evidence is uncertain.[1] But when Alice Kipling came for her children in March 1877, and the doors of Lorne Lodge finally swung open, they opened upon such a world as the twelve-year-old boy could scarcely have imagined:

By the end of that long holiday I understood that my Mother had written verses, that my Father 'wrote things' also; that books and pictures were among the most important affairs in the world; that I could read as much as I chose and ask the meaning of things from anyone I met. I had found out, too, that one could take pen and set down what one thought, and that nobody accused one of 'showing off' by so doing. I read a good deal; *Sidonia the Sorceress*; Emerson's poems; and Bret Harte's stories; and I learned all sorts of verses for the pleasure of repeating them to myself in bed.[2]

The loving care now lavished upon him by his mother was one antidote to his five years' deprivation. Later he would attach himself to the Anglo-Indian community, his lost home. But in the meantime reading and writing were the most important things in his life. He had a family claim upon the world of letters, and he was prepared to work towards the day when he would be able to take his place among the poets.

[1] James McGregor Stewart, *Rudyard Kipling: A Bibliographical Catalogue*, ed. A. W. Yeats (Toronto, 1959), p. 4. The Stewart Collection at Dalhousie University possesses the MS. of a short poem on the wreck of the *Carolina*. The paper carries an 1876 watermark, but this is the only evidence that points to the poem's having been written before Kipling went away to school.

[2] *Something of Myself*, p. 20.

IV

Rudyard and Trix spent the better part of a year with their mother in Epping Forest and London. When the time came for Alice Kipling to return to Bombay, the family circle was broken again. Trix went back to Lorne Lodge, and in January 1878, Rudyard entered the United Services College at Westward Ho! on the Devon coast.

The United Services College was only four years old when Kipling arrived as a new boy.[1] It had been founded by a group of officers to provide the sons of servicemen with a public school education at the same time as it prepared them for the Army Examinations; in general tone and outlook, the school appears to have fallen between the cynical pragmatism of the London 'crammers' and the complacency of the older public schools. It has been argued that Kipling's later claims for the United Services College are sentimentally exaggerated, but in fact the school seems to have been run with a singular degree of good sense. The students knew what they were there for; the teachers at their best must have been very good indeed; the geographical situation was open, wild, and healthy; and, unhampered either by traditions or by conservative old boys, the Headmaster could both act freely himself and allow a good deal of freedom to the masters and boys under his charge. In the seventies and eighties, the English public schools enjoyed unparalleled prestige: in effect, they were exempt from outside criticism.[2] But by modern educational standards — and psychological and moral standards as well — the schools were doing a

[1] Conditions at the College in Kipling's time have been extensively discussed by professional and amateur scholars. See, for example, the third chapter of Prof. Carrington's *Rudyard Kipling* and William M. Carpenter's informative *Kipling's College* (Evanston, 1929).

[2] According to Edward C. Mack, the seventies and eighties 'witnessed the greatest up-surge of passionate adoration to which the schools had ever been subjected'. See his *Public Schools and British Opinion since 1860* (New York, 1941), p. 134.

less and less satisfactory job as the century waned. Athleticism, linked to a pseudo-Arnoldian ideal of 'character', was becoming dominant throughout the older establishments, bringing with it a widespread suspicion of individuality and intellect.[1] In contrast to the general trend, the U.S.C. had no organized fagging, played games with rough and ready enthusiasm, discouraged excessive piety, and easily made room for such resolute individualists as Rudyard Kipling and his two particular friends, L. C. Dunsterville ('Stalky') and G. C. Beresford ('M'Turk'). Kipling later called the U.S.C. a 'school before its time': to the extent that the College was out of step with contemporary public schools, he was undoubtedly correct.[2]

The character of the school and Kipling's happy experiences there were due in large measure to the Head, Mr. Cormell Price. Price's advantage over most other headmasters of the period lay in the breadth and type of his interests. He had been a member of the Morris–Burne-Jones circle, had lived abroad, was a layman, and maintained his connections with artists and intellectuals in London. The school prospered from his ability to see pupils through the Army Examinations, but it was the other aspect of his life, his friendship with the Burne-Joneses, that recommended his school to the Kiplings. This time Rudyard's parents chose wisely. Price took a special interest in their son and in many ways, some overt and some carefully concealed, fostered his intellectual

[1] Ibid., p. 124.

[2] Compare chapter II of *Something of Myself* with Prof. Carrington's view that the school was entirely *of* its time, not in advance of it (*Rudyard Kipling*, p. 24). In so far as the U.S.C. was a superior crammer's establishment, Carrington is correct, but this aspect of the school was relatively unimportant to Kipling, who admired the rough freedom of the place and the students' many opportunities for out-of-doors adventures. These qualities are more admired nowadays than they were in the seventies, in part, perhaps, because of *Stalky*, as well as Kipling's direct influence on Baden-Powell's Boy Scout movement.

growth.[1] Without appearing to grant favours, Price trained the boy in précis-writing and modern languages, gave him free access to a large and fascinating library, revived the school paper for Rudyard to edit, and unobtrusively guided him towards the beginnings of a literary career. Whatever Cormell Price's merits as a headmaster, he was the ideal mentor for Rudyard Kipling; in particular, he represented the very antithesis of Mrs. Holloway and all she stood for.

During the four years he spent at Westward Ho!, Kipling took several steps towards becoming a writer. But his artistic development has been obscured by the popularity of *Stalky & Co.*, the fictional re-creation of his schooldays, which has focused the attention and curiosity of readers upon the external details of life at the United Services College.[2] As Kipling's biographer has pointed out, however, the boy inhabited at least two worlds during his schooldays, and only one of them is reflected in *Stalky*.[3] Thus, if we are to understand Kipling's growth as a writer, we must examine *Stalky* as a set of deliberate choices, a pattern of conscious distortions and suppressions, designed not to give a full account of its author's early life but to argue a particular case.

'While we were at Torquay', Kipling wrote, 'there came to me the idea of beginning some tracts or parables on the education of the young. These, for reasons

[1] The Kiplings' anxious concern over their son's schooling is illustrated in a series of letters they wrote to Cormell Price, recently sold at Sotheby's in London. See the Sotheby *Catalogue of Nineteenth-Century and Modern First Editions*, sale of 30 November and 1 December 1964 (London, 1964), pp. 93–94. Twenty-five of the letters were written while Kipling was at school.

[2] See, for example, two books by Kipling's schoolmates, written in response to this curiosity: George C. Beresford, *Schooldays with Kipling* (London, 1936); and Lionel C. Dunsterville, *Stalky's Reminiscences* (London, 1928). A considerable bibliography of articles about the school could be assembled: Stalky's adventures, whatever their value as literature, seem to have generated more interest than any other phase of Kipling's work.

[3] Carrington, *Rudyard Kipling*, p. 28.

honestly beyond my control, turned themselves into a series of tales called *Stalky & Co.*'[1] It was in the early spring of 1897 that Kipling began to write about Beetle, Stalky, and M'Turk. He had left Vermont the previous summer and was entering a period of his life marked by vociferous patriotism and a growing concern for England's lack of military preparedness. The pride and optimism of 'A Song of the English' (1893) had darkened to the warning tones of 'Recessional' (1897) and would shade still further into the magisterial criticism of 'The Islanders' (1902). Rough and entertaining though they might be, the 'Stalky' stories were designed to show the English how a certain kind of public school training could best produce young men capable of safeguarding and extending the British Empire. Kipling made his point most clearly in the earliest of the stories, the two parts of 'Slaves of the Lamp', which appeared in April and May 1897: Stalky, the master tactician of Number Five Study, employs the same stratagem to win a frontier campaign that he used to take revenge on Mr. King, an officious master at the College. After a year's lapse, Kipling resumed the series; he didn't need to draw the moral so baldly in the remainder of the stories, but none of them strays very far from the parabolic intentions that were in his mind at the start.

In order to prove his point, Kipling altered the circumstances of life at Westward Ho! with considerable freedom. To some extent these changes were simply exaggerations: ordinary schoolboy pranks were blown up to heroic proportions. But Kipling also made a systematic effort to give the United Services College the lineaments of a more conventional public school; fagging, bullying, and flogging — none of which seems to have played much part in Kipling's school life — become the order of the day, and the gentle, withdrawn Price is turned into 'Prooshian' Bates, a conventionally severe Victorian headmaster. It may seem odd that Kipling, who remained

[1] *Something of Myself*, pp. 134–5.

fiercely loyal to the school as it really was, should have changed its fictional counterpart into something like the stereotypes of contemporary school fiction, but in fact he had to do so in order to make his parables generally applicable.[1] After the old boys have finished discussing Stalky's military exploits, Dick Four exclaims: 'There's nobody like Stalky.'

> 'That's just where you make the mistake,' I said. 'India's full of Stalkies — Cheltenham and Haileybury and Marlborough chaps — that we don't know anything about, and the surprises will begin when there is really a big row on.'
>
> 'Who will be surprised?' said Dick Four.
>
> 'The other side. The gentlemen who go to the front in first-class carriages. Just imagine Stalky let loose on the south side of Europe with a sufficiency of Sikhs and a reasonable prospect of loot. Consider it quietly.'[2]

In other words, *Stalky & Co.* argues on behalf of a particular sort of boy even more than a particular sort of school. Stalky, the man of action, fills the centre of the canvas; Kipling's portrait of himself as Beetle is characteristically modest and unassuming. There are, to be sure, several

[1] Naturally, the Stalky stories have room for many other interpretations besides this one, but it is unjust to Kipling not to take his explicit intentions into account. Reading the stories for their autobiographical content alone, Mr. Edmund Wilson concludes: 'The important thing is that he [Kipling] suffered.' This may or may not be true of the boy Rudyard, but the stories, for all their violence, have very little to say about suffering: had Kipling wanted to create a sense of his unhappiness at school, he could have used the techniques of 'Baa Baa, Black Sheep', but instead he created a world of wild, coarse humour, in which beatings and practical jokes are as empty of real pain as the smack of slapsticks in a farce. Cf. Edmund Wilson, 'The Kipling That Nobody Read', in *The Wound and the Bow* (Boston, 1941), pp. 105–81. The best treatment of the Stalky stories I have yet seen is Steven Marcus's introduction to *Stalky & Co.* in the Collier Books edition (New York, 1962). Professor Marcus is one of the handful of critics who have taken Kipling at more than face value and read him as a serious and relevant modern author; his essay deserves a wider circulation than it has received.

[2] 'Slaves of the Lamp: Part ii.'

glimpses of Beetle in his role of school *littérateur*, writing lampoons of the masters or declaiming Browning and Swinburne against the roar of the breakers, but in general Kipling shows us Beetle as he might have appeared to his schoolmates: a harmless poetaster, ineffectual when it came to football or the organization of elaborate practical jokes. It is boys like Stalky and his counterparts — 'Cheltenham and Haileybury and Marlborough chaps' — who will grow up to do the work of the Empire.

To his actual schoolmates, however, Kipling was a more impressive phenomenon than the 'Stalky' stories imply; in Dunsterville's later judgment, 'Beresford and I had our fair share of brains, but Kipling had a great deal more than his fair share, and added to it the enormous asset of knowledge — intuitive and acquired.' [1] He may have lacked Dunsterville's ingenuity and Beresford's imperturbable façade, but he made up for it by playing to the hilt the part of school intellectual.

The source of Kipling's 'intuitive' knowledge was the family background that made him an heir to the culture and attitudes of his Pre-Raphaelite relatives and their friends; of this background his schoolmates remained largely unaware. During the holidays Kipling returned to the world into which he had been introduced after leaving Southsea, a world in which Mr. Cormell Price became 'Uncle Crom', in which the poets he read with avidity at Westward Ho! might turn up as fellow guests of his Uncle Ned and Aunt Georgie. His parents, still true to their independent principles, did not ask Rudyard's aunts and uncles to take responsibility for him during school holidays; instead, Lorne Lodge was replaced by a far more sympathetic environment, the London house of Mrs. Winnard and the two Miss Craiks, friends of the family who became for Rudyard and Trix the three dear ladies of Warwick Gardens. They were gentle and interested critics to whom the Kipling children later took pleasure in sending the books they wrote in

[1] Dunsterville, *Stalky's Reminiscences*, p. 26.

India. It was, Kipling recalled, 'a house filled with books, peace, kindliness, patience and what today would be called "culture"'.[1] The ladies were proud of their acquaintance with Jean Ingelow, with Christina Rossetti, with the de Morgans. 'All the people one was taken to see either wrote or painted pictures.'[2]

On the wall of this house hung two clay pipes once smoked by Carlyle; enshrined, they epitomize the atmosphere of the literary world Kipling was discovering. The generation of writers who had come of age in the eighteen-thirties was now a race of almost legendary giants. Dickens and Thackeray were dead; Carlyle would follow in 1881; Tennyson had been laureate for thirty years; Browning was deep in the obscurity of his late poems. For five decades these men had dominated English literature. Their successors, who can roughly be grouped together as the Pre-Raphaelites, were no longer the subversive rebels they had seemed in the fifties and sixties. They were now the older generation, the contemporaries of Kipling's parents, uncles, and teachers, so that the boy found himself guided by his elders towards Rossetti, Swinburne, the *Rubá'iyát*, *The City of Dreadful Night*. In fact, Rudyard probably had more guidance than was altogether good for him. The path was being laid down too carefully; he was being introduced to a world of other people's pious memories — 'of years when all the planets were little newlit stars trying to find their places in the uncaring void, and he, the Head, knew them as young men know one another' — instead of being granted the young man's right to discover new gods for himself.

In and out of school Kipling read voraciously and with such speed that his schoolmates would try to trap him by quizzing him on what he read; it did them no good: they found his comprehension a match for his rapidity.[3] The books he remembered fall into no very striking pattern, except that nearly all of them lie in the domain of belles-

[1] *Something of Myself*, p. 21. [2] Ibid., p. 22.
[3] Beresford, *Schooldays*, p. 131.

lettres. He read for enjoyment, not instruction, and in consequence was less apt at his schoolwork than his evident precocity would lead one to expect; instead of Virgil and Horace he spent his time with Carlyle and Ruskin, Mark Twain and Bret Harte, Pushkin and Lermontov, Donne and Crashaw, Alexander Smith and Lydia Sigourney. The tenor of his later writings occasionally led critics to the conclusion that Kipling was a literary barbarian, unread and unsophisticated; but a taste for the abstruse in literature remained with him throughout his life and continually impressed his friends and associates: he could dispute French and English letters with no less a man than the omniscient Saintsbury and win that formidable reader's friendship and respect.[1] And yet, though he did not try to conceal his reading from his schoolmates, he kept his intellectual life separate from his other activities. The alliance he formed with Beresford and Dunsterville foreshadows the mature Kipling, who chose his closest friends from among technicians and men of action rather than commit himself wholly to literature. Similarly, although the books Kipling read at Westward Ho! had a perceptible effect on his early verse style, in other ways they had surprisingly little influence on him as a writer. A skilful parodist at eighteen, Kipling never lost his ability to imitate the mannerisms of other authors, but he never fully developed the gift of assimilation: unlike Joyce and Eliot and Pound, he never learned to use the work of earlier writers in such a way as to make it his own.[2]

If we accept the evidence of the 'Stalky' stories, Kipling often discussed *Sartor Resartus* and *Fors Clavigera*

[1] Carrington, *Rudyard Kipling*, pp. 478–9. Ann M. Weygandt's *Kipling's Reading and Its Influence on His Poetry* (Philadelphia, 1939) gives a sense of the scope and depth of Kipling's interest in recherché books.

[2] For example, it is surprising to discover that Kipling was an enthusiast of John Donne and at one time considered Rabelais the greatest of realists. For Rabelais, see Kipling's revealing fantasy 'The Last of the Stories' (15 September 1888).

with his friends, but he kept his own poetry strictly to himself. His schoolmates knew his head was full of rhymes — he would copy them out on note-paper in the form room, under the pretext of writing letters to his family — but they were a private affair, confided only to little leather-covered notebooks and to his parents in India. Even Beresford, in most things his confidant, recognized that Kipling's poetry was forbidden territory. He recalled in *Schooldays with Kipling* that 'inspection of the verses inscribed in his Russia-leather, gilt-edged, cream-laid MS. books would not have been at all welcomed; and, in fact, these sanctuaries were never violated, never opened by careless or unworthy hands. The leather-bound books were guarded by a taboo; one of the few sacred words honoured by schoolboys covered them with its protection: "Private".'[1] There were sound reasons for privacy; as Beresford points out, Kipling would have laid himself open to the ridicule of his masters and friends by allowing his verses to circulate.[2] But Beresford did not know what inquisitions Kipling had been forced to undergo at Lorne Lodge. There, he had surrounded Crusoe's trading-post with a magic fence in order to protect his imaginary realm from the intrusion of Mrs. Holloway. He had not lost, nor would he ever lose, a profound desire to shut the world out from the charmed circle of his most intimate family and from the workings of his own mind.

But unlike his schoolmates, Kipling's family did have a part to play in his development as a writer. Doubtless remembering the literary ambitions of her childhood, Alice Kipling encouraged her son to write verse, and the other Macdonald sisters helped to foster his talent. In 1879, after the end of his second year at school, Rudyard joined the Burne-Jones and Morris children in making up a handwritten magazine called 'The Scribbler'; some of his contributions, signed 'Nickson', still survive.[3] A

[1] Beresford, *Schooldays*, p. 284. [2] Ibid., pp. 286–8.

[3] Stewart, *Bibliographical Catalogue*, p. 3.

year later Alice was writing anxiously to her friend Miss Plowden: 'I wish when Ruddy sends you any verses you would let me have a copy. He promised I should have all he did — but he is not sending them — and as time and distance do their fatal work I am sure that his Mother will know less of him than any other woman of his acquaintance.'[1] But Alice had little reason to complain, for when Rudyard did write, his letters were delightful: he not only included poems but decorated the pages with vividly funny sketches illustrating his Stalky-esque scrapes.[2] Unknown to him, his mother was carefully preserving the poems he sent her, and towards the end of 1881, when Rudyard was approaching his sixteenth birthday, she had twenty-three of them privately printed in a little volume called *Schoolboy Lyrics*. Rudyard didn't find out about the book till after his return to India.[3] As his mother might have foreseen, he was more annoyed than grateful; the poems were meant for family reading only. Alice's gesture was well meant but symptomatic of her constant pressure on Rudyard to make the most of his abilities.

Because they are derivative and conventional, the poems in *Schoolboy Lyrics* do not give a very clear picture of Kipling's mind, but a few salient features can be made

[1] Quoted in Baldwin, *The Macdonald Sisters*, p. 127.

[2] See, for example, an autograph letter signed 'Ruddy', from Rudyard Kipling to his mother, dated 9 March 1882, in the W. M. Carpenter Collection at the Library of Congress. Four years earlier, on 24 January 1878, Alice had written to Cormell Price about Rudyard's epistolary habits: that day she had no letter from her son; the day before, four. She hastened to reassure Price that she wasn't encouraging him to be so prolific; on the one hand, she felt he hadn't made close friends at school and was still relying heavily on his mother for sympathy and interest; on the other, she reminded Price that the son inherited his parents' facility with the pen. The letter mixes maternal anxiety and pride in such a way as to echo the tone of Alice's later letter to Miss Plowden; taken together, the letters suggest a good deal about Rudyard's relationship with his parents. (See Sotheby's catalogue of the 1 December 1964 sale of letters, p. 93.)

[3] Carrington, *Rudyard Kipling*, p. 50.

out. Undated, the verses differ so strikingly in quality that they must represent the fruits of a rapid development in skill: a poem written for the 1879 'Scribbler' — 'The Dusky Crew' — is quite childish in comparison with other poems that could have been composed no more than two years later, and another, 'The Song of the Sufferer', is an undistinguished piece of schoolboy humour, a fragment from the world of Stalky and his friends.

The rest of the poems, however, form patterns that help us to infer the state of Kipling's mind during his third and fourth years of school. Browning was evidently his favourite poet. Kipling found his rough and colloquial diction easy to imitate, but, more significantly, the form of the dramatic monologue allowed him to remain impersonal, to take refuge behind the masks of speakers not himself. In general, the *Schoolboy Lyrics* are more objective than one would expect adolescent poems to be; diffident about speaking in his own person, Kipling puts speculations about life, love, and death into the mouths of an ancient Roman on the banks of the Styx, a front door, a newly buried corpse. The speculations, to be sure, are predictable, but the manner of their presentation is not. Similarly, most of the poems are anti-romantic, even cynical, in tone. Certain commonplaces recur: fame is a delusion; beauty, a matter of false hair and paint; love comes too late to be of any use. The cynicism is to be expected — schoolboys aren't noted for their tolerance of romantic sentimentality — but in these poems the commonplaces also suggest that Kipling is on the defensive; he is perhaps more concerned with love, beauty, and fame than he is willing to admit. Cynicism cooperates with the objectivity of the Browning-esque monologue to prevent the *Schoolboy Lyrics* from becoming passionate adolescent effusions; Kipling keeps his verse under careful control.

Another rather surprising aspect of the poems is the extent to which they dwell on the lives of the mean and sordid. A servant-girl tells her love in Cockney dialect;

'ferret-eyed women and keen-faced men' anxiously await the reading of the will; 'red hands may be raised to kill', and a dull lover will commit a crime of passion for the sake of a woman 'weak-mouthed and chalky-white, limping, and stuttering too'. These dreary creations not only reinforce the anti-romantic tendency of the volume but also anticipate Kipling's lifelong interest in derelicts and outcasts. One poem, 'Overheard', is particularly striking. For once, the young poet makes carelessness into a virtue and achieves a vividly casual opening:

So the day dragged through,
And the afternoon brought the spangles,
    The sawdust smell, the tights,
    The flickering, flashing lights, . . .

'It was hot, too, and I felt bored.' What the speaker overhears fits his mood: a young prostitute is soliciting a potential customer.

'Took to the streets for a life.
                Entre nous,
It's a terrible uphill strife,
Like all professions — too filled.
And now I'm in lodgings hard by,
Au quatrième, up in the sky.
    Visit me by and by,
They're furnished, but oh — so cold,
                So cold!'

The poem, as these extracts suggest, oscillates in and out of sentimentality and finally collapses into adolescent moralizing, but at the same time it looks forward to Kipling at his least sentimental, to the Kipling who would, like Yeats's horseman, 'cast a cold eye on life, on death' in his finest Simla stories.

When 'Overheard' was reprinted many years later, Kipling added the subtitle 'Supposed To Be after Browning', but in fact there is little in the poem beyond its colloquial diction to suggest the debt. Although grotesque and sordid characters throng Browning's poems, they are either frayed but charming Bohemians or actors in moral dramas; Kipling presents his prostitute, in spite of sentimental lapses, with a detachment, a sense of moral disengagement, that reminds us less of Browning than of naturalistic fiction. Had Kipling written 'Overheard' in 1890, it would be easy to claim that he had been dining at the troughs of Zolaism, but in 1880 the naturalists were virtually unknown in England: Maupassant had not yet begun to publish, Zola was untranslated, and the famous Vizetelly obscenity trials were still several years in the future. Nevertheless, Kipling may have been well in advance of his countrymen. His father had taught him to read French fluently and in those days, as Kipling wrote later, 'knowledge of it connoted leanings towards immorality'; what more natural than for the accomplished schoolboy to have dipped into Zola to see what he and other young persons were being protected from.[1] Subdued, perhaps, by a strain of Puritanism in his make-up, Kipling was more than usually reticent in his published works about his knowledge of Zola and his followers, so that the question of influence remains open; but it is pleasant to speculate that in one area, at least, he was reading books that hadn't been urged on him by his staid and protective elders.

Schoolboy Lyrics gave Rudyard's family access to a private life that he kept from his school friends, but he inhabited another world so closely guarded that even Lockwood and Alice Kipling seem to have found it inaccessible. For all his poetical scoffs at romance, Rudyard had fallen in love. The girl's name was Florence Garrard. Rudyard met her in 1880, at Lorne Lodge, the scene of his early sorrows, where she and Trix were fellow boarders.[2] Little is known of Florence beyond a few bare facts: she was a year or two older than Rudyard — perhaps fifteen or sixteen when they met; she wanted to be a painter and studied art in Paris and, later, at the Slade

[1] *Something of Myself*, p. 25.

[2] Carrington, *Rudyard Kipling*, pp. 41–42.

School in London; she seems to have been a good deal more sophisticated than her young admirer.[1] Otherwise, we know her only through the impression she made on Rudyard. But that impression was a strong and lasting one. There can be no doubt that Kipling drew her portrait as Maisie, the heroine of *The Light That Failed*, for she had re-entered his life by the time he wrote that novel and was much in his thoughts.[2] Self-contained and unresponsive, Maisie corresponds to what little we can surmise about Florence's personality, just as the first chapter of *The Light That Failed* seems to portray the mood and atmosphere of Rudyard's meetings with Florence on the mournful beaches at Southsea. Though we have no clue to Florence's state of mind, Rudyard's can be inferred from numerous hints in his published and unpublished writings. He was in love with a girl who was essentially unsympathetic and elusive, he strongly suspected that this love would lead nowhere, and yet he was helpless to do anything about it.[3] Later, when he read *Manon Lescaut*, he found in Des Grieux's unhappy passion the fictional correlative of his own, and he put something of both into *The Light That Failed*.[4] But in that curious novel personal experience and literary allusion were so

[1] An interesting sketch-book of Florence's is now in the Berg Collection, New York Public Library. It contains some sketches by Rudyard of Florence: they show a sturdy figure in the long skirts of the period setting out to paint with easel and paraphernalia, chased by a bull, starting a forest fire with a discarded cigarette. The pictures give little or no impression of Florence's appearance, but the cigarette, at least (it was the early eighties), suggests a certain degree of sophistication and independence.

[2] A valuable essay on the connection between Florence and Maisie is Professor Carrington's 'Some Conjectures about *The Light That Failed*', *Kipling Journal*, xxv, no. 125 (March 1958), 9–14.

[3] Baldwin, *The Macdonald Sisters*, p. 124, mentions the effect that the strength of Rudyard's attachment had on his young Aunt Edith.

[4] *Something of Myself*, pp. 227–8. J. M. S. Tompkins discusses the novel's debt to *Manon Lescaut* in her excellent study, *The Art of Rudyard Kipling* (London, 1959), p. 13.

'metagrobolized', to use Kipling's own term, that the personality of the fictitious Maisie scarcely emerges, let alone that of the real Florence. Kipling's first love remains even more elusive to us than she must have seemed to the boy whom she so fascinated.

Permitted by the exigencies of school life to see Florence only at intervals, Rudyard compensated as best he could by writing love poems, which he copied into one of his Russia-leather manuscript books and sent to Florence. This book, called 'Sundry Phansies', has survived and can be examined at the Berg Collection in the New York Public Library. It contains thirty-two poems, only eight of which have been published: three appeared in *Schoolboy Lyrics* (1881) and the remaining five in *Echoes* (1884) and *Quartette* (1885), so that 'Sundry Phansies' looks both backwards and forwards in time, and helps bridge the gap between Kipling the schoolboy and Kipling the Anglo-Indian poet.

At first glance Kipling's verse appears to have taken a new and predictable direction. The pressure towards objectivity so marked in *Schoolboy Lyrics* has been relaxed; in more than half the unpublished poems the poet allows himself to speak in what might be his own voice. Death and romantic love dominate the book and introduce a note of adolescent melancholy that is absent from the 1881 volume and, indeed, very rarely to be found in any of Kipling's extant writings. Browning's influence is still strong but no longer paramount; he has been replaced by Rossetti, Swinburne, and Morris. 'Overheard' has not been included, nor do any of the new poems suggest an interest in French naturalism. In short, the cynical cosmopolitan of *Schoolboy Lyrics* has given way to a new poetic voice whose tone is often passionate, melancholy, and romantic.

It is tempting to label the author of 'Sundry Phansies' a young man in love and let the matter end there, but to do so would be to overlook the real significance of the volume. Undeniably personal, undeniably the fruits of his love for Florence, these poems are also the deliberate experiments of a young artist who is attempting to control his experience by putting it into forms provided for him by his predecessors. The tone of his poetry has changed but his underlying intention has not. For example, a number of the 'Sundry Phansies' poems are technical exercises pure and simple; unrelated to his feelings about Florence, they are attempts to discover a style through the imitation of the styles of others. 'How the Goddess Awakened' — the meditations of a statue of Venus that finds itself worshipped as an image of the Virgin — is a moderately skilful imitation of Swinburne's paganism; 'How the Day Broke', later subtitled 'Drawing-Room Song', is a drawing-room song; 'Waytinge' and 'Conspiracy' half-playfully test the effects of archaic spelling and diction. Swinburne's mannerisms in a few instances completely submerge the poet's own personality. '*For as flame that flickers and flies, / Our memory comes and goes*': the all-too-imitable rhythm and alliteration point unmistakably to the author of *Poems and Ballads*. Unassimilated Morris appears in the superficial medievalism of 'The Page's Song' and 'The Page's Message', which purport to be 'Translated from the French of the Garde Ysoude'; and the tutelary spirit of 'The House of Life' hovers over the introductory lines of 'A Visitation':

> There came to me one at midnight, on golden pinions and said
> 'Lo! I am Love and I bring thee a Passion back from the dead.'[1]

But imitation is a legitimate mode of experiment. Rossetti, Swinburne, and Morris not only suited Kipling's state of mind better than Browning: in the early eighties they represented the advance guard of modern poetry, the chief fertilizing influence on Kipling's generation.[2]

[1] Compare the opening lines of 'Passion and Worship' (Sonnet ix of 'The House of Life'): 'One flame-winged brought a white-winged harp-player / Even where my lady and I lay all alone'.

[2] In this connection, it is important to keep in mind that Kipling was born in the same year as W. B. Yeats and that the fathers of both writers

To the extent that 'Sundry Phansies' is imitative, it stands as evidence of Kipling's early and deliberate choice of the artist's vocation.

But there is more to 'Sundry Phansies' than the barren pastiche that my examples seem to suggest. In several of the poems Kipling assimilates the poetry of his predecessors rather than merely copying it: his own experiences, his own state of mind take on significance when he views them through the glass of Morris's or Rossetti's poetry. The Pre-Raphaelite 'Ballad of the King's Daughter', for example, provides a glimpse of the unattainable Florence in the mysterious, incantatory verse of some of Morris's poems:

> Many came to her over the water,
> Princes all, and the King stood by
> But she gave them the scorn of a Monarch's daughter,
> Coldly, strangely, and haughtily.

Florence was at Southsea, we recall, and when Rudyard visited her there, they must have wandered along the melancholy beach that he later described in the first chapter of *The Light That Failed*. That beach occurs, quite vividly realized, in 'How It Seemed to Us':

> A grey flat lying out against the sea,
> Where the strait guts are choked with weeded wood
> And tangled cordage, moving aimlessly.

The movement of the verse echoes Rossetti: the beach is Kipling's own, but it is also, I think, the beach of Rossetti's 'Sudden Light' and 'The Sea-Limits'; the poet has taught the boy to see that bleak landscape with an eye for the emotional significance of visual details. Similarly, when the boy stands at the sea's edge and asks the waves to bring him a message from his lady, we recognize the

were professional artists of a more or less Pre-Raphaelite persuasion. The influence of Rossetti, Swinburne, and Morris on Yeats's generation has often been discussed; a particularly lucid analysis of it is to be found in Graham Hough, *The Last Romantics* (London, 1947).

situation of Rossetti's poem 'The Stream's Secret', yet the effect of Kipling's poem — 'By the Sea' — is to make that situation real and his own: we are given a boy's sense of frustration at being trapped in a school, on the Devon coast, infinitely far from 'the low sand dunes where my heart is set', the sand dunes of Southsea.

The moment at which an apprentice poet ceases merely to imitate and begins to assimilate the work of others can mark a decisive point in his career. In 1882, on the eve of his departure for India, Kipling seems to have been preparing to join the poets whom Graham Hough has termed 'the last romantics': he was following the same path as his coeval, William Butler Yeats, from whom he was later so widely to diverge. This affinity with the Pre-Raphaelite tradition is clearest in 'The Story of Paul Vaugel', the longest, most ambitious, and in some ways the most interesting poem in 'Sundry Phansies'. A dramatic monologue, 'Paul Vaugel' recounts the experiences of a Norman peasant: according to Kipling's prose heading, the poem tells 'how he took to himselfe an unfortunate [i.e., a prostitute], and maintained her, and how she died, and how he buried her in the Pol-lourdesse and of the evil that came on him'. The poem's mood and form owe a good deal, I think, to Morris: the action produces an effect similar to that of 'The Haystack in the Floods', the effect of an intensely vivid fragment whose outlines blur into vagueness. Curiosity as to time, place, and circumstance is aroused but never satisfied, so that we move in a dreamlike world where perceptions and emotions, for all their intensity, are divorced from any intelligible surroundings.

The verse form Kipling chooses reinforces the poem's effect. 'Paul Vaugel' is written in loose, four-beat iambics that suggest, through their relaxed monotony, automatic writing or poetry dictated in a dream. Given another context, this somnambulistic verse might appear only to reflect the poet's lack of skill, but here the monotonous iambics, the 'and . . . and . . . and . . .' of the compound sentences, are surprisingly effective in creating a sense of the speaker's numbed, uncomprehending mind.

> And then was rest when the day was over,
> And hope and love were high in the heart,
> For her white arms closed round me, her lover
> And her kiss was worth all pain and smart
>
> And the heat and toil of a little day,
> At the sound of her voice would pass away
>
> And I thought that what is would always be
> And that hope and Love should rule i' the heart,
> But God's hand took her love from me
> And I alone bore the pain and the smart
>
> For the plague that summer brings to our town
> Seized her and held, and threw her down.

The poem proceeds in this manner for about one-third of its length. But when the girl dies, the pace slows still further, and we follow Vaugel step by step as he carries her body out to the beach, digs a grave for her in the dunes, and buries her there. Whatever significance that mournful sea-coast had for Kipling at the conscious level, here it seems to have broken free and taken on the quality of a dream landscape: haunting and portentous, yet seen with intense clarity.

> And I plucked sea poppy and wind dried heather,
> And wove them into a wreath together
> And I set the wreath on her brows as night
> Came, and shut them out of my sight.
> Then I piled the sand over face and hair
> Till I left no whit of the body bare
> For I felt in the dark lest foot or hand
> Should be uncovered by the sand.
> And I staked up gorze till my fingers bled,
> Lest the sheep should pasture over head.
> And I weighted the bushes with boulder clay,
> And I sat on the dunes and wept till day.

And a great mist rose from the dim St. Lo,
And an inland wind on the full tide's flow
And all night long the sea-mist passed
In a thousand shapes before the blast
And all our past Life shewed to me
Till morning broke on the sullen sea.

Strange in itself, this fragmentary dream of an imagined sorrow seems doubly strange when we recall the characteristic later work of the boy who wrote it. The glib parodies of *Echoes*, the social comedy of *Departmental Ditties*, and the vigour of the *Barrack-Room Ballads* are far removed from the Pol-Lourdesse and Vaugel's buried mistress. And yet, 'Paul Vaugel' does look forward to the writings of an older Kipling. The next example of this aspect of his art, however, will be not poetry but the remarkable 'Gate of the Hundred Sorrows', which he wrote in India some two years later. Nor did Kipling ever return to this poetic mode; the visionary qualities that remind us of 'Paul Vaugel' recur in his stories, not his verse. 'Sundry Phansies' faintly hints at the kind of poet Kipling might have become — an 'aesthete' of the nineties, a *triste* Georgian, a thin and minor version of the early Yeats. But that road Kipling was destined, for a variety of reasons, not to travel.

V

On one occasion Kipling's most energetic teacher, the fiery Mr. Crofts, could not restrain his irritation at his most promising student and 'literally threw' a copy of Browning's *Men and Women* at Kipling's head.[1] Fifteen years later Kipling worked the incident into *Stalky*: Mr. King refers sarcastically to Beetle as 'Gigadibs, the literary man', just as Crofts had done years before.[2] The epithet

[1] *Something of Myself*, p. 34.

[2] 'Slaves of the Lamp, Part i', in *Stalky & Co.*; Carrington, *Rudyard Kipling*, p. 33.

is apt in some ways, though its relevance to the young Kipling is in other ways sharply restricted.

> You, Gigadibs, who, thirty years of age,
> Write statedly for Blackwood's Magazine,
> Believe you see two points in Hamlet's soul
> Unseized by the Germans yet — which view you'll print —[1]

By the age of thirty Kipling had become the most popular major author England had seen since Dickens, a far cry from Browning's impoverished critic. And even at sixteen he had known hate and love, had been forsaken and reunited. He considered himself a successful lover, informally engaged to Florence Garrard.[2] He had filled pages with verse, and much of it had seen print in India; he had even had a sonnet accepted for publication in an English paper.[3] And yet, though there was no Blougram to unsettle what convictions he had formed, he was, like Gigadibs, 'Outward-bound': not for Australia, with 'settler's-implements (enough for three)', but for a job on an up-country newspaper in the distant Indian Empire.

Like the Punch of 'Baa Baa, Black Sheep', Kipling had come to England as an alien, an Anglo-Indian, his head filled with wrong ideas about how to behave. Now, a decade later, he had adapted himself to English ways: he must have viewed his departure with mixed feelings. On the one hand, he had to leave Florence behind; we can recognize a younger self in Kipling's portrait of Dicky Hatt, the miserable hero of 'In the Pride of His Youth' (5 May 1887); and earlier, when his memory was fresher still, Kipling described the departure from Gravesend in the guise of an 'echo' of William Morris:

1 Robert Browning, 'Bishop Blougram's Apology', *The Poetical Works*, ed. Augustine Birrell (New York, 1900), i. 541.

2 Carrington, *Rudyard Kipling*, p. 42.

3 The sonnet was 'Two Lives', 8 November 1882. It was first identified by William M. Carpenter, '"Kipling about" in London for a Week: By a Hustling American', *Kipling Journal*, no. 7 (Oct. 1928), 9–16.

And Estunt turned him landward, and wan hope
Grew on his spirit as an evil mist,
Thinking of loving lips his lips had kissed
An hour since, and how those lips were sweet
An hour since, far off in Fenchurch Street.[1]

On the other hand, his thoughts must have turned often to the literary world of London, which he was being forced to abandon. 'He had rather wished to stay in England', according to the recollections of his schoolmate Beresford. 'He looked upon this expedition as rather a wild adventure. . . . London, he considered, would be his natural socket, where he thought he fitted in.'[2] For England had become a significant part of Kipling's experience, not only the bleak coast at Southsea and Westward Ho! but the glare of London, where he hoped some day to make his name as an author. Places were always to be of the greatest importance to Kipling: his life was to be punctuated by critical arrivals and departures, each marked by emotions as ambivalent as they were strong.

[1] 'Estunt the Griff', *Echoes*, November 1884. (The title is Anglo-Indian slang: 'Estunt' is a corruption of 'Assistant'; 'Griff' is for 'griffin', an eighteenth-century word meaning 'greenhorn'.)

[2] Beresford, *Schooldays*, p. 315.

2. Homecoming

I

In the earlier nineteenth century, when family interest could obtain a young man a position in the East India Company, John Lockwood Kipling might have found it easy to establish his son in India. But since the Mutiny and the transfer of India to the Crown, the Civil Service had become more interested in a man's capabilities than in his family. Unless one had been trained to do a specific job, his chances of making a success of an Indian career were slight. John Kipling was a designer; he had been hired as an architectural sculptor and charged with overseeing the ornamentation of several new public buildings in Bombay. A man of charm as well as ability, he had been looked upon with favour by the Government and had risen to positions of increasing responsibility. The time had come for him to set his son upon the road to similar accomplishments.

It was a trying moment. Left to himself, the boy would probably choose to slip into a carefree and disorderly life on the fringe of literary London. He had some talent for poetry, but such talent is not uncommon at sixteen; it would hardly serve to support a young man in the city. And there were more compelling reasons for bringing Rudyard to India. Cormell Price, who had outlived the days of his Pre-Raphaelite wild oats, may have intimated to the Kiplings that Rudyard, though mature in some ways, was not entirely trustworthy when left to himself. And there was Florence to be taken into account. The family knew the strength of Rudyard's attachment. The prospect of their son's eking out a living in Bohemia, in full view of censorious aunts and uncles, with such a companion — perhaps, even, such a wife — must have given the parents more than one restless night.[1]

But if Rudyard was to be brought out to India, what was he to do there? Unlike his father, he was master of no craft. His poor eyesight ruled out the possibility of a career in the Army or Navy. The family could not afford to send him to a university, nor had he demonstrated any aptitude for scholarship. An attempt at competing for the Indian Civil Service would have been absurd, for the examinations tempted some of the cleverest and most ambitious young men in the realm. Commerce was out of the question. Planters and merchants had to adopt the East as a permanent home; Kipling was unwilling to make such a commitment. And those who settled in India lost caste *vis-à-vis* the civilians: it was not unusual for them to marry Indian women — by now a sure path to ostracism from the European community — and they were apt to be considered by some as differing but little from the despised Eurasians.[2] With the professions, the military, the civil service, and the business world closed, only journalism was left.

It has been said that Kipling was born a journalist, but clearly this is a judgment after the event.[3] It must have been no easy matter to convince the proprietor of an Indian newspaper that the schoolboy had promise. Normally, an Indian editor would hire only a man who had mastered the basic techniques of journalism — one

[1] Edmonia Hill, 'The Young Kipling: Personal Recollections', *Atlantic Monthly*, clvii (1936), 408. 'It seems that after his school days he went to London and stayed with his aunt and uncle. They felt that he was seeing too much of life about town.'

[2] For example, Phil Garron in '"Yoked with an Unbeliever"' (7 December 1886), who began 'more and more to look upon India as his home. Some men fall this way, and they are of no use afterwards.'

[3] Abel Chevalley, *Le Roman anglais de notre temps* (London, 1921), p. 148.

who had worked, for example, for one of the larger provincial papers in England. An untrained hand could easily involve the paper in damage suits, nor could he be depended upon to take the editor's place when the latter went on leave or caught fever.[1] But Lockwood Kipling numbered several journalists among his friends.[2] Like many officials he had contributed irregularly to the *Pioneer* since his Bombay days. A friend of his, Sir George Allen, had founded that paper at Allahabad and raised it to a position of power and distinction; two other family friends, the Punjabi financiers James Walker and William Rattigan, had ventured into journalism in the early 1870's, using the *Civil and Military Gazette* as a base for expansion. Within ten years the *Civil and Military* had absorbed four older papers of the region, and shortly before Kipling's departure from England the owners added the *Pioneer* to their organization.[3]

We do not know precisely when and how Lockwood Kipling suggested to his friends that they hire his son, but later nearly everyone connected with the *Pioneer* and the *Civil and Military* came forward to claim the honour of having accepted his suggestion. Allen probably played the largest role: Kipling's friend Mrs. Hill was told — presumably by Kipling himself — that Allen had wired from London, to conclude the negotiations, 'Kipling will do.' [4] Rudyard's protests went unheard.[5]

[1] J. P. Collins, 'Rudyard Kipling at Lahore', *The Nineteenth Century and After*, cxxi (1937), 84. Arnold Wright, *Baboo English as 'Tis Writ* (London, 1891), p. 10.

[2] Charles Carrington, *Rudyard Kipling: His Life and Work* (London, 1955), p. 48; and John Harry Rivett Carnac, *Many Memories of Life in India, at Home and Abroad* (Edinburgh, 1910), p. 226.

[3] Margarita Barns, *The Indian Press* (London, 1940), pp. 276–7; Carrington, *Rudyard Kipling*, p. 48.

[4] Hill, *Atlantic Monthly*, p. 408; William M. Carpenter, '"Kipling about" in London for a Week: By a Hustling American', *Kipling Journal*, no. 7 (Oct. 1928), 11–12.

[5] George C. Beresford, *Schooldays with Kipling* (London, 1936), pp. 315–16.

Here was a remarkable opportunity for an untrained schoolboy. Better still, from his parents' point of view, he could live at home; the family would not only save the cost of his room and board but could guard against the possibility of a successor to Florence. 'I am sure', wrote Lockwood after Rudyard's arrival, 'he is better here . . . where there are no music-hall ditties to pick up, no young persons to philander about with, and a great many other negatives of the most wholesome description. All that makes Lahore profoundly dull makes it safe for young persons.' [1]

Socially and intellectually, Lahore was dull by comparison with London; and Kipling's post as sub-editor of the *Civil and Military* provided none of the excitement of metropolitan journalism. The work was hard, and Kipling found himself restricted to his office desk. 'Our local news is comparatively limited', he later told an American interviewer. 'The ubiquitous reporter is unknown with us. . . . He is not needed.' [2] The newspaper served a local community of about seventy Europeans, not counting the military personnel. So small a group could provide an occasional social note, scandal, or crime, but local news could come nowhere near filling the eighteen pages published daily. World and Indian news came in over the wires from Reuter's or the Indian capital, but telegrams rarely filled more than half a column on the front page.[3] The rest of the day's copy came from a variety of sources: there were official notices of appointments, awards, and promotions, there were exchange items from papers located all over the world, letters from subscribers, essays on subjects ranging from Indian administration to Milton's poetry, stories, verse, and occasional correspondence by a full- or part-time

[1] Carrington, *Rudyard Kipling*, p. 50.

[2] From an interview with Kipling printed in the *San Francisco Chronicle*, 2 June 1889; transcribed in the Chandler 'Special Edition' of Kipling's works at the Library of Congress.

[3] Barns, *The Indian Press*, p. 277.

member of the staff.[1] Kipling's tasks were editorial and supervisory rather than literary and reportorial; for a year and a half he was concerned with preparing other men's writings for publication, with translating foreign articles, with proof-reading, correcting, skimming through other newspapers, guarding against libels and hoaxes.[2] His responsibility as sub-editor was relatively large, but the entire operation, like that of most Anglo-Indian newspapers, took place on a small scale.[3]

Kipling's chief at the *Civil and Military* made no effort to analyse his young assistant's talents or to give them any scope. Stephen Wheeler, editor of the Lahore paper, appears to have been the only person connected with Walker and Rattigan's organization who never claimed to have launched Rudyard Kipling's career. To one who knew him Wheeler was 'a man of model patience and few words, a fine judge of literature, Persian and English, a writer of force and capacity'; but Lockwood Kipling described him as 'very tetchy and irritable'.[4] Rudyard himself, who hated to speak ill of anyone who had been kind to him, admitted that he owed his chief a debt but remembered how he had felt years before: 'My Chief took me in hand, and for three years or so I loathed him. He had to break me in, and I knew nothing.'[5] As Carrington suggests, the editor probably resented having to train a boy fresh from school, imposed upon the paper through family influence, rather than the experienced apprentice he had a right to expect.[6] At any rate, the

[1] The Anglo-Indian editor 'courts the amateur contributor, and is only too glad to open his columns to any one who has a story to tell and the power to clothe it in a pungent or graceful style'. Francis Henry Skrine, *Life of Sir William Wilson Hunter* (London, 1901), p. 100.

[2] Rudyard Kipling, *Something of Myself for My Friends Known and Unknown*, 'Library Edition' (London, 1951), pp. 48–49.

[3] Skrine, *Hunter*, pp. 99–100.

[4] Collins, *The Nineteenth Century and After*, p. 88. Carrington, *Rudyard Kipling*, p. 50.

[5] *Something of Myself*, pp. 40–41.

[6] Carrington, *Rudyard Kipling*, p. 48.

taciturn, scholarly Wheeler showed no interest in taking advantage of Kipling's literary talent. His successor, E. Kay Robinson, who used that talent brilliantly, summed up Wheeler's policy in a memoir of Kipling's days as a young journalist:

It is almost pathetic to look through the 'Civil and Military Gazette' of that time and note where Kipling's bright humor only flashed out in the introdudtory lines to summaries of government reports, dry semi-political notes, and the side headings of scissors-and-paste paragraphs. This, however, was the maximum of literary display usually allowed to him. . . . My predecessor in the editorship of the 'Civil and Military Gazette' had done his best to make a sound second-rate journalist out of the youngster.[1]

It was a decided change of milieu for 'Gigadibs, the literary man', who had so recently been the leader of the intellectual *avant-garde* at the United Services College. At first, Kipling was delighted with India and his new job. 'I found myself at Bombay where I was born,' he wrote, 'moving among sights and smells that made me deliver in the vernacular sentences whose meaning I knew not. . . . There were yet three or four days' rail to Lahore, where my people lived. After these, my English years fell away, nor ever, I think, came back in full strength.'[2] All the paraphernalia of an Anglo-Indian's daily routine seemed the new and wonderful symbols of a young man's entry into adult life and responsibilities: 'I had my own room in the house; my servant, handed over to me by my father's servant, whose son he was, with the solemnity of a marriage-contract; my own horse, cart, and groom; my own office-hours and direct responsibilities; and — oh joy! — my own office-box, just like my Father's.'[3] But he was soon to find that with responsibilities came drudgery and boredom. 'I never worked less than ten hours and seldom more than fifteen per

[1] E. Kay Robinson, 'Kipling in India', *McClure's Magazine*, vii (1896), 100–1.

[2] *Something of Myself*, p. 39.

[3] Ibid., p. 40.

diem; and as our paper came out in the evening did not see the midday sun except on Sundays. I had fever too, regular and persistent, to which I added for a while chronic dysentery. Yet I discovered that a man can work with a temperature of 104, even though next day he has to ask the office who wrote the article.'[1]

In one sense, it was a harsher way of life than any Kipling had yet experienced: Edmund Wilson goes so far as to speak of 'these years . . . of newspaper work, with all their warping and thwarting influences', during which the young man 'worked his head off for a chief he detested'.[2] In India, however, Kipling responded to the strenuous conditions of his life and work in a way quite different from that of his earlier years. At Mrs. Holloway's and at school he had struggled to remain aloof from his surroundings: he had fought Aunty Rosa's efforts to break his spirit and had avoided becoming the hard-working, games-playing stereotype of the English public school boy; without undertaking an active rebellion, he had managed to steer an individual course. But when he returned to India, his attitude towards his surroundings underwent a change. It is evident from the general tenor of his autobiographical and fictional writings that he soon came to think of himself as an Anglo-Indian of the Anglo-Indians. 'My English years fell away, nor ever, I think, came back in full strength.' Documents from Kipling's first year or two in India — letters, diaries, and published writings — are so scarce that we cannot ascertain the reasons for this change. It may be that he had never felt at home in England, even among relatives and friends: his vivid recollection of Punch's sense of alienation suggests that he remained spiritually a foreigner on English soil. It may be that his being treated more or less as a peer by older men led him to adopt wholesale the values they espoused. It may be that reunion with

[1] *Something of Myself*, p. 41.

[2] Edmund Wilson, 'The Kipling That Nobody Read', in *The Wound and the Bow* (Boston, 1941), pp. 118, 114.

his family after so long a time reconciled the young man to the world in which his parents moved.

Whatever the reason or reasons may have been, we can discover his complex attitude towards Anglo-Indian life in an allegorical poem that he composed for the first English edition of *Departmental Ditties* (1890). It is called 'The Galley-Slave', and the galley is clearly India, with her wealth of goods and humanity, her constant threat of disease and death:

> Our bulkheads bulged with cotton and our masts were
> stepped in gold —
> We ran a mighty merchandise of niggers in the hold. . . .
>
> Our women and our children toiled beside us in the
> dark —
> They died, we filed their fetters, and we heaved them
> to the shark.

Even the Anglo-Indians' perpetual concern with the chance of another Mutiny is made part of the allegory:

> Yet they talk of times and seasons and of woe the
> years bring forth,
> Of our galley swamped and shattered in the rollers of
> the North;
> When the niggers break the hatches and the decks are
> gay with gore,
> And a craven-hearted pilot crams her crashing on the
> shore.

But Kipling strains his allegory to the limit, for this slave, instead of concluding with a song in praise of his new-found freedom, looks back on his servitude with nostalgia and regret:

> It may be that Fate will give me life and leave to
> row once more —
> Set some strong man free for fighting as I take awhile
> his oar.

But today I leave the galley. Shall I curse her
service then?
God be thanked! Whate'er comes after, I have lived
and toiled with Men!

In fact, once he had adapted himself to the fundamental axioms of Anglo-Indian society, Kipling never seriously questioned them. He may have found Lahore 'profoundly dull', as his father predicted, and he certainly found Stephen Wheeler a harsh and unsympathetic task-master, but when Kipling looked back at those years, it was with affection and a tough, stoic pride.

II

'This was the setting', Kipling wrote, 'in which my world revolved. Its centre for me — a member at seventeen — was the Punjab Club, where bachelors, for the most part, gathered to eat meals of no merit among men whose merits they knew well.'[1] These bachelors, the 'Men' of 'The Galley-Slave', held to the standards and beliefs of Anglo-Indian society in general, the axioms of thought and behaviour to which Kipling rapidly accommodated himself. If we are to understand Kipling's views of politics and society, we must begin by understanding British India; we must realize that Kipling thought and behaved like an Anglo-Indian, that he adapted himself to modes of thought and feeling which were in existence long before he arrived on the scene and which had come about through the action of great historical forces working over the course of centuries.

Anglo-Indian attitudes changed and developed from one generation to the next. Some of these changes were reflections of changing social conditions in England, while others were limited to India.[2] The Company's merchants,

[1] *Something of Myself*, pp. 42–43.

[2] I have relied for factual information about the British raj largely upon Alfred Comyn Lyall, *The Rise and Expansion of the British Dominion in India*, 5th ed. (London, 1910), and William H. Moreland and Atul

from the time of their arrival until around the middle of the eighteenth century, had established a way of life of their own; although they seldom troubled to learn the Indian vernaculars, they felt little racial or religious hostility towards the native inhabitants, who were their suppliers, customers, and sometimes nominal overlords. They adopted native customs when it suited them, smoked hookahs, drank arrack, and married or kept Indian women, for few Englishwomen went out to the East at that time. With no tradition of stunning military victories behind them, they had a solid respect for the power of the native princes.[1] Morally and religiously, these Nabobs shared the easy-going tolerance of their age.

Clive's conquest of Bengal brought about immense social changes. Faced with the necessity of governing millions of native subjects as well as waging war on the borders, the English found they could not simply place themselves at the head of the government; they felt themselves required to fill more and more of the administrative and judiciary posts from their own numbers. The resultant growth of the Anglo-Indian community was the greatest cause of the social changes that followed Plassey.[2] The newly arrived official was apt to have a wife and family who wanted only to reproduce on Indian soil the appearance and institutions of the English village.[3]

Chandra Chatterjee, *A Short History of India* (London, 1936). For social history I have followed, where possible, T. G. P. Spear, *The Nabobs: A Study of the Social Life of the English in Eighteenth Century India* (London, 1932). Other less useful books are: Hilton Brown, ed., *The Sahibs: The Life and Ways of the British in India as Recorded by Themselves* (London, 1948); Dennis Kincaid, *British Social Life in India, 1608–1937* (London, 1939); C. T. Buckland, *Sketches of Social Life in India* (London, 1884); and R. Pearson, *Eastern Interlude: A Social History of the European Community in Calcutta* (Calcutta, 1954).

[1] Kincaid, *British Social Life*, p. 199.

[2] Spear, *The Nabobs*, p. 142.

[3] Ibid., pp. 34 and 142. Cf. Buckland, *Sketches*, p. 2, where the author points with pride to the fact that 'over the whole length and breadth of India there is now a large and continually growing colony of

The Englishwoman neither wanted nor was allowed any contact with a native aristocracy that hid its own women from the view of strangers.[1] Her husband found he had a new and irrational source of fear: the notion of his family's danger at the hands of the natives he had known and respected before.[2]

With due allowance for the work of outstanding Anglo-Indians, we can begin at this period to trace the development of the melancholy pattern that was to characterize British India throughout the nineteenth century: the passage of time brought with it an increasing estrangement between the races. The general awakening of religious conscience in England around the end of the eighteenth century brought to India the first wave of missionary Evangelicalism. Before that time, the Company had succeeded in discouraging missionaries, viewing them as an unnecessary cause of friction between the rulers and their Hindu and Moslem subjects; but now, although the missionaries were unable to make many conversions among the natives, their denunciation of the local religions as ignorant and disgusting superstition served to strengthen the Anglo-Indians' growing sense of their own innate superiority.[3] The rulers could draw further conclusions from the corruption of the native magistrates. In order to eliminate that corruption, Lord

English families, who endeavour to maintain their old home feelings and to keep all those old surroundings which remind them of the land of their birth, to which they all hope in due course to return'.

[1] There was, moreover, 'no Indian "society" in the sense which the word bears in English', no 'numerous body of persons . . . meeting openly on the common ground of similarity of outlook on life, in religion and politics, in art and recreation'. Moreland and Chatterjee, *Short History*, pp. 362–3.

[2] Spear, *The Nabobs*, p. 141.

[3] It is easy to see in Kipling's dislike of missionaries the survival of a viewpoint that antedates the Evangelical movement. Religious enthusiasm never caught the Anglo-Indian imagination, though it led to a general reform of the manners and morals of the Nabob era. See Spear, *The Nabobs*, pp. 108–25; Kincaid, *British Social Life*, pp. 136–7, 177.

Cornwallis took the extreme step of closing the upper ranks of the judiciary to natives; he thereby sealed off the principal channel by which well-born Indians could achieve participation in the work of the Government. Thus, at the beginning of the nineteenth century the British community in India presented characteristics familiar to readers not only of Kipling but of E. M. Forster and other liberal critics of Empire. By and large, the rulers distrusted their subjects and held their abilities and traditions in contempt. Neither the Government nor English society provided any means for assimilating native Indians.[1]

Although racial distrust provided the background for the next hundred and fifty years of British rule, two new forces determined the course of Anglo-Indian history during the eighteen hundreds: the pressure of the Indians towards national unification with complete self-government and the countervailing pressure of the English national conscience towards more efficient and beneficent government of the Indians. At first the subjects seemed prepared to accept the benefits of subservience; in the 1830's, we are told, 'the attitude of those Indians who came into direct contact with Englishmen was receptive, and to some extent imitative, rather than critical or hostile'.[2] Characteristic of the reforming spirit of this period were such actions as the prohibition of suttee (1820), the revision of the Company's charter (1833), the suppression of the Thugs (1836), the abolition of slavery as a legally recognized institution (1843), and a growing concern with the establishment of native education and journalism. Yet it was considered an offence to the dignity of the Governor-General that

[1] 'The effect of the closing of the avenues of official and especially legal appointments was to drive the old governing classes into seclusion and to leave none but the clerk, the banian and the shroff to represent Indian character and culture to the average Englishman.' Spear, *The Nabobs*, p. 138.

[2] Moreland and Chatterjee, *Short History*, pp. 339–40.

Indians should be allowed to visit his house otherwise than on foot.[1] Similarly, the brilliant administrator Dalhousie provided India in the early 1850's with a postal service, the beginnings of a rail system, and the first thorough analysis of the needs and possibilities for universal free education.[2] And yet the Mutiny, the most savage racial conflict of Victorian times, followed hard upon Dalhousie's departure for England and can in part be attributed to his policies.

One cause of the Mutiny had been an uneasy sense on the part of the Indians that old cultural and religious values were under attack. Macaulay had predicted that, after a few generations of Western education, only skin-colour would distinguish an upper-class Indian from his English counterpart; but a century later Gandhi was to preach the rejection of Western culture, the return to a mythical golden age of unsoiled Hinduism. Reforms that seem nowadays and to us the most incontrovertibly humanitarian — the rescue of Hindu widows from slavery and degradation, for example, or the protection of child-brides by a raising of the age of consent — were successfully magnified by agitators into plots to subvert Hinduism itself. It is, in short, only too easy for us to see now that the Indians would be satisfied by nothing less than independence on their own terms, terms which seemed to the English to promise an immediate relapse into anarchy and barbarism.

Thus, Kipling returned in 1882 to an India which appears to have reached an impasse; there was nothing further for the Anglo-Indians to do but try to improve the efficiency of their government, veiling their growing uneasiness with an increasing reliance upon the undoubted material, and even moral, benefits of their regime. Ruler of India at that time was George Frederick Samuel Robinson, first Marquis of Ripon, Viceroy from 1880 to 1884. Scion of a wealthy and influential Whig family,

[1] Spear, *The Nabobs*, p. 140.

[2] Moreland and Chatterjee, *Short History*, pp. 354–9.

he had risen quickly to the rank of Lord President of the Council in Gladstone's 1868 cabinet. He was thoughtful, earnest, and idealistic: as a young man he had disturbed his Christian Socialist friends by writing a pamphlet they found too radical for publication, and in 1873 he caused Gladstone acute distress by becoming a Roman Catholic.[1] His predecessor in the Viceroyalty, the flamboyant Lord Lytton, had been one of the victims of Gladstone's Midlothian crusade; 'more Disraelian than his hated chief',[2] Lytton was the 'Great Ornamental' of a contemporary satirist, 'something floating loosely about in wide pantaloons and flying skirts, diffusing as he passes the fragrance of smile and pleasantry and cigarette'.[3] The man whom Gladstone called from political retirement to carry the ideals of Midlothian to India could hardly have supplied a greater contrast. No longer was the subcontinent to be governed 'by repressive measures and tinsel shows'.[4]

In some ways the early 1880's appeared to be a halcyon period for British India. The year 1881 saw the publication of two formal assessments of the Indian situation, both by distinguished and articulate Anglo-Indian administrators. R. C. Temple, criticized in some quarters for being over-optimistic, announced: 'Certainly I feel the pride which all Englishmen have felt on contemplating the wondrous achievements of our countrymen in the East. But if by optimism is meant the disposition to

[1] Before his conversion Ripon had been Grand Master of the English Freemasons and does not seem to have been entirely conscious of the antagonism between that organization and his new church; he was indeed a perplexing mixture of qualities. The standard biography is Lucien Wolf, *Life of the First Marquess of Ripon*, 2 vols. (London, 1921).

[2] Ibid. ii. 3.

[3] George Aberigh-Mackay, *Twenty-One Days in India*, 2nd ed. (London, 1880), p. 3.

[4] The words are Ripon's, quoted from manuscript sources by Sarvepalli Gopal, *The Viceroyalty of Lord Ripon: 1880–1884* (London, 1953), p. 117.

E

observe the bright parts only of the picture, and not its shadows, then I have no intention at all of being an optimist.'[1] The shadows, however, were in large measure the administrative problems to which the civil service was more and more devoting its attention. Temple never seriously questioned the right of the British to hold India nor the overall benefits of British rule.[2] And W. W. Hunter — eloquent, informed, and devotedly liberal — likewise found himself compelled to repudiate a charge of optimism. He wrote in the preface to a group of four lectures that the first two 'gave rise to a too favourable . . . view of our position'.[3] In order to counterbalance their effect, he lectured further on India's meagre food supply and the difficulty of maintaining good government without sufficient revenues: problems, once again, purely administrative rather than political or moral. Weighing the benefits of British rule, he draws his conclusion without hesitancy: 'If . . . we find that our countrymen have not failed in their splendid and difficult task; if we find that British rule in India means order in place of anarchy . . . then I think that Great Britain may with a firm heart continue to accept the great responsibility which has fallen to her, and that she may calmly face each new duty which that responsibility involves.'[4]

Is it entirely accurate, then, to say with Noel Annan that Kipling found upon his arrival in India 'a society which politically, nervously, physically, and spiritually quivered on the edge of a precipice'?[5] The answer

[1] Richard C. Temple, *India in 1880*, 3rd ed. (London, 1881), p. vi.

[2] Temple lists in his preface the causes for alarm that he discusses in the text. The majority deal with matters of agriculture, education, and the like. He refers in several places to native disaffection but discounts the possibility of another Mutiny, the only contingency that seems to occur to him. Ibid., pp. vi–viii *et passim*.

[3] William Wilson Hunter, *England's Work in India* (London, 1881), Preface.

[4] Ibid., p. 2.

[5] Noel Annan, 'Kipling's Place in the History of Ideas', *Victorian Studies*, iii (1960), 327–8.

depends on how one takes Professor Annan's words. In one sense they are quite true, though the British raj 'quivered' for nearly seventy years before going over the brink. The fact that conscientious Anglo-Indians were in 1880 largely unaware or contemptuous of the forces that were to drive them from India does not mean that those forces did not then exist. The Mutiny, whose spectre sometimes rose in their thoughts, had been a last gesture of the warriors and aristocrats of an older India. Modern Indian historians have tried to give it the colouring of a national revolt, but it would be fair to say that the nationalism it expressed was different in kind from the idea that motivated Gandhi generations later. That sort of nationalism was in 1880 in the process of becoming a weapon of the new and ignored middle-class intelligentsia, oriental cousin of the clerisy that had carved national states out of Imperial Europe not long before. No one but Wilfrid Scawen Blunt appears to have listened to the babus, and even he did not foresee that within two decades the Anglo-Indians would be forced to deal, not with disaffected princes and armed sepoys, but with revolutionary newspapers, home-made bombs, student riots, and all the other paraphernalia of a modern middle-class uprising.[1]

But the Anglo-Indians were unaware of the precipice that gaped beside them. Subject as individuals to severe anxiety concerning their health and careers, they were, as a social group, the opposite of anxious. On the contrary, Kipling's contemporaries are more apt to strike us

[1] Cf. Wilfrid Scawen Blunt, *Ideas about India* (London, 1885). Blunt visited India briefly in 1879, then more extensively in the winter of 1883–4. By that time relations had worsened under the impact of the Ilbert Bill controversy, but Blunt still was one of the very few to read the handwriting on the wall. The most enlightened Indian thinkers, he wrote, 'still trust to the English people [as distinguished from the Anglo-Indians] if they could only make them hear. But they are beginning to doubt the possibility of attracting their attention, and they are very nearly in despair' (p. 72).

as remarkably thick-skinned: it is not until somewhat later that we find symptoms of the imperialist malaise, the sense of frustration and discomfort that marks the British India of the twentieth century.[1] But if the Anglo-Indians ignored the great question of whether they had a right to be in India, they are not entirely to be blamed, for as a social group they had been sorted out and conditioned by the ineluctable processes of history: they were not in a position to exercise free choice. If one went to India as a visitor — a 'globe-trotter', in the contemptuous phrase of the Anglo-Indian — one could perhaps criticize objectively the axioms of British India. But once a man committed himself to the Anglo-Indian endeavour, as did Kipling, he found that the processes of history had determined for him a way of thinking and acting; he found himself caught up in the dilemmas of a century of British occupation with no hope of resolving them. Kipling took the old metaphor of the Ship of State and converted it, so to speak, from sail to steam: 'the first glimpse of the naked machinery of the Great Indian Government, stripped of its casings, and lacquer, and paint, and guard-rails, impresses even the most stupid man'.[2] One was, in other words, aboard a vast mechanical contrivance of admirable power and speed, but one could not hope to influence the vessel's course: one could only choose to disembark at one of the predetermined ports of call. Under such circumstances, it is small wonder that those who were committed to British India had no patience with critics who sided with Indian agitators against the principle of British dominion. If a man had to remain aboard such a vessel, he was better off admiring its power and speed than worrying about where it was going.

[1] Cf. Susanne Howe [Nobbe], *Novels of Empire* (New York, 1949), pp. 34–37. A brilliant study of the imperialist malaise is Archibald P. Thornton, *The Imperial Idea and Its Enemies: A Study in British Power* (London, 1959).

[2] 'Consequences' (9 December 1886).

III

The Marquis of Ripon had arrived in a season of hope. Educated Indians looked to Gladstone's representative for the foundation of a new order, for a redress of grievances still reparable by a humane and generous Government. Some of the rulers regretted that Lytton had been turned out of office, but the majority of the officials were aware of the failure of his regime. Afghanistan continued to smoulder. An enormous error in computing the cost of the Afghan campaigns destroyed Anglo-Indian confidence in the skill of the Viceroy's financial advisers. Had Lytton stayed on for a few months longer, however, his Afghan policy might have justified its sponsor, for Ripon arrived to inherit what appeared to be a rapidly improving situation and began his viceroyalty with a resounding success: General Roberts marched victoriously to Kandahar, and Abdurrahman, pro-English and strong enough to rule his kingdom, ascended the Afghan throne. With the glow of this success upon him, Ripon turned to social reform and before the end of 1882 had won the confidence of the Indians by instituting factory legislation and repealing Lytton's hated Vernacular Press Act. When young Rudyard Kipling stepped ashore on 18 October 1882, he returned to an India that seemed ready to justify the confidence of the Richard Temples and William Hunters.

In fact, the appearance of calm was illusory. Within a matter of months after Kipling's arrival British India was rent by a violent controversy that forced the young editor to take sides, to show publicly that he considered himself committed to the values of the average Anglo-Indian. For by the middle of 1882 Lord Ripon's forthright Liberalism had become a matter of concern to the more authoritarian elements of the British population, especially to the planters, who had a traditional antipathy to the civil service and its policy of unselfish and responsible government.[1] In 1882 one of the few Indians to have attained high rank in the civil service called attention to an anomaly in the judicial structure of the country. Although Indians were in theory guaranteed the right to compete against Europeans in the civil service, they were debarred from achieving full judicial authority outside the three Presidency towns, Bombay, Madras, and Calcutta. Specifically, they were not permitted to try Europeans in the provinces, the so-called 'Mofussil'. Each interested group viewed this provision of the law in a different light. To the aspiring Indian magistrate, it meant that he might be offered a post carrying a nominal advancement in salary and prestige, but in fact less authority than he enjoyed in an inferior position. To the legally minded civil servant, it represented a blemish on the intricate and otherwise consistent judicial system. To the more liberal European, it was not an anomaly so much as an injustice, a betrayal of the principle of equal opportunity without regard to colour. But to the majority of Anglo-Indians, the law guaranteed protection against falling into the hands of a member of an alien and hostile race, a race which treated its women as chattels, was susceptible to bribery, and had not yet learned to honour truth above all things. The privilege of trial by a European judge was of particular importance to the planters, who not only lived at great distances from centres of British authority but had in many cases given their Indian neighbours and employees cause to detest them.

Early in 1883 Ripon set out to remove what he considered an inconsistency from the Judicial Code. He consulted the heads of the provincial governments and found, surprisingly, that none of them anticipated any difficulty over the impending legislation. On 2 February Sir Courtenay Ilbert, Legal Member of the Council, presented a bill designed to bring about the necessary

[1] Cf. George Otto Trevelyan, *The Competition Wallah* (London, 1864), 'Letter X: The "Anglo-Saxon" Party in India', pp. 328–66.

changes in the judicial structure. Here was the opportunity Ripon's opponents had been waiting for. At first the planters, then soon the entire European community, rose up in horror and fury against the so-called Ilbert Bill. Before the end of the month there were angry rallies in Calcutta; 'I could hear', wrote Sir Mortimer Durand, 'from my room at Government House, and so could [Ripon], the shouts of applause and wrath at the Town Hall close by, where his opponents were denouncing him.'[1] Ripon found himself nearly alone. The Home Government supported him, as did some of his most powerful civilian colleagues, but for the most part the officials joined the planters in what amounted to an orgy of hysterical denunciation.

The Anglo-Indian press led the attack on the Viceroy, keeping public opinion in a state of constant agitation, and the *Civil and Military*'s young sub-editor found himself in the thick of the fight. 'Our paper, like most of the European Press, began with stern disapproval of the measure, and, I fancy, published much comment and correspondence which would now be called "disloyal".'[2] Stephen Wheeler was no Liberal; he later described the Indian agitator for home rule as a place-hunter, pure and simple, whose profession of lofty aims was merely a cover for his ambition to be employed by the Government in a profitable post.[3] But the *Pioneer*, so closely bound to the smaller *Civil and Military*, was in a vulnerable position. Wherever the sympathy of the proprietors might lie, the journal's success depended on its close links with government sources of information, links that Allen had had to pay large sums of money to establish.[4] The *Civil and Military Gazette* retreated, therefore, from its extreme

[1] Sir Mortimer Durand, *Life of the Right Hon. Sir Alfred Comyn Lyall* (Edinburgh, 1913), p. 280.

[2] *Something of Myself*, p. 50.

[3] Stephen Wheeler, 'Home-Rule for India', *Macmillan's Magazine*, lix (1888–9), 294.

[4] Barns, *The Indian Press*, p. 291.

position, and that night Kipling was hissed at the Punjab Club. 'It is not pleasant', he wrote later, 'to sit still when one is twenty while all your universe hisses you.'[1] Though it was soon pointed out to the offended members that Kipling had no responsibility for his paper's policies, it is clear from *Something of Myself* that the affair made a deep impression on the young man. 'The demonstration tailed off,' he wrote, 'but I had seen a great light. . . . I was a hireling, paid to do what I was paid to do, and — I did not relish the idea.'[2]

There is no indication, however, that Kipling was paid for any writing during that year which could be construed as being pro-Ripon. He succeeded in having five brief items printed in the *Civil and Military* during the autumn of 1883, and all of them snipe in one way or another at liberal attitudes.[3] He began in August with 'Lord Truro and Indian Crime' (9 August 1883), a sarcastic paragraph directed against a speech in the House of Lords that appears to have claimed that habitual criminals in India were motivated by starvation and misery; then he turned in 'The Dasera Festival' (2 October) and admonished the natives of Lahore for the element of childish display in their religious processions. Later in the month he exploded a pair of squibs under the Viceroy, then concluded his prose work for the year with a brief attack on William Morris's socialism.[4] The last of these items becomes more interesting than the others when we recall the strength of Kipling's Pre-Raphaelite associa-

[1] *Something of Myself*, p. 51. He was, in fact, only seventeen.

[2] Ibid., p. 51.

[3] We are able to identify these early 'scraps' because Kipling sent copies of them to Mr. Crofts at the United Services College. The Crofts Collection thus provides one of the most reliable means of identifying Kipling's early newspaper work.

[4] 'The Volcanic Explosion in Java' (2 October 1883) and 'The Vice-Regal Tour in Cashmere' (16 October 1883) poke fun at the Viceroy; the Morris piece is 'William Morris's Poem "The Day is Coming"' (7 November 1883).

tions. Morris, he wrote, has only the vaguest idea of the London workman, seeing him 'as through a rose-coloured glass, darkly'. 'He sketches . . . the millennium, when everybody's property shall belong to everyone else; when there shall be no trade competition — as a pushing and energetic manufacturer of carpets and stained glass, Mr. Morris's sentiments on this head seem scarcely natural; — and nobody shall become richer than his neighbour.' Morris publishes 'the haziest of programmes. . . . He tells us — *apropos* [*sic*] to nothing at all — that "o'er the weltering tangle, a glimmering light is shed". It would need far more than a glimmering light to unravel the "weltering tangle" of Mr. Morris's verse.' Now the Viceroy of India was no Socialist, but the animus of this short review indicates the young Kipling's need to assert his loyalty to the conservative ideals that were in the ascendancy throughout his little world during that critical season.

After nearly a year of strife and bitterness Lord Ripon and his supporters capitulated, and in January 1884 a compromise was reached and a modified form of the Bill, innocuous enough to satisfy Anglo-Indian opinion, was passed. The Viceroy had not been well advised by his subordinates, men whose experience should have led them to predict the opposition of the European community, but at the same time Ripon did not possess the strength of character needed to ride out the storm. The effects of the controversy, however, did not end with the Viceroy's defeat: the Indians soon realized not only that a limit had been set to the amount of responsibility they would be allowed to attain, but also that the Government could not muster enough power to overcome a group determined to employ all the resources of riot and violence in order to achieve its purposes. The Europeans demonstrated to the Indians how to resist authority; the Indians learned their lesson quickly and well.[1]

[1] Sarvepalli Gopal, *The Viceroyalty of Lord Ripon* (London, 1953), pp. 165–6.

Kipling claimed that the Ilbert Bill controversy had revealed to him the extent to which the Government could control the lives of its servants: 'I followed under shrewd guidance, often native, the many pretty ways by which a Government can put veiled pressure on its employees in a land where every circumstance *and* relation of a man's life is public property.'[1] In view of the Government's defeat, it would be odd if this were all he had learned. Rather, I think we may conclude that the Bill's chief effect upon Kipling was to confirm his commitment to the views of the Punjab Club: views which he saw no reason to abandon later in his life. Towards the end of 1884, when Ripon was about to leave India to make way for Lord Dufferin, his successor, the young sub-editor found in the occasion his first opportunity to publish the sort of political verse that was to add so much to his later fame. Lord Ripon is imagined musing — in the metre of 'Locksley Hall' — upon his departure:

> I shall leave it in a little — leave it ere my turn has run,
> Of the millions that I govern who will wish me back? Not one.
> Curse the land and all within it. As of old, the papers scoff —
> Dreary columns of invective, read by stealth at Peterhoff. . . .
> Yes! I see you [Dufferin] old and soured (as you will be in a year),
> Playing skittles, just as I did, with the rights men hold most dear.[2]

Even fifty years later Kipling's mature judgment echoes the newspaper rhetoric of his youth: Ripon becomes 'a circular and bewildered recluse of religious tendencies', and his ideals, 'Liberal "principle", which so far as I have observed ends not seldom in bloodshed'.[3] As far as we know, Kipling had been virtually without political

[1] *Something of Myself*, p. 52.
[2] 'Lord Ripon's Reverie', 15 September 1884.
[3] *Something of Myself*, pp. 49–50.

views before his arrival in India.[1] Less than a year later, the Punjab Club had become the centre of his world; the view from that centre had become his view, and it was to remain his for the rest of his life.

1 The first of his patriotic poems, 'Ave Imperatrix', has been cited as an example of Kipling's early bent, but he spoke in many voices: there is no reason to believe that that particular verse represents a confirmed position. Cf. Carrington, *Rudyard Kipling*, p. 40, and Beresford, *Schooldays*, pp. 104–5 and 289–93. It is clear that Professor Ferguson erred in blaming Kipling's later political views on the United Services College, which he claims to have 'instilled in Kipling-Beetle the whole law and gospel of the Tories'. See J. De Lancey Ferguson, 'The Education of Rudyard Kipling', *Education*, xlv (1924), 179–80.

3. Digressions from Office Work

I

KIPLING's new sense of membership in the Anglo-Indian community had various effects on his career as a writer. Sooner or later, for example, he was to realize the potential value of British India as a subject for fiction; he would then set himself the task of showing the Anglo-Indians to themselves in his stories. But an earlier and equally profound consequence of his return to India is to be discovered in his poetry — specifically, in the differences between the Pre-Raphaelite experiments of 'Sundry Phansies' and the self-assured light verse of *Departmental Ditties*. Among the many reasons for such a drastic change in style and intention, none seems more important than the alteration of Kipling's relationship to his audience. As a schoolboy, Kipling had shown an awareness of three separate audiences, each with its influence on the kind of poetry he wrote: he had published light verse for the readers of the school newspaper, had sent poetic exercises to his parents in Lahore, and had written love poems for Florence Garrard. Now that all his readers were either very much nearer or very much farther away, Kipling had to make adjustments in his attitude towards them, and these adjustments helped determine the kind of poet he eventually became.

Rudyard's love for Florence Garrard had culminated in some sort of informal engagement, but their understanding did not long survive Kipling's departure, for Florence wrote to break the engagement in the early summer of 1884.[1] Kipling seems to have realized all along that he

[1] Charles Carrington, *Rudyard Kipling: His Life and Work* (London, 1955), p. 55.

and Florence had nothing to look forward to, but the actual parting was a shock and put an end to the love poetry that had been so characteristic a feature of 'Sundry Phansies'. After the summer of 1884 Kipling's verse reflects his lack of an emotional attachment. He flirted at Simla, for he was a susceptible young man. His friend Robinson reports that 'Kipling was never without friends of the other sex' and adds that 'intellectual women, who are proportionately numerous in India, were especially fond of his society': soon he would be drawn into the world of Mrs. Hauksbee and her circle.[1] And even before the rift with Florence, he was celebrating less passionate attachments in such graceful verse as the following lines to 'A. E. W.':

> There is one greeting for all —
> One salutation,
> When Birds flit or Flowers fall,
> Or the Maid quits the Station:—
> Come back, with the cooler Spring Wind,
> For the land lieth lonely;—
> Come back — for ye leave us behind
> Sweet memories only.[2]

---

[1] E. Kay Robinson, 'Kipling in India: Reminiscences by the Editor of the Newspaper on Which Kipling Served at Lahore', *McClure's Magazine*, vii (1896), 109.

[2] Untitled poem in Kipling's autograph, dated 14 February 1884. It is reproduced in the *Sale Catalogue of the G. M. Williamson Collection* (New York: Anderson Galleries cat. 1140, 1915), p. 16. Unable to locate the manuscript, I have emended 'dand' to 'land' in the sixth line; Kipling's 'l's' are like 'd's'. 'A. E. W.' is probably Evelyn Welford; if so, two related items are the following: (1) 'Saint Valentine his Day. To You.' Verse letter in Kipling's autograph, sent to Miss Welford before 1884; the manuscript is at the Pierpont Morgan Library. (2) 'The Memory of a Maiden's Sympathy.' Autograph poem of three stanzas in a copy of *Echoes* inscribed 'Evelyn, from R. K. Sept. 1884'; reproduced in facsimile in Maggs Bros. cat. 200 (London, 1918). See James McG. Stewart, *Rudyard Kipling: A Bibliographical Catalogue* (Toronto, 1959), pp. 15, 529.

Under the influence of distance and novelty, the spell cast by Florence Garrard was breaking.

After a separation of some four years, Rudyard was now reunited with his family; between the ages of seventeen and twenty-two he lived with his parents in Lahore, where his sister Trix joined him in 1884. Thus, for five years Kipling was exposed to a group of strong and distinct personalities, all of whom were keenly interested in his artistic development.

In a number of ways Lockwood and Alice Kipling stood apart from their Anglo-Indian contemporaries. A member of the Indian Educational Service, Lockwood was a talented specialist who could not easily be fitted into the tripartite Anglo-Indian scheme of civilian, military, and commercial; his vocation — to acquaint the Indian peoples with their own traditional arts and crafts — further distinguished him from most of his colleagues, whose goal was to impose upon India the culture of Europe. Nor was Alice content to play the role of the conventional mem-sahib. Like her husband, she wrote for local newspapers; and her satiric wit — the source of such uneasiness to her family in England — gave delight to the predominantly masculine society of the hill-stations, a society in which Alice was to make a notable mark. 'They both, from the first, took a very intelligent interest in everything connected with the people and country', a friend of those days wrote later, 'and even in their Bombay days were better informed on all matters Indian — religion, customs, and peculiarities — than many officials who had been long in the country.'[1] If Lockwood was an acknowledged expert on Indian crafts and customs, Alice surely had her own sphere of expertise: the ballrooms of Simla that Rudyard later came to know so well. For one whose lifelong concern was to know, to see the world around him with new eyes, to penetrate the surface of things, to speak the language, Kipling's

[1] John Harry Rivett Carnac, *Many Memories of Life in India, at Home and Abroad* (Edinburgh, 1910), p. 226.

parents could hardly have been better suited, by temperament and accomplishments, as guides.

And yet, though Kipling's parents assisted his intellectual growth to an incalculable extent, it is easy to exaggerate the benefits he derived from living with them. The tone of the household, one imagines, was strenuous. Lockwood's immense sympathy and charm are attested by a number of acquaintances: one young man remembered him as 'without exception, the most delightful companion I had ever met', and another guest doubted 'if I ever enjoyed walks and talks with any man as much as those I had with him'. Mrs. Kipling made a rather different impression: what her guests remembered was not so much her sympathy as her 'sprightly, if occasionally caustic wit', 'her quickness of intellect and skill in selecting striking phrases'.[1] She was, in her brother's words, 'keen, quick, and versatile beyond anyone I have known, saw things at a glance, and dispatched them in a word'. Lockwood's mind, by way of contrast, 'moved more slowly, and was patient and meditative to a degree that for her was impossible'.[2] Evidently the tense, rebellious Alice Macdonald had developed into a brilliant and formidable matron, unwilling to play a passive role either in society or amongst the members of her family.

In 1881, when Rudyard was just turning fifteen, Alice had written to her friend Miss Plowden: 'Ruddy thirsts for a man's life with man's work & if our plan be carried out he will get both when he is eighteen.'[3] The plan had indeed been carried out, but Rudyard was by no means as independent as Alice's words would seem to imply. Two months before his wife's letter to Miss Plowden,

[1] Kay Robinson, 'Kipling in India', pp. 99–100; and J. C. Rimington, 'Westward Ho Reminiscences', *Kipling Journal*, no. 59 (Oct. 1941), 12–13.

[2] Frederic William Macdonald, *As a Tale That Is Told* (London, 1919), p. 115.

[3] Quoted in Arthur Windham Baldwin, *The Macdonald Sisters* (London, 1960), p. 128.

Lockwood had written to Cormell Price, Rudyard's headmaster, in quite different terms. He claimed that India would present few temptations to a young man, particularly a young man living at home with his parents; then, rather surprisingly, he expressed his 'dread' of a 'breakout' on 'the moral side' — a fear lest Rudyard prove unequal to whatever temptations Lahore might have to offer.[1] What sort of 'breakout' the Kiplings dreaded is difficult to conceive. But we must recall that, although they had abandoned the Methodist piety of their parents, Lockwood and Alice Kipling could by no stretch of the imagination be labelled Bohemians. Like so many of their Victorian contemporaries, they possessed an earnestness that outlived the religious faith of their childhood. Whether it was Rudyard's attachment to Florence that dismayed them or merely his laziness in school, they were determined to watch over him with kind but firm solicitude.

Nor was their concern merely for the moral side of Rudyard's nature: they were equally determined to foster his literary career with co-operation and advice. Near the end of his life, Kipling wrote: 'I think I can with truth say that those two made for me the only public for whom then I had any regard whatever till their deaths, in my forty-fifth year.'[2] With all respect to Kipling's own judgment, we must nevertheless recognize the disadvantages to a young writer of having to exercise his talents under the constant supervision of such accomplished parents. If Rudyard needed a line of poetry, his mother could supply it; if he wanted the details of an Indian ceremony or costume, his father could advise him; and if he wrote a story too close to the edge of

[1] Quoted in Sotheby's *Catalogue of Nineteenth-Century and Modern First Editions*, Sale of 30 November and 1 December 1964 (London, 1964), p. 93. This and other letters in the series express Lockwood's worry about his son's desultory and easy-going ways; journalism, he thought, might help to cure Rudyard's bad habits.

[2] *Something of Myself*, 'Library Edition' (London, 1951), p. 89.

impropriety, he was willing to let his mother suppress it.[1] Indeed, Lockwood and Alice were so close to their son that they became, from time to time, participants in the creative process rather than commentators and observers; not only did the family collaborate on a number of publications, but they shared devices of style that have raised numerous difficulties in the attribution of unsigned newspaper pieces.[2] 'The Mother was at hand', Kipling wrote in his autobiography, 'with now and then some shrivelling comment that infuriated me. But, as she said: "There's no Mother in Poetry, my dear."'[3] If we may be permitted to shift the sense of her words, however, it can be claimed that there was a good deal too much Mother in Kipling's life and poetry at this time: the parents, for all their good intentions, were not making it easy for Kipling to develop a young man's proper independence. Though he never admitted it, Kipling needed a critical audience beyond the family circle: a symptom of his dissatisfaction, perhaps, is that not long after his arrival in India he began to send his work home to his former teacher William Crofts, who had always treated Rudyard's literary pretensions with good-humoured derision.

Thus, Kipling found that his position with respect to his two private audiences had changed significantly as a result of his return to India. With respect to his public audience the change was even more important. To be sure, the group at the Punjab Club, the readers of the *Civil and Military*, stood in somewhat the same relation

[1] Ibid., pp. 72, 89–90.

[2] Among the pieces whose authorship is in dispute may be cited a number of the 'Plain Tales from the Hills' that appeared in the *Civil and Military* during 1886 and 1887: these include 'Love-in-a-Mist' (2 November 1886); 'Love: A "Miss"' (26 November); and 'A Pinchbeck Goddess' (10 December). For evidence as to the authorship of these and other pieces, see Appendix III, 'Kipling's Uncollected Newspaper Writings', below.

[3] *Something of Myself*, p. 206.

to his poetry as had his acquaintances at school: they were prepared to be amused by witty newspaper verses but were hardly the audience for 'By the Sea' or 'Paul Vaugel'; in order to please them Kipling had only to continue a line of development he had already established through his contributions to the U.S.C. *Chronicle*. And yet, such a development could not have been entirely satisfying to the young man. In the first place, his attitude towards his Anglo-Indian readers was quite different from his attitude towards his Westward Ho! schoolmates. At school his impulse had been away from the conventional, whether conventional behaviour took the form of skill at games or devotion to Latin and mathematics; holding his schoolmates in low esteem, he published what suited him without caring whether or not they admired it. Publication in the *Pioneer* or the *Civil and Military* was not to be taken so lightly. Even Kipling's factual reporting was subject to rigorous scrutiny by his elders; as he recalled many years later, 'I was almost nightly responsible for my output to visible and often brutally voluble critics at the Club. They were not concerned with my dreams. They wanted accuracy and interest, but first of all accuracy.'[1] We have seen that Kipling was quick to adopt the political views of those about him: we may assume that when he wrote for either of the two Anglo-Indian papers, he was acutely concerned with the impression he was making upon the Punjab Club.

In the second place, now that his private audience was so drastically changed, Kipling began to search for a way to synthesize his private and public writings. If his poetic impulse could no longer be satisfied by writing love poems for Florence and exercises for the approval of his mother, then he would have to find a way to adapt his talent to his Anglo-Indian audience. If he could not pursue the line of development that had led to 'Sundry Phansies', he would have to experiment until he found

[1] *Something of Myself*, p. 205.

a new line that would satisfy both himself and the readers of the *Pioneer* and the *Civil and Military Gazette*.

II

A number of extant presentation copies of *Echoes*, published in November 1884, illustrate Kipling's uncertainty about the audience for whom he was writing. One of the little books went to Florence, but now that she had rejected its author she could not expect to be the only recipient of dedicatory verses. Into her copy went the following lines:

> I wrote you verses two years syne
> When I was yours and you were mine
> Will you accept these rhymes I send
> If I but call myself your friend
> And should my foolish songs discover
> Some traces of your girlhood's lover
> Forgive me — two long years apart
> Still leaves me [*sic*] mistress of my heart.[1]

Still suffering under Florence's recent change of heart, Kipling protested to his young aunt Edith Macdonald: 'I haven't sent you a line since you acknowledged the receipt of *Echoes* and so wildly mistook the dedication thereof. No dear I did *not* write those verses for Flo, and if I had should certainly not have sent you a duplicate.'[2] More than anyone else in the family, Edith had been Rudyard's confidante during his courtship of Florence: small wonder that she misunderstood the inscription he sent her —

[1] J. McG. Stewart reports the existence of 'a copy inscribed to "F. G. from R. K. Sept. 1884", with an autograph poem commencing "I wrote you verses two years syne"'. (*Bibliographical Catalogue*, p. 15.) I reproduce the lines from a typed copy in one of Flora V. Livingston's scrapbooks, now in the Houghton Library at Harvard University. Neither Stewart nor Mrs. Livingston gives the location of the manuscript.

[2] Quoted in Carrington, *Rudyard Kipling*, p. 58.

Though the 'Englishman' deride it,
Though the captious 'Statesman' chide it,
Your dear judgement shall decide it
Yours alone.
For the good that in each line is,
From the title page to Finis,
Is your own.[1]

A number of his other correspondents also received poems along with the books, and several of these have survived.

To 'the Ladies of Warwick Gardens' — the Misses Craik, with whom he and Trix had boarded in London — he wrote:

For even now, as then, we feel
The rhyming *brochure* we submit
Will reach, when you have studied it,
Our Court of Ultimate Appeal.[2]

He addressed the U.S.C. Common-Room in much the same vein:

Placetne, Domini? — in far Lahore
I wait your verdict, 'mid the palms and roses
Much as I did those judgments writ of yore
Upon my 'proses'.[3]

Nor did these three graceful — and almost identical — compliments complete the tale, for he gave his mother, away at that time on a visit to England, to understand that the book was for her alone:

Who is the Public I write for?
Men 'neath an Indian sky

[1] Quoted in Baldwin, *The Macdonald Sisters*, p. 226.

[2] Poem in Kipling's autograph in the flyleaf of a copy of *Echoes* in the Berg Collection, New York Public Library.

[3] 'Inscribed in a Presentation Copy of "*Echoes*" to the Common-Room', reprinted in the U.S.C. *Chronicle* on 27 March 1889 and in *Verse Early* (volume xvii of the 'Outward Bound Edition' of Kipling's works).

Cynical, seedy and dry
Are these then the people I write for?
No, not I.

How should they know whom I write for
Papers that praise me or scoff? —
More than six thousand miles off
Lives the dear Public *I* write for,
Under an English sky.[1]

There is a good deal of Kiplingesque humour in this proliferation of epistles dedicatory, but beneath it lies a fundamental uncertainty of intention — a real doubt about the identity of his public — that is reflected in the contents of the volume itself. These contents, for example, Rudyard treated as entirely his own in a number of the dedications, though *Echoes* was in fact a collaboration between himself and his sister, one of those joint efforts so characteristic of the family.[2] But the chief significance of *Echoes* is that it looks both backwards and forwards: it marks the dividing line between Kipling's juvenile verse and the beginning of his career as an Anglo-Indian poet. Verse that had been written two or more years earlier and either copied into 'Sundry Phansies' or put aside was here presented for the first time to the public, set forth side by side with the parodies — or 'echoes', as Rudyard and Trix preferred to call them — that made up the bulk of the volume. Since

[1] From a facsimile reproduction of the holograph poem, in Ellis Ames Ballard's *Catalogue Intimate and Descriptive of My Kipling Collection* (Philadelphia, 1935), p. 16.

[2] Completed in the summer holidays of 1884, when the family spent a month together at the hill-station of Dalhousie, *Echoes* was published anonymously in the autumn. As Trix wrote only eight of the thirty-nine poems in the original volume, Rudyard was justified in treating the book as his own. Fifteen years later he included 'Jane Smith', one of Trix's poems, in *Early Verse*; at that time, neither of the authors was very clear as to who had written what, but Trix's authorship of this poem is attested by a note in her handwriting in the copy of *Echoes* sent to the Misses Craik.

the poems were undated, readers would not have known that the echoes rather than the original verse represented a new phase of the young writer's career.

Of the poems culled from the manuscript book, only 'Failure' strikes a personal note. 'How the Day Broke', 'The Ballad of the King's Daughter', and 'How the Goddess Awakened' are objective and conventional — the reason, perhaps, why Kipling included them in a published volume. But some of the verses that postdate 'Sundry Phansies' recall the melancholy of his schoolboy lyrics:

Bear me with thee, O River —
 On the rush of thy flood to the sea —
I am sick of this smooth, green land;
 I long for the breeze off the sand.
Take me away with thee
To the shifting face of the sea,
 And the low, wind-bitten strand.
('Land-Bound' [1])

It's cruel seeking in London,
 Boundless London,
For a face that'll never come —
 For the face of a friend,
The face of my lost, lost friend,
 Lost in London.
There's no God in London,
 Your terrible London!
('London Town')

But these attempts to return to the state of mind of 1882, of schooldays, London, yearnings for Florence Garrard, stand as a valedictory to the earliest stage of Kipling's poetic development. We look in vain in later collections for that mournful seacoast and that recurring hopeless quest for an elusive love until we come to *The Light That*

[1] Kipling noted in a copy of *Echoes* that 'Land-Bound' had been written at school; see Stewart, *Bibliographical Catalogue*, p. 15

Failed, in which a much older Kipling revisits the beaches of Southsea and Westward Ho! and disposes of them once for all.

Echoes is usually referred to as a collection of parodies, and indeed seventeen of the poems are printed in the *Early Verse* volume of later collected editions with the names of the poets whose styles they mimic. Nevertheless, a distinction must be made if we are to perceive the importance of the echoes: Kipling is not treating parody as an end in itself; rather, he is using the imitative mode in order to achieve certain purposes of his own. In the melancholy schoolboy poems he first borrowed, and then assimilated, the techniques of his predecessors, with the aim of writing poetry in the nineteenth-century romantic tradition; in the echoes he is borrowing, but not assimilating, with the intention of freeing himself from that tradition.

Thus, the echoes may be said to begin in pure parody, but not to end there. 'The Flight of the Bucket' gives us the story of Jack and Jill in the style of *Sordello*: it is an amusing comment on Browning's ability to make a plain narrative unintelligible, but in substance it is nothing more than a verbal exercise. In most of the echoes Kipling's aim is less simple. Several of the poems, for example, use another writer's style to give distance to emotions that were probably Kipling's own at the time *Echoes* was written. 'Estunt the Griff', to which I have referred in an earlier chapter, not only imitates William Morris but surely describes Kipling's gloomy departure from England. 'His Consolation', though it claims to echo Browning, much more vividly suggests the rejected lover of Florence Garrard.

> So be it; you give me my release,
> And let me go. Yes, I am free.
> But think you that a love will cease
> By bidding merely? Can yon sea
> Stop at the tide's increase? . . .

You cannot, *cannot* understand?
  Go forward, then. The time will be
When, lip to lip and hand to hand,
  By some far-distant planet's sea
    We meet — and *I* command.

Browning may or may not be looking over the young poet's shoulder, but the emphasized words, the woman who cannot 'understand', the inevitable seaside are unmistakable legacies from 'Sundry Phansies'.[1]

But most of the poems in *Echoes* are neither pure parody nor devices for covertly presenting Kipling's personal woes; rather, they are adaptations of the style of well-known poets to Indian subjects and, as such, are Kipling's first Anglo-Indian writings in either verse or prose. Their most striking characteristic is their tough, sardonic tone. As if in reaction to the melancholy of his schoolboy love poems, Kipling here refuses to take himself seriously. Time after time he allows the fact that he is imitating a famous style to undercut the gravity of his subject; he confronts Anglo-Indian life, but indirectly rather than face to face.

At one extreme he writes bitter and amusing 'Nursery Rhymes for Little Anglo-Indians':

Sing a Song of Sixpence
  Purchased by our lives —
Decent English gentlemen
  Roasting with their wives

In the plains of India,
  Where like flies they die.
Isn't that a wholesome risk
  To get our living by?

Elsewhere his motives are not quite so simple. Tennyson's 'Vision of Sin', for example, becomes 'A Vision of India':

[1] But compare Ann M. Weygandt, *Kipling's Reading and its Influence on His Poetry* (Philadelphia, 1939), p. 107.

Mother India, wan and thin,
  Here is forage come your way;
Take the young Civilian in,
  Kill him swiftly as you may. . . .

Brown and Jones and Smith shall die;
  We succeed to all their places,
Bear the badge of slavery,
  Sunken eyes and pallid faces.

Laughter that is worse than tears
  Is our portion in the land,
And the tombstones of our peers
  Make the steps whereon we stand.

The parody of Tennyson's 'Vision' is not especially important, nor is the poem meant to be funny; the speaker is making an assertion about his own ability to face the dangers of Indian life without flinching, and the element of parody has become a rhetorical device to heighten our sense of the speaker's lack of 'poetic' sentiment about life and death. It is as if Kipling were turning back to the adolescent cynicism of *Schoolboy Lyrics*, bypassing the sentimentalities of the intervening 'Sundry Phansies'. At the other extreme from the 'Nursery Rhymes' is 'Laocoon', which is supposed to echo Matthew Arnold:

So, under Indian skies,
Compassed by many ills,
Weary workers abide,
Neither joyed nor afraid
Waiting the unseen doom.
Only, at times, when a friend
Falls at their side and is lost
Out of his place in their life,
Lift they their hearts aloft,
Crying aloud: 'If a God
Govern the ways of men,

Spare us this last for a space —
Not for ourselves, indeed,
Seeing that this is our right,
But for our children and wives!'

Parody has all but vanished from these lines. Read in isolation, they might be taken for the work of a serious Anglo-Indian poet under the influence of Arnold's tone and style; but elsewhere in the poem Kipling betrays the fact that he is still 'echoing', and 'Laocoon' is thereby shifted back in the direction of parody. The ultimate effect is not of sober concern but of the bravado we find in 'A Vision of India' and throughout *Echoes*. If we re-examine the dedicatory verses, we can see through Kipling's assertions about his imagined audience.

Who is the Public I write for?
Men 'neath an Indian sky
Cynical, seedy and dry
Are these then the people I write for?

The answer, I think, must be 'Yes'. The attitude Kipling adopts towards life and death in India — an attitude sustained by the element of parody in his poems — is clearly a reflection of the tough, humorous talk he heard at the Punjab Club; and the echoes are designed, at least in part, to show the 'brutally voluble critics at the Club' that the youngest member is a sophisticated and amusing yokefellow.

A friendly reviewer greeted *Echoes* in the January 1885 issue of the *Calcutta Review* as 'a most quaint, original and altogether charming little volume of Anglo-Indian verse'. The critic, evidently more impressed with the anonymous authors' youth than their sophistication, may have surprised Rudyard and Trix with the fatuity of his remarks: 'What particularly phenomenal children these two little ones must be. The surroundings of child-life in India are, as a rule, sad, monotonous, and prosaic enough, not very rich, we should imagine, in materials for humorous verses. But sunny natures can throw sunshine on the gloomiest and dullest aspects of their surrounding circumstances.'[1] But in spite of the patronizing tone of his first review, Kipling was delighted at being welcomed to the ranks of Anglo-Indian poets. 'Saw very good review in Calcutta review of Echoes', he noted in his diary, 'wh. pleased me highly.'[2]

III

As *Echoes* marked Rudyard Kipling's debut as an Anglo-Indian poet, it remains to discover what status poetry had in the British India of the 1880's. Kipling's immediate public may have been the Punjab Club and the *Civil and Military*'s subscribers, but what of the wider audience his poems were soon to reach? To what Anglo-Indian poetic tradition could he attach himself?

The circumstances of the British in India were hostile to literature. The reading public was scattered throughout an enormous area: no one city could fill the role of an Anglo-Indian cultural centre, where theatres, universities, and publishing enterprises could stimulate enthusiasm for the arts. Nor was there any place in the structure of Anglo-Indian society for the independent, self-supporting artist; such imaginative writings as did appear in local newspapers and magazines were contributed by men whose lives were professionally dedicated to some other calling, to governing a province or editing a daily paper. Holding themselves aloof from the life of India, the British found themselves neither mere visitors nor bona fide residents. Cut off from the indigenous culture, unable to form a rich and varied culture of their own, the Anglo-Indians could hardly have been in a worse position to cultivate the arts.

Nor did the Anglo-Indians constitute the kind of reading public favourable to the writing of distinguished poetry. To be sure, Kipling's friend Robinson could

[1] Anonymous review of *Echoes*, *Calcutta Review*, lxxx (1885), p. lv.

[2] Kipling's manuscript diary for 1885 is in the Houghton Library.

label them 'the most cultured audience to which an English writer can appeal'. As he pointed out, 'In Anglo-India there are no uneducated readers, for ninety-nine per cent of the men out there have passed difficult competitive examinations to get there.'[1] But another contemporary of Kipling's, also arguing in defence of his fellows, lets slip a revealing phrase; the civil servants are, in his words, 'the best educated bureaucracy in the world'.[2] Whatever their educational qualifications, bureaucrats are not noted for enthusiastic patronage of the arts.

One of the few men with the credentials to judge the intellectual climate of British India left no doubt of his opinion. In 1856, just after his arrival in Calcutta, Alfred Comyn Lyall wrote to his family: 'I have no talents that would be of use out here, where a man of business gets on best, and where, as a very clever man told me a few days ago, any acquaintance with books is not the slightest use.'[3] Fortunately for his career — and for India — Lyall had a wider range of talents than he was willing to admit; he rose to a position near the summit of the administrative hierarchy and retired full of honours. But unlike his fellow bureaucrats he also pursued a literary career: besides a distinguished history of the British conquest of India, he was the author of one of the better volumes of Anglo-Indian verse and was called upon to contribute a study of Tennyson to the 'English Men of Letters' series. In spite of his many successes, however, Lyall never changed the opinion he had formed on his arrival. 'No situation', he wrote in 1899, 'more unfavourable to the development of imaginative literature could be found than that of a few thousand Europeans isolated, far from home, among millions of

[1] 'Kipling in India', p. 109.

[2] Arnold Wright, *Baboo English as 'Tis Writ: Being Curiosities of Indian Journalism* (London, 1891), p. 10.

[3] Quoted in Sir Mortimer Durand, *Life of the Right Hon. Sir Alfred Comyn Lyall* (Edinburgh, 1913), p. 33.

Asiatics entirely different from them in race, manners, and language.' 'Cut off from the culture which is essential to the growth of art and letters', he explained, few of the overworked civilians 'have either leisure or inclination for that picturesque side of things which lies at the source of most poetry and romance'.[1] We need not accept Lyall's old-fashioned emphasis on the picturesque in order to admit the force of his indictment: that for the most part the Anglo-Indians were highly competent Philistines, too busy running the affairs of a continent to give much thought to the life of the mind.

Lyall's pessimism is borne out by the poetry of Kipling's Anglo-Indian predecessors and contemporaries.[2] Since the days of Sir William Jones and the revival of Sanskrit studies, there had always been a few enthusiasts for Indian culture whose poetic output ranged from scholarly translations of the epics to Sir Edwin Arnold's *Light of Asia*; but it is fair to say that most Anglo-Indians found the literature of their subjects as tedious and obscure in English translation as in the original Sanskrit.[3] Lyall himself tried to break new ground by putting Browning-esque monologues into the mouths

[1] 'The Anglo-Indian Novelist', in his *Studies in Literature and History* (London, 1915), p. 121. (The essay first appeared in the *Edinburgh Review* in October 1899.)

[2] I am indebted in this section to two works by Edward Farley Oaten: *A Sketch of Anglo-Indian Literature* (London, 1908) and 'Anglo-Indian Literature', *CHEL*, xiv. 331–42.

[3] I do not intend to minimize the splendid work of certain Anglo-Indians in helping to recover the treasures of Indian culture and history; this is set forth in Sir Atul Chandra Chatterjee's *British Contributions to Indian Studies* (London, 1943), and represents one of the most sympathetic chapters in the story of Indo-British relations. Nevertheless, such scholarly pursuits were nearly always undertaken by individual amateurs in the face of adverse general opinion, opinion that ranged from the outright hostility of some missionaries through the self-confident insularity of Macaulay's famous Minute on education to the good-natured satire of Kipling's 'Wressley of the Foreign Office'.

of native Indians, but the absence of any imitators testifies to the fact that his Anglo-Indian readers preferred not to take their Oriental neighbours quite so seriously.[1] For the rest, poets wrote about British India; and by far their favourite theme was homesickness for England. In 'Aliph Cheem's' *Lays of Ind*, a book of predominantly humorous verse, there are four of these 'exile's laments'; John Leyden had struck the tone as early as 1805; Lyall fitted his 'Land of Regrets' to the tune of Swinburne's 'Dolores'; and Kipling, leafing through files of Anglo-Indian newspapers, discovered that the Company's anonymous young factors had spoken the same language at the end of the eighteenth century.[2] One of the sad ironies of the British raj is that nearly two hundred years of triumph and suffering produced in the realm of poetry little more than sentimental effusions of *Heimweh*.

Writers of satiric verse did not face such serious obstacles. Though Anglo-Indian official society lacked culture, it had homogeneity and a certain stability of shared aims and assumptions: fruitful conditions for the writing of satire. All over India Englishmen were doing the same kind of work under similar conditions; they had been prepared for their careers in similar ways, looked forward to, or had passed through, the same grades of the civilian or military hierarchy, lived in similar houses in similar towns and villages, suffered from the same maladies and discomforts, spiritual and

[1] Sir Alfred Comyn Lyall, *Verses Written in India* (London, 1889); see especially 'Meditations of a Hindu Prince', 'The Old Pindaree', 'The Amir's Message', and 'A Sermon in Lower Bengal'.

[2] See 'The Letter from Home', 'The Benedict's Dream', 'Homeward Bound', and 'A Christmas Reverie' in 'Aliph Cheem' [pseud. of Walter Yeldham], *Lays of Ind*, 6th ed. (Calcutta, 1879); 'Ode to an Indian Gold Coin' in *The Poetical Works of John Leyden* (Edinburgh, 1875); 'Land of Regrets' in Lyall, *Verses Written in India*; and Rudyard Kipling, 'Departmental Ditties', in *My First Book*, ed. Jerome K. Jerome (London, 1894), p. 95.

physical. Thus work — the civilizing mission of the English — had for many of Kipling's contemporaries a nearly mystical importance; for that very reason its ministers were made to serve as butts for ridicule.[1] All Anglo-Indians were uncomfortably aware of the Government and its power; it, too, was made ridiculous in consequence. Anglo-Indians were supposed to be concerned with the misfortunes and strivings of their native subjects: hence, 'Aliph Cheem' and his like could earn widespread popularity by holding up for general laughter the pretensions of 'Rajah Kistnamah Howdie Doo', 'Cardozo, the Half-Caste', and 'The Sensitive Fakeer'. Dedication, in other words, walked hand in hand with triviality, because all knew that the comic versifier at bottom accepted the axioms of his society. When readers laughed, it was with the laughter of good fellowship, not savage mockery, for British India produced no Swift, no satirist so profoundly disturbed by the very basis of Anglo-Indian life that he was prepared to abandon the whole affair in favour of a new and Houyhnhnm-like social order. In view of the prevalence of satire, the absence of such a figure is a trifle surprising; perhaps the explanation is simply that all had too large a stake in things-as-they-were; it was easier for the fundamentally dissatisfied to pack up and go home.

Viewed against the background of British India's poetic tradition, then, *Echoes* can be seen as the first product of Kipling the Anglo-Indian writer: by abandoning the lyric style of his schooldays and devoting himself to light verse, Kipling placed himself in the main stream of Anglo-Indian poetry. As he later took pains to point

[1] Compare Susanne Howe [Nobbe], *Novels of Empire* (New York, 1949), p. 73. The influence of the Utilitarians on British policy in India has long been recognized; but in the Punjab (and elsewhere) during Kipling's time Carlyle's Gospel of Work seems to have been in the ascendancy. Perhaps late nineteenth-century India was one of the last battlegrounds of those great Victorian antagonists, Carlyle and Mill: the matter deserves further investigation.

out, he was the heir of a tradition dating back to the times of Hickey's *Bengal Gazette*. 'I was in very good company', he wrote, 'for there is always an undercurrent of song, a little bitter for the most part, running through the Indian papers. . . . Forty years ago, the men sang of just the same subjects as we did — of heat, loneliness, love, lack of promotion, poverty, sport, and war.'[1] It is possible to find analogues to nearly all of Kipling's Anglo-Indian light poems in such a book as *Lays of Ind*, but it would be a waste of effort to hunt sources in the face of Kipling's testimony as to the range and ubiquity of his predecessors.[2]

IV

Elsewhere in the same essay — a memoir of the genesis of *Departmental Ditties* — Kipling describes the form his poetic impulse took during his Indian years. 'All my verses', he wrote, 'were digressions from office work. They came without invitation, unmanneredly, in the nature of things; but they had to come, and the writing out of them kept me healthy and amused.'[3] Kipling's words recall his friend Beresford's descriptions of the ease with which his schoolmate wrote verses, but we must not take Kipling's self-deprecatory remarks at face value, for even within the confines of light verse he shows a substantial development in art and skill between *Echoes* and the first of the 'Departmental Ditties'. His earliest Indian poems lack satirical force and narrative structure; the poems that did not appear in *Echoes* attempt merely to display an attitude or characterize a

[1] Kipling, in *My First Book*, p. 95.

[2] The same sense of homogeneity is conveyed by an anonymous contemporary article: 'Some Anglo-Indian Poets', *The University Magazine* (Dublin), v (May 1880), 513–24. The poets dealt with are just such anonymous newspaper versifiers as those Kipling describes. See also Oaten, *A Sketch*, chap. v, 'Humorous and Satiric Verse'.

[3] Kipling, in *My First Book*, p. 92.

well-known feature of Anglo-Indian life. '"The May Voyage"' (23 May 1884) and 'The Descent of the Punkah' (10 October 1884), for example, have no other motive than to celebrate the arrival and departure of the hot weather. 'The Story of Tommy' (29 September 1884), which describes the crime and death of a young soldier, is indeed a narrative, but it deals superficially with a way of life in which an older Kipling was to find the materials for comedy and tragedy. Although the poem distantly foreshadows the soldier stories and *Barrack-Room Ballads*, Kipling seems to have judged it an unsuccessful experiment, for he avoided making another attempt at such a subject for three years. Instead, he contented himself with an occasional amused glance at Anglo-Indian courtship and love ('The Moon of Other Days', 'To the Unknown Goddess', 'My Rival'); with good-humoured criticism of the Government ('"Laid Low"', 'Lord D–ff–r–n's Clôture'); and with the conventional sentiments evoked by memories of dead comrades and thoughts of Home ('Possibilities', 'In Springtime').

In 1885, during the long summer at Simla, Kipling hit upon the notion of writing a series of comic verses for the *Pioneer*, the journal which had published most of his miscellaneous poetry of the previous winter and spring. He gave the series the title of 'Bungalow Ballads' and saw them in print during the latter half of August.[1] The six poems have little merit — only two achieved even the small dignity of republication in *Departmental Ditties* — but they represent Kipling's first attempt at writing a group of pieces bound together by similarities of length or style. With the exception of 'Divided Destinies' they are humorous narratives:

[1] The 'Bungalow Ballads' are: 'The Tale of Two Suits' (15 August), 'Divided Destinies' (19 August), 'The Legend of the Lilly' (22 August; collected as 'The Mare's Nest'), 'A Tale of Yesterday's Ten Thousand Years' (27 August), 'Revenge: A Ballad of the Fleeter' (31 August), and 'The Legend of the Pill' (5 September).

exercises, probably in emulation of 'Aliph Cheem', in what we would now call situation comedy. A wife is deluded into thinking her husband keeps a mistress, but 'Lilly' turns out to be a race horse; a lover murmurs sweet nothings into the ear of the wrong lady; another lover hoodwinks his rival into a disastrous ride on an uncontrollable horse. The stories hinge, as do many of Kipling's, on delusions, mistakes, and sly tricks played on the unwary. In point of style, however, they are regressions from the ease and metrical skill of some of his earlier pieces. A few lines from 'Revenge: A Ballad of the Fleeter' will demonstrate the sort of prolixity of which an older Kipling would have been incapable:

> Two lovers to one maid. Aye! It was so.
> O aye! Aye O! Two knights to one ladye.
> Two lovers, — for the world is managed so
> On principles of curst economy;
> And sometimes it is two and sometimes three,
> Four, five, six, seven, as the case may be.

Since most of the 'Bungalow Ballads' were never included in a collection of his work, Kipling must have written them off as a failed experiment. It would be hard not to agree with him. And yet only five months separate 'The Legend of the Pill' from 'Army Headquarters'. The latter is the first of the 'Departmental Ditties', and, whatever the absolute merit of the 'Departmental Ditties', it is generally admitted that they accomplish what they set out to do — they are good light verse. The 'Bungalow Ballads', on the other hand, are not good light verse, for they lack compression and point: not only are they diffuse in style; they fail to suggest that the author's intellect is at work. Nor are there any published verses between September 1885 and February 1886 that can be assigned a transitional role, no works that modulate between the dullness of one set of poems and the sparkle of the other. *Quartette*, in fact — which was published in December 1885 — contains at least one poem that is worse than any of the 'Ballads': the vulgar 'Tragedy of Teeth', which extracts what comedy it can from the theft of a woman's false teeth by a monkey.

If Kipling's style did undergo a swift development that winter, it might be well to ask whether the later verses differ in other ways from the earlier, whether they differ, for example, in structure and content. At least one comic device persists; the characters in both series have ludicrous Dickensian names — Rattleton Traplegh, Jane Austen Beecher Stowe de Rouse, Sleary, Minnie Boffkin. And both sets of verses are predominantly narrative; they reflect Kipling's growing interest in story-telling. But the later group of narratives is concerned with issues larger than the tragedy of Lucretia MacWhone's teeth. 'Bungalow' becomes 'Departmental'; Kipling moves from the domestic to the official; the new poems illustrate and display, attack and defend, aspects of political India. And yet it is not just the political element in these poems that represents a new departure. In an earlier chapter we saw that Kipling began his career as a newspaper writer by attacking the political philosophy of Lord Ripon, and we have seen him return to political verse during this period of experimentation. What is new in the 'Departmental Ditties' is the synthesis of political comment with narrative. Now that he is telling stories that have a point to make, Kipling achieves a new succinctness and compression. Two developments, stylistic and thematic, coincide, and the result is the earliest verse of Kipling's that is in any way memorable.

Properly speaking, the original 'Departmental Ditties' are ten in number, published in the *Civil and Military* between 5 February and 13 April 1886. They supplied the germ from which grew *Departmental Ditties and Other Verses*, a volume which, in the course of its four earliest editions (1886–90), provided a conveniently elastic vehicle for putting Kipling's poems before the public. As the various editions of the book succeeded one another, the original coherence of the 'Departmental' series became lost, a change indicated by one of the few revisions Kipling made in these tight, polished verses: the verse heading to 'A Code of Morals' (the ninth of the series to appear in the *Civil and Military*) originally read, "'Tis *my ninth* / Unmitigated misstatement'.[1] Likewise, readers who are familiar with the poems from their arrangement in the 'Definitive Edition' of Kipling's verse will doubtless have been perplexed by an introductory poem labelled 'Prelude (To "Departmental Ditties") 1885', which reads, in part, as follows:

> I have written the tale of our life
> For a sheltered people's mirth,
> In jesting guise — but ye are wise,
> And ye know what the jest is worth.

Perplexing indeed, for none of the 'Departmental Ditties' appeared before 1886, nor was such a prelude included in the first edition. It appeared, in fact, in the first English edition, that of 1890, a fact which explains its puzzling and misleading implications.

For the whole point of the 'Departmental Ditties' lies in the fact that they were not written 'for a sheltered people's mirth' but for Kipling's fellow Anglo-Indians. They define a position within the Anglo-Indian hierarchy; it is for others within that hierarchy that they are intended. They are the rueful plaints of a young man looking up at an administrative structure both vast and absurd, an inept colossus. The adventures of Ahasuerus Jenkins, Potiphar Gubbins, Sleary, and Exeter Battleby Tring show how the Government and the old men who are its representatives can be discomfited by younger men with sharp wits and no excess of scruple: '*No tangle's so tangled it cannot improve / If the Lover has brains.*' The exceptions to this narrative pattern are consistent with the attitude the pattern expresses. Rustum Beg of Kolazai may win no more than a dis-

[1] Rudyard Kipling, *Departmental Ditties and Other Verses* (Lahore, 1886). My italics.

appointing C.I.E., but his behaviour exposes the naïve good faith of the Foreign Office. Although 'The Story of Uriah' appears to have been based upon a true incident, the poem indicts not so much an individual as the 'Fear, Favour or Affection' that appear, especially from below, to be built into the system.[1] Of the individuals who come into conflict with the system, only Boanerges Blitzen, 'The Man Who Could Write', suffers a justifiable comic punishment for his presumption. We may take that poem as a sort of strategic apology for the whole series, a cautionary tale aimed, with Kipling's habitual irony, against himself. '*Men who spar with Government need, to back their blows, / Something more than ordinary journalistic prose.*' Is this not a rite of propitiation offered to 'the Little Tin Gods on the Mountain Side'?

In the introduction to his *Choice of Kipling's Verse*, T. S. Eliot explains why he has not included in his collection poetry from the 'Departmental Ditties' period:

It is obviously the work of a clever young man who might go far in journalism, but neither in feeling nor in rhythm does most of it give any hint that the author would ever write a memorable poem. It is unnecessary to say that it is not poetry: what is surprising and interesting is that it does not pretend to be poetry, that it is not the work of a youth whom anyone would suspect of any aspiration to write poetry. That he is gifted, that he is worth watching, is obvious when you know how young he is: but the gift appears to be only for the ephemeral, and the writer appears to aim at nothing higher. . . . Kipling was not trying to write poetry at all.[2]

---

[1] Thus Kay Robinson explains the effect this poem had on his first readers: 'The poems that made up his "Departmental Ditties" were personal and topical in their origin, and gained tenfold in force for readers who could supply the names and places. . . . Those who had known the real "Jack Barrett", good fellow that he was, and the vile superior and faithless wife who sent him "on duty" to his death, felt the heat of the spirit which inspired Kipling's verse in a way that gave those few lines an imperishable force.' 'Kipling in India', p. 106.

[2] T. S. Eliot, 'Rudyard Kipling', in *A Choice of Kipling's Verse*, ed. Eliot (London, 1941), p. 8.

The irony of Mr. Eliot's words is that, to the student of Kipling's early writings, they are truer than their author realized. Before he came to India, Kipling had been trying to write poetry: the youth whom no one 'would suspect of any aspiration to write poetry' had entertained just such an aspiration. Why he abandoned it will never be entirely clear. To some extent it seems evident that he succumbed to the sterility of the Anglo-Indian poetic environment, the sterility that prevented a distinguished Anglo-Indian poetry from coming to birth; but we must also take account of the element of free choice involved. Kipling chose to write deft, inconsequential verse like that of his Anglo-Indian contemporaries, just as he chose to support the conservative forces in the Ilbert Bill controversy. As in politics, the decision proved far-reaching. The verse Kipling wrote during the rest of his life can be seen as a development predictable from the 'Departmental Ditties' but not as an outgrowth of *Schoolboy Lyrics* and 'Sundry Phansies', for Kipling never followed Yeats, his great coeval, into the forest of symbolism; though incomparably finer than anything in the 'Departmental Ditties', the best of Kipling's mature poems remain public rather than private, rhetorical *tours de force* rather than explorations of the mind's intricate geography. Mr. Eliot's essay goes on to characterize Kipling's best work as 'great verse' rather than poetry. The phrase has been criticized as a blurring of issues, but it suggests a quality of Kipling's poetry that is hard to deny.[1] For Kipling, the admirer of Browning, did not heed Browning's message; like

[1] Several reviewers of Eliot's *Choice* took issue with the critic's attempt to defend Kipling's poetry as 'great verse'. Two severe attacks on both Eliot and Kipling are: Boris Ford, 'A Case for Kipling?' *Scrutiny*, xi (1942–3), 23–33; and Lionel Trilling, 'Mr. Eliot's Kipling', *Nation*, clvii (1943), 436–42. When he reprinted his essay in *The Liberal Imagination*, Professor Trilling somewhat moderated the severity of his attack. The essay has recently reappeared in Andrew Rutherford's collection, *Kipling's Mind and Art* (London, 1964), with a comment by

Andrea del Sarto, he attempted only what he knew he could accomplish. Whatever its merits, the Kipling canon is homogeneous. Earlier than most, Kipling learned what he could do as a poet and from that point on avoided what he thought he could not do: the canon is a record of distinguished accomplishment, but it is not a record of trials, failures, syntheses, and unpredictable triumphs.

Professor Trilling that if he were writing on Kipling now, he 'would do so less censoriously and with more affectionate admiration' (p. 85).

4. Something more than Ordinary Journalistic Prose

I

EVER since his schooldays at Westward Ho! Rudyard Kipling had intended to become a writer. But by the end of 1884, after two years in India, he had little reason to expect that his ambition would be fulfilled. The stultifying routine of the newspaper office seemed to lead nowhere; he was publishing competent verse, but he had clearly abandoned any attempt to write serious poetry. Tied to an office desk by the demands of his job, how was he to master the difficult art to which he had committed himself?

Only one solution to the dilemma seemed possible: he would have to divide his energies between his editorial work and his literary apprenticeship. This decision meant, in practical terms, that he would have to write by and for himself in the hours he could spare from the *Civil and Military*. And so, during 1884 and 1885, Kipling carried on a double life: since Stephen Wheeler discouraged 'literary' newspaper work, his assistant editor devoted his free time to a laborious struggle with prose fiction, writing stories that he never expected to see printed in his own newspaper.

This stimulation gave rise to a peculiar division between two types of prose in the work that Kipling published between the end of 1884 and the middle of 1886. On the one hand, there are a few grotesque and fantastic tales, all in the form of the dramatic monologue, and a portion of an unfinished novel, now lost, called 'Mother

Maturin'; on the other, a series of sketches of local scenes and events told from the point of view of a first-person narrator-observer. The grotesque monologues Kipling wrote in private: they were independent projects that seemed to offer a way of escaping from journalism into literature. What Kipling only gradually realized, however, was that the true path of his development lay not with these tales but in and through his routine newspaper assignments. By looking about him and writing of what he saw, heard, and smelled, the young editor not only mastered a unique prose style but also created a form, a type of short story, that enabled him to combine precise delineation of external detail with a personal and imaginative vision of Anglo-Indian life. Thus, the years from 1884 through 1886 were crucial to Kipling's development, for in them he learned, by a series of experiments, the techniques that came to maturity in *Plain Tales from the Hills*. And the pages of the *Civil and Military*, contrary to the young man's expectations, provided the laboratory in which those experiments were carried out.

II

On 26 September 1884, about three months before his nineteenth birthday, Kipling published his first short story. We cannot tell why he turned to prose fiction at this time; he had not attempted it since his school-days and had achieved very little then. During most of the summer of 1884 he found himself alone in the house at Lahore. It was an evil season: cholera was abroad in the city, and Rudyard himself, suffering from gastric pains, relied on opiates given him by his bearer to pull him through a time of discomfort and insomnia.[1] Opium dreams, midnight walks through Lahore, and a fascination with the life of outcasts and derelicts: these provide

[1] Charles Carrington, *Rudyard Kipling: His Life and Work* (London, 1955), p. 57.

the background for 'The Gate of the Hundred Sorrows', an evocation of the mind of an opium addict slipping down towards death.

'The Gate of the Hundred Sorrows' is an exercise in texture and mood. It has no plot, no possible source in anecdote, but weaves together a number of related motifs — death, money, darkness, the Black Smoke, decay — into a compelling vision. Everything outside the confines of the opium den is vague and uncertain: Gabral, the Eurasian narrator, will not reveal where the house stands, he does not know how Fung-Tching, the original proprietor, came there ('They say that he murdered his wife'), he struggles to evade the memory of why and when his own wife died. 'It is very hard to keep count of time in the Gate, and, besides, time doesn't matter to me. I draw my sixty rupees fresh and fresh every month.' The rupees act as a refrain; they are Gabral's only link with the world outside, and they are turned into Black Smoke — his euphemism for the drug — whenever they arrive. They are all the nourishment Gabral needs; though dead, they are 'fresh and fresh', timeless, and will continue to be paid to the Gate's proprietor after Gabral himself has died and ceased to need them. And yet the Gate itself, though Gabral wants to think of it as outside time, is, on his own admission, decaying as he draws nearer death. It used to be a '*pukka*, respectable opium house, and not one of those stifling, sweltering *chandoo-khanas* that you can find all over the City'; 'it was clean, and quiet, and not crowded'. But now Fung-Tching is dead, and his nephew has relaxed the old standards. He and his half-caste mistress 'let in all sorts of low people, niggers and all, and the Black Smoke isn't as good as it used to be'. Hell itself has declined under new management: 'Nothing matters much to me — only I wish Tsin-ling wouldn't put bran into the Black Smoke.'

Although impressive in its own right, 'The Gate of the Hundred Sorrows' is perhaps most interesting for what it can tell us about the state of Kipling's mind and art. We note, in the first place, the author's neutrality towards his material. Kipling could easily have used the tale as ammunition in the perennial Anglo-Indian dispute over whether the British were morally justified in maintaining an official opium monopoly. He later sided with the Government on this issue, but in spite of the fact that his last prose writings had been tendentiously political, he refrained in his first story from making any explicit comment on the use of the drug. And, though Gabral Misquitta is a Portuguese Eurasian, Kipling does not clutter 'The Gate' with any of the crude and irritating racial theories that mar 'His Chance in Life', published three years later (2 April 1887).

Although Kipling refused to take sides on particular issues, it is clear that the subject and milieu of 'The Gate of the Hundred Sorrows' exercised a powerful fascination upon him. This is Kipling's first exploration of the Asian underworld and may have helped to set the pattern for a whole class of stories that deal with Europeans and Eurasians who go to pieces in the Far East: Conrad wrote masterpieces in this genre; Maugham and lesser writers turned the pattern into a stereotype. But Kipling, like Conrad, wrote from direct observation. Early in his life, during a visit to London that followed his release from the House of Desolation, Kipling had a memorable experience. As he recalled in his memoirs: 'Here, for the first time, it happened that the night got into my head. I rose up and wandered about that still house till daybreak, when I slipped out into the little brick-walled garden and saw the dawn break. . . . I did not know then that such night-wakings would be laid upon me through my life; or that my fortunate hour would be on the turn of sunrise, with a sou'-west breeze afoot.'[1]

[1] Rudyard Kipling, *Something of Myself for My Friends Known and Unknown*, 'Library Edition' (London, 1951), pp. 18–19. The importance of this passage was brought to my attention by Professor C. A. Bodelsen's illuminating study, *Aspects of Kipling's Art* (Manchester, 1964), pp. 1–6.

These night-wakings were to be habitual with him; while he was in India, they showed him a side of life in Lahore that Europeans of more regular habits never saw. Here is his own description of the night world that so caught his imagination:

Often the night got into my head as it had done in the boarding-house in the Brompton Road, and I would wander till dawn in all manner of odd places — liquor-shops, gambling- and opium-dens, which are not a bit mysterious, wayside entertainments such as puppet-shows, native dances; or in and about the narrow gullies under the Mosque of Wazir Khan for the sheer sake of looking. . . . One would come home, just as the light broke, in some night-hawk of a hired carriage which stank of hookah-fumes, jasmine-flowers, and sandalwood; and if the driver were moved to talk, he told one a good deal. Much of real Indian life goes on in the hot-weather nights.[1]

Thus, seeing himself as a modern Dante with spectacles and a notebook, he wandered through sordid urban Infernos in Lahore, Calcutta, Hong Kong, San Francisco, and London.[2]

Kipling had some acquaintance with the dark underside of Indian life, but in fact verisimilitude is the least important aspect of 'The Gate of the Hundred Sorrows', for instead of foreshadowing Kipling's later fiction, in which verisimilitude is a principal aim, the story shares

[1] *Something of Myself*, pp. 53–54.

[2] '"And where next?"' the reporter asks. '"To the lowest sink of all", say the Police after the manner of Virgil when he took the Italian with the indigestion to look at the frozen sinners. . . . They lead and they lead and they lead, and they cease not from leading till they come to the last circle of the Inferno — a long, long, winding, quiet road.' Rudyard Kipling, *The City of Dreadful Night* (London, 1891), p. 40. The text differs somewhat from that of the *From Sea to Sea* version. For Kipling's Hong Kong and San Francisco adventures, see *From Sea to Sea*, chaps. viii and xxiv. London Infernos are not so explicitly described, but in *Something of Myself*, pp. 80–82, Kipling recalls his experience of pubs and music halls, an experience that finds expression in 'The Record of Badalia Herodsfoot' (November 1890) and elsewhere in his later writings.

several characteristics with his schoolboy poem 'The Story of Paul Vaugel'. Both pieces are dramatic monologues in which Kipling seeks objectivity by choosing speakers whose circumstances are nothing like his own. And yet, although both pieces are superficially remote from Kipling's experience, each can be seen as reflecting the state of its author's mind at a particular time: in the earlier case, the sorrows of first love; in the later, ill health and the discomfort of a summer in Lahore. The two pieces are most clearly linked, however, by the tone or atmosphere they share, for both take place in a timeless, dreamlike setting; in neither do we find the open daylight that characterizes Kipling's later stories, but rather a night world, some of whose details are illuminated with intense, disquieting vividness. Although 'Paul Vaugel' was written as early as 1881 or 1882, no published narrative intervenes between it and 'The Gate of the Hundred Sorrows', so that the 1884 story provides a link between the schoolboy poet and the Anglo-Indian storyteller. Faced with the problem of writing a prose story, Kipling reverted to one of his most recent experiments in the narrative art and took over into prose its technique and atmosphere.

In his next story, 'The Dream of Duncan Parrenness' (25 December 1884), Kipling again sought objectivity by using a speaker who cannot be confused with the author himself: this time, the action takes place at the end of the eighteenth century, when Hastings was Governor-General. The tale gave Kipling a good deal of trouble. 'It has only taken me three months', he wrote his aunt in November, 'and is only six pages long but I've never fallen in love with any tale of my own fashioning so much — not that it has any merit.' [1] Evidently Kipling's affection was no passing fancy, for he collected the story many years later in *Life's Handicap* (1891), where it consorts oddly with stories in Kipling's maturer style. It is hard to tell what endeared the story to its author, unless

[1] Quoted in Carrington, *Rudyard Kipling*, p. 58.

its mood of wasted youth and blank despair reflected his personal feelings at the end of a year of hard work. Although 'Duncan Parrenness' recalls the dreamlike remoteness of 'The Gate of the Hundred Sorrows', it is neither as subtle nor as moving as the earlier story. The action is mechanically allegorical, and the narrator's language is an awkward and self-conscious attempt to suggest the idiom of Hastings's time: these unpromising elements are used to support a Christmas ghost story, an Anglo-Indian variant of Dickens's *Christmas Carol*, in which the hero confronts his own future and sees the waste land that lies before him.

Although both 'The Gate of the Hundred Sorrows' and 'The Dream of Duncan Parrenness' appeared in the *Civil and Military Gazette*, it is likely that neither had any formal connection with Kipling's regular newspaper work. As to 'Duncan Parrenness', he wrote in the same letter to his aunt, 'I'm trying to work it off on some alien paper to get myself pice thereby.' I have found no such direct references to his plans for 'The Gate of the Hundred Sorrows', but in the previously quoted passage about night walks there is a suggestive comment: 'I did not supply my paper with many accounts of these prowls.'[1] More decisive is the fact that these two stories resemble nothing else that Kipling published during 1884; rather, they look forward to two literary projects that were certainly undertaken as independent artistic efforts. Less than a month after completing 'Duncan Parrenness' Kipling noted in his diary: 'Mem. to finish handsomely the "Village of the Dead" which was taken in hand three days ago.'[2] This story, later entitled 'The Strange Ride of Morrowbie Jukes', refused to be finished off: it grew so much longer than either of the earlier tales that the following February, after three months of work, it was still incomplete.[3] And on 7 March 1885 he conceived

[1] *Something of Myself*, p. 54.

[2] Kipling's manuscript diary for 1885, entry for 8 December 1884.

[3] The diary's last reference to the story occurs on 20 February 1885.

the notion of writing a full-length Anglo-Indian novel. 'The idea of "Mother Maturin",' he noted in his diary, 'dawned on me today.'

By the middle of the summer both projects seemed to be well in hand. A letter of 30 July to his aunt Edith Macdonald sounds a note of elation, for the *Calcutta Review* was planning to publish 'a long ghost story of a wholly novel type' — probably 'Morrowbie Jukes' — and the novel was growing steadily. He wrote:

I have really embarked to the tune of 237 foolscap pages on my novel — Mother Maturin — an Anglo-Indian episode. Like Topsy 'it growed' while I wrote and I find myself now committed to a two volume business at least. It's not one bit nice or proper but it carries a grim sort of a moral with it and tries to deal with the unutterable horrors of lower class Eurasian and native life as they exist outside reports and reports and reports. . . . Trixie says its awfully horrid; Mother says its nasty but powerful and I know it to be in large measure true. It is an unfailing delight to me and I'm just in that pleasant stage where the characters are living with me always.[1]

But despite Kipling's optimism neither project bore fruit in the way that he anticipated. The *Calcutta Review* never published his story: 'Jukes' had to await the publication of *Quartette* at the year's end. As for 'Mother Maturin', though its persons and incidents haunted his mind for many years, Kipling was unable to finish it. A hint of what his manuscript contained may be found in 'To Be Filed for Reference' (January 1888), which is, among other things, a sort of advertisement for the forthcoming book; and parts of *Kim*, according to Professor Carrington, were quarried from 'Mother Maturin' in 1899 and 1900.[2] As late as 1923 Kipling was still trying to give shape to the material that had once caught his imagination. There are reports of a film scenario in which he had a hand: a peculiar mélange of elements

[1] Quoted in Carrington, *Rudyard Kipling*, pp. 66–67.
[2] Ibid., pp. 358–9.

from 'The Gate of the Hundred Sorrows', 'To Be Filed for Reference', 'The Ballad of Fisher's Boarding House', and 'Mother Maturin', all mingled together with spiritualism and an unconvincing love story.[1] Fortunately, the film was never made; by this time Kipling had lost his imaginative sympathy with 'the unutterable horrors of lower class Eurasian and native life', and all that was left of 'Mother Maturin' was a hodge-podge of sentimental clichés.

III

Kipling was never to achieve unqualified success as a novelist.[2] But even as he worked at 'Mother Maturin' he was laying the foundations for his future successes in the short story. Although Kipling looked forward to a literary career, he never held his journalistic duties in contempt: he might not enjoy working for Stephen Wheeler, but he was the son of a craftsman of the Ruskinian school, and he shared his father's pride in sound workmanship. If he had to mark time as a journalist, Kipling was determined to be as good a journalist as possible: he would make the *Civil and Military Gazette* his workshop. Consequently, by examining his early newspaper pieces, we can trace in some detail the development of the young craftsman's skill at the art of prose. For ultimately the lost 'Mother Maturin' was to be less important to him than the dull assignments he slaved over in the hot Indian nights, when he discovered 'that a man can work with a temperature of 104, even though next day he has to ask the office who wrote the article'.[3]

[1] A summary of the scenario is provided by the indefatigable R. Thurston Hopkins in *Rudyard Kipling: The Story of a Genius* (London, 1930), chap. viii.

[2] Some interesting speculations as to the reasons for Kipling's failure as a novelist may be found in the first chapter of J. M. S. Tompkins, *The Art of Rudyard Kipling* (London, 1959).

[3] *Something of Myself*, p. 41.

The second of the articles Kipling sent home to Mr. Crofts at Westward Ho! is dated 9 October 1882. Its subject, the Dasera Festival at Lahore, makes it a convenient point of departure for our investigation, for it is the earliest of Kipling's many sketches of Indian life. Not surprisingly, 'The Dasera Festival' is a conventional exercise: it lies within a popular Anglo-Indian genre, the amused, often supercilious report of native life and its quaint customs. Kipling had evidently been reading such contemporary essayists as A. J. Bamford or the pseudonymous 'Ali Baba' and 'Eha'.[1] What chiefly strikes him about the festival is the disparity between a grandiose legend and the clumsiness of this local commemoration of its heroes. 'To the great delight of the people,' he tells us, 'Ramchandra and his brothers, attired in the traditional costume and head-dress, were mounted aloft and held the mighty bow, the breaking of which shook the world to its centre. But it must be admitted that Sita, uncomfortably astride a broad-backed wicker-work bull, supported by an uneasy Rama, buried in tinsel and attended by bearers . . . was a spectacle more comic than imposing.' Doubtless it was, but irony at the expense of such a provincial ceremony comes rather cheap; an older Kipling would never have told us the spectacle was comic without making it appear so. But for that matter, an older Kipling wouldn't have been content to remain so detached and disdainful a bystander.

The texture of the young man's prose betrays uncertainties of technique and attitude. Summarizing his impressions, he writes: 'But it may occur to some, that a city, which has had an Oriental College, teaching Oriental

[1] Cf. A. J. Bamford, *Turbans and Tails; or, Sketches in the Unromantic East* (London, 1888); George Aberigh-Mackay, *Twenty-One Days in India: Being the Tour of Sir Ali Baba, K.C.B.*, 2nd ed. (London, 1880); and 'Eha' [pseud. of Edward Hamilton Aitken], *Behind the Bungalow*, 2nd ed. (Calcutta, 1889). I have found no evidence that Kipling read these particular books, but they suggest a well-defined tradition of satirical writing that he must have been aware of.

poetry in its midst for many years, might have acquired a taste for more artistic completeness and propriety, in one of its most interesting and popular manifestations.' The putative connection between an Oriental College and a popular festival reveals the weakness of Kipling's grasp of the Indian character, just as the final 'its', dubious as to antecedent, suggests an uncertain command of English syntax. Similarly, the observed details of the procession dissolve into the annoying vagueness of 'artistic completeness and propriety' and 'interesting and popular manifestations', so that we miss altogether the visual clarity of Kipling's later art. In fact, what makes this sketch most useful for our purposes is its very anonymity: without the testimony of the Crofts Collection, no one would identify it as Kipling's. Evidently, then, Kipling did not simply inherit an individual prose style; he achieved it through a process of experiment over a period of several years.

The prose experiments of 1884 have not been identified. Kipling felt, no doubt, that the poems in *Echoes* were more representative of his best than his newspaper pieces, for he sent none of the latter to Mr. Crofts during 1884. Towards the end of the year, however, we can pick up the trail again, because in his 1885 diary Kipling kept track of his special assignments, adding up at the end of the year the extra money these 'specials' had earned for him.

In December 1884 and January 1885 Stephen Wheeler sent Kipling to cover two local events for the paper. The events were unimportant — a celebration arranged for the native community of Lahore and a provincial exhibition — but they gave Kipling an opportunity to write professionally of what he saw about him and he rose to the challenge. He caught the sensation of the crowd's pressure at Proclamation Day: 'The *vis a tergo* drove the front ranks forward like so many sheep to the slaughter and movement of any kind was absolutely impossible. The packed masses advanced slowly but steadily — after the manner of glaciers — perfectly aware of the justice of each execration, but entirely unable to stir hand or foot.' The Biblical phrase 'after the manner of' reminds us of an older Kipling, but more important is the fact that here he no longer observes native India from a distance but mingles with the crowds and sympathizes with their discomfort. Later in the day he observed a child entranced with a crude merry-go-round and used him to express not only the gay atmosphere of the fête, but a new perception of the relation between reality and illusion among the Indians: 'He begged or borrowed no less than three several rides on a peagreen thing with two legs and no head. Yet he sat for all that, as though mounted on a fiery and untameable steed, with the jauntiest air in life.' The situation is quite close to that of 'The Dasera Festival', but already Kipling's attitude has become richer and more complex. Similarly, at the exhibition of arts and sciences, the response of the individual attracts his attention and sums up the experience of the mass. Here, peasants stand fascinated before tiny models of farm animals: 'Presently the bolder spirits among them would put out a horny finger, and carefully touch one of the bullocks. Then as the animal was evidently constructed of nothing more terrible than clay . . . the whole hand would be drawn gently over its form; and, after an appreciative pat, the adventurous one would begin a lengthy dissertation to the bystanders at large.'

These special assignments by no means accounted for the bulk of Kipling's writing during 1885, for, as his diary testifies, he was principally occupied with reports of the week in Lahore, translations from Russian journals (published in French, not Russian), book reviews, and miscellaneous columns of what he called 'scraps'. Furthermore, he spent several months in Simla, both on holiday and as special correspondent for the paper, so that for a substantial part of 1885 he was too absorbed in the social and official life of the summer capital to give full attention to his writing. When he returned from Simla, he contributed two pieces to the *Civil and Military* that indicate the tendency of his experiments with prose. Both sketches — '"The City of Dreadful Night"' (10 September) and 'The City of Two Creeds' (19 and 20 October) — depict Lahore at night. They are companion-pieces: in the earlier, Lahore lies dead and silent, paralysed by the summer heat; in the later, the city is violently alive, swept by Hindu and Moslem crowds on the verge of riot. And both are descriptive exercises filled with fine writing and stylistic devices of a kind that Kipling later stripped from his prose. 'Overhead the white moonlight struggled with the glare of the torches and red lights. To the right and left lay the black darkness of deserted alleys and courtyards, and as far as one could see in front and behind, stretched a sea of tossing turbans and white garments. The *taboots* [floats carried by the Moslem marchers], tossing like galleons at sea, glittered bravely in the light of the torches; or died away in less vivid hues as the moonlight touched them.' The self-conscious attention to effects of light and the simile of the tossing galleons are characteristic of both sketches. Kipling later avoided metaphor and simile in his prose, but in '"The City of Dreadful Night"' we find bones 'like mother o' pearl', 'sleeping men who lay like sheeted corpses', 'the unwinking eye of the moon', a road 'straight as a bar of polished steel', a leper like a 'rigid silver statue', — all within two pages. 'Doré might have drawn it!' the watcher exclaims, and indeed the manner in which Kipling renders the sleeping city recalls the murkiness and rhetoric of the French illustrator. And yet, in spite of his tendency to over-write, Kipling was discovering the fascination of the world around him. '"The City of Dreadful Night"' is overblown by comparison to 'The Gate of the Hundred Sorrows', but it takes Kipling several steps nearer the commonplace, the everyday world of British India, where he found the atmosphere and subject matter of his later stories.

IV

The two 'City' sketches, with some other prose pieces of 1885, fall into a special category; written with the *Civil and Military* in mind, they are neither routine assignments nor independent literary projects. In order to clarify the development of Kipling's prose fiction, we must turn from these sketches to the two substantial short stories he published in *Quartette* at the end of 1885: these are the first fruits of his determination to become a writer of fiction rather than a journalist.

'The Strange Ride of Morrowbie Jukes' — the story he worked on during the early months of 1885 — is, like the 1884 stories, a dramatic monologue relating a grotesque experience. Its source is probably Poe's 'The Pit and the Pendulum', for both tales deal with man-made traps and the futile attempts of the victims to extricate themselves, and both end with fortuitous and unexpected rescues which allow the narrators to tell their stories afterwards. Both Poe and Kipling use for background the disciplinary arm of an alien religion — in one case the Inquisition and in the other, a nameless Hindu sect. But in each story the trap, not the shadowy trappers, compels our attention. Through the eyes of its victim we must be made to see each of its ingenious details, to foresee avenues of escape and then suffer the victim's horror and disappointment when he finds that his discovery has been anticipated by his captors.

But Jukes is not merely the victim of a trap. He is in the first place a Civil Engineer, and it has been noted that his precise and matter-of-fact air stands in ironic contrast to his grotesque situation.[1] But he is, aside from his profession, an arrogant Anglo-Saxon, a self-styled 'English gentleman' who prides himself on his freedom from unmanly weaknesses like 'moping'. He shows the proper concern for his horse, and his horror at the fate of the dead Englishman he finds there becomes, under the

[1] Tompkins, *The Art of Rudyard Kipling*, p. 199.

circumstances, an absurd exaggeration of the conventional Anglo-Indian sense of brotherhood: '[Good God! Gunga Dass!] For pity's sake, tell me all you know about him. Who was he? When did he come, and when did he die?' [1]

The sand-pit — a grim enough place for the Hindu outcasts it harbours — becomes a living hell for Jukes, the pukka sahib. He gets a taste of what is in store when he first approaches his fellow-victims: 'Even in these days, when [the Ilbert Bill and] local self-government [have] destroyed the great part of a native's respect for a Sahib, I have been accustomed to a certain amount of civility from my inferiors, and on approaching the crowd naturally expected that there would be some recognition of my presence.' Recognition there is, but it takes a disconcerting form: 'They cackled, yelled, whistled, and howled as I [rode] into their midst; some of them literally throwing themselves down on the ground in convulsions of unholy mirth.' Shocked beyond measure, Jukes loses control of himself and hits out at these helpless starvelings, who collapse like ninepins under his blows. From that point on his problem is twofold: he has not only to escape, but to maintain his identity as 'a representative of the dominant race', though 'helpless as a child and completely at the mercy of his native neighbours'. Jukes is sorely tried. He must depend for food and shelter upon Gunga Dass, a scarred Brahmin for whose disfigurement Jukes himself, in some unexplained manner, has been responsible. He must eat literal crow and sleep in a hole in the sand-bank whose 'sides had been worn smooth and greasy by the contact of innumerable naked bodies, added to which it smelt abominably'.

Morrowbie Jukes finds, in other words, that he is a

[1] Kipling made numerous revisions in 'Morrowbie Jukes' and 'The Phantom 'Rickshaw' between their first appearance in *Quartette* and their republication in *The Phantom 'Rickshaw* (December 1888). In order to indicate the kind of revisions he made, I have placed the wording of the earlier version in square brackets here and elsewhere.

sahib for whom a hundred years of British rule in India have suddenly become undone. The trap at the bottom of the sand-hills is a world where none of the customary rules of decent behaviour can be applied, where the Englishman must eat and sleep, not only in the manner of his fellow-victims, but in a way that differs little from that of many Indian paupers in the normal world outside. He realizes that he must fight with beggars for scraps, 'that in the accursed settlement there was no law save that of the strongest; that the living dead men had thrown behind them every canon of the world which had cast them out'. Gunga Dass, delighted to have this particular sahib at his mercy, passes sarcastic judgment in the language of an anglicized babu: '"We are now Republic, Mister Jukes, and you are entitled to a fair share of the beast [i.e. of Jukes's dead horse]. If you like, we will pass a vote of thanks. Shall I propose?"' Hilton Brown objects to the story on the grounds that such a settlement is melodramatic 'balderdash', that there could be no such thing in the real India.[1] But that is not the point. The village of the dead is not the realistic picture of a curious ethnic survival. In this tale Kipling has gone beyond a mere imitation of Poe and created a genuine Anglo-Indian nightmare, a vision of what it would be like to be one of the least of the ruled instead of one of the rulers.

The other major story in *Quartette* is 'The Phantom 'Rickshaw'. Kipling wrote it more quickly and easily than 'Morrowbie Jukes'; his 'Personal Daemon', he wrote, 'came to me early when I sat bewildered among other notions, and said: "Take this and no other." I obeyed, and was rewarded. . . . Some of it was weak, much was bad and out of key; but it was my first serious attempt to think in another man's skin.'[2] Like the earlier tale, it is the narrative of a man undergoing a weird and frightening experience and has some affinities to Poe's

[1] See Hilton Brown, *Rudyard Kipling* (New York, 1945), p. 170.

[2] *Something of Myself*, p. 209.

'The Tell-Tale Heart' and 'The Black Cat'. But once again Kipling has improved upon his models, for 'The Phantom 'Rickshaw', instead of taking place in the vaguely Gothic world of the conventional nineteenth-century tale of terror, is firmly based in Kipling's Simla. Just as Jukes's matter-of-fact engineer's mind makes vivid his nightmare, so the Simla milieu and the conventions of an Anglo-Indian flirtation give substance to this tale of a blackguard and his pathetic demon-lover.

At first glance the story is simple. Jack Pansay, the narrator, has terminated a monotonous love affair. The shock so wounded his mistress that she died; her spirit has returned together with the 'rickshaw and servants she used when alive, and the phantoms are hounding Pansay into his grave. But this is Pansay's version: in order to leave us in doubt of the truth, the author puts into the mouth of Pansay's doctor the more plausible theory that Mrs. Keith-Wessington and her 'rickshaw are the products of his patient's diseased brain. The ambiguity must have appealed to Kipling, for he made it more explicit in the introductory pages he added in 1888 when the story was reprinted. The narrator of this introduction reports that the doctor 'laughs at my theory that there was a crack in Pansay's head and a little bit of the Dark World came through and pressed him to death'. The doctor claims merely that '"overwork started his illness, kept it alight, and killed him, poor devil"'. The ambiguity is, of course, functional, as Dr. Tompkins points out; we are not supposed to eliminate one possibility in favour of the other, but to remain suspended between them.[1]

Nor is this ambiguity the only reward that 'The Phantom 'Rickshaw' offers. The story does not allow us to see Mrs. Wessington solely as a frightening revenant, for in a moment of startling perception, Kipling has Pansay pay tribute to the reality of the vision that haunts him:

[1] *The Art of Rudyard Kipling*, p. 199.

The second and most tormenting of my moods of sickness had suddenly laid hold upon me, and, like the Prince in Tennyson's poem, 'I seemed to move among a world of ghosts.' There had been a garden-party at the Commander-in-Chief's, and we two joined the crowd of homeward-bound folk. As I saw them it seemed that *they* were the shadows — impalpable fantastic shadows — that divided for Mrs. Wessington's 'rickshaw to pass through. . . . It was a ghastly and yet in some indefinable way a marvellously dear experience. Could it be possible, I wondered, that I was in this life to woo a second time the woman I had killed by my own neglect and cruelty?

With a single phrase — 'in some indefinable way a marvellously dear experience' — Kipling changes and deepens the tone of the story; and in so doing he foreshadows nearly all of his later excursions into the supernatural. Again and again in the ghost stories of his maturity, supernatural phenomena, sources of mere fright in the work of a less perceptive writer, demand of those who experience them a response that mingles apprehension with a powerful nostalgia for the unseen world.

In some ways the most successful of Kipling's four grotesque monologues, 'The Phantom 'Rickshaw' is also the last of them. Having worked in a tradition that demanded a grotesque situation or supernatural event as the basis for a story, Kipling was preparing himself, towards the end of 1885, for the adoption of a new fictional mode. His conversion may be illustrated by the way he revised 'Morrowbie Jukes' and 'The Phantom 'Rickshaw' when he republished them in 1888. His verbal revisions indicate the direction of his stylistic development: he consistently made phrases more concise and substituted understatement for exaggeration. Even then he was not satisfied. For he added to both stories introductory paragraphs in which an 'I' recounts how he learned of Jukes's and Pansay's adventures. The 'I' in both cases sounds suspiciously like an older Kipling apologizing for the stylistic inadequacies of his younger self: Jukes, he says, 'wrote this quite straightforwardly at first, but he has touched it up in places and introduced Moral Reflections'; and Pansay 'was in a high fever while he was writing, and the blood-and-thunder magazine diction he adopted did not calm him'. But Kipling's revisions were not restricted to style; the introduction of the 'I' put both stories into frames and brought them into conformity with the narrative technique he used during the next phase of his career. Thus, the four monologues, into which Kipling put at least as much effort as he gave to his regular work, turned out to be a false start: it was through newspaper sketches, not grotesque tales, that the main course of his development was to lie.

V

The stories of Kipling's next phase grew directly out of his newspaper work. Kipling had too lively an imagination to remain content with the mere reporting of events. The more ambitious of his newspaper sketches outgrow their reportorial format; they continually transform themselves into something else: if not stories, then pieces that lie in a nameless region between the story and the essay. 'East and West' (14 November 1885) provides an early example of this intermediate, quasi-fictional type. The narrator meets an anglicized Afghan on a train; the two fall into conversation, and Kipling uses the Afghan to dramatize his own views on the differences between Europeans and Asians.

> 'What I say is this; and this I do not say to all Englishmen. God made us different — you and I, and your fathers and my fathers. For one thing we have not the same notions of honesty and of speaking the truth. That is not our fault, because we are made so; and in a land where most men are liars, it is just the same as if most men were truth tellers. And look now what you do. You come and judge us by your own standard of morality — that morality which is the outcome of your climate and your education and your traditions.'

The Afghan is not really a fictional character, and yet we learn enough about his tastes and habits in the course of the sketch so that he becomes more than simply an essayist's mouthpiece. Here, as in 'The Phantom 'Rickshaw', Kipling is thinking in another man's skin, with the result that 'East and West', neither essay nor story, sharing aspects of both, represents a bold advance in imaginative sympathy over his previous sketches of the Indian character. Moreover, like so many of his suppressed newspaper pieces, 'East and West' looks forward to more substantial works of Kipling's later years. The Afghan's critique of English politics, for example, recurs in the scathing 'One View of the Question' (1890), and the concluding sentence of the 1885 sketch irresistibly suggests Kipling's most famous lines on the subject of East and West: 'Literally and metaphorically we were standing upon different platforms; and parallel straight lines as every one does *not* know, are lines in the same plane which being continued to all eternity will never meet.' These foreshadowings are of more than passing interest: they prove that in his early sketches Kipling's imagination was beginning to work upon themes and techniques that would occupy him for many years to come.

The looseness of this quasi-fictional form enabled Kipling to experiment freely with prose styles and narrative techniques; most of his prose writings prior to the 'Plain Tales from the Hills' display a variety of approaches without ever becoming stories. 'Twenty Years After' (9 January 1885), for example, is an exchange of imaginary letters that satirizes the Punjab Police; '"Dis Aliter Visum"' (4 July 1885) presents the spirits of well-known figures of Anglo-Indian history commenting on the degeneracy of their descendants; 'His Excellency' (8 October 1885) is an elaborate and fanciful tribute to the child of some Simla acquaintances. In several of the 1886 pieces Kipling exercises his command of the English language by means of amusing verbal experiments. 'At that time', Kipling later wrote, '. . . the French Press was not nationally enamoured of England. I answered some of their criticisms by what I then conceived to be parodies of Victor Hugo's more extravagant prose.'[1] 'The History of a Crime' (5 February) well illustrates the sheer verbal fun that so often marks Kipling's writing: 'Sir Colvin made calembours. He was encountered by statements. Worse still, by letters which were brutal. They were *exposés*. They demonstrated the Crudity. They mangled the Necessity. They annihilated the Logic. They made clear the Unwisdom. They made Hay.' 'A Nightmare of Rule' (3 September) mocks the pedantries of the Theosophists: 'I prevailed upon the Mahatma, by the memory of the Cracked Tea Cup and the Missing Brooch, that he should perform the last Incantation of Materialization.' These gay experiments all point to Kipling's increasing mastery of prose. In the process of forging his own style, he fills the air with verbal sparks.

VI

But these pieces, whatever their promise, are still non-narrative sketches: Kipling needed to take a further step, a step that would enable him to bring to fiction the keen observation and verbal brilliance he had been developing in his newspaper essays. Published side by side with 'Morrowbie Jukes' and 'The Phantom 'Rickshaw' in the 1885 Christmas annual *Quartette* is an inept, forgotten tale that marks the transition. The plot of 'My Christmas at the Ajaibgaum Exhibition' is trivial: sent to cover a provincial exhibition like the one Kipling had described about a year before, the narrator is mistaken for an important personage with the same name, and various farcical misadventures ensue. What makes the story important is that it first employs the 'I' of the earlier newspaper sketches to narrate fictional events; it intro-

[1] Rudyard Kipling, *Souvenirs of France* (London, 1933), p. 11.

duces the ubiquitous first-person narrator of nearly all Kipling's later Indian stories. We may appropriately call this narrator 'the reporter'. The word carries a useful double meaning, for the narrator is both a reporter of events and, from time to time, explicitly a newspaper reporter by profession. And it is helpful to maintain in this way the distinction between Kipling the man and the 'I' who tells the stories. We shall have more to say about the distinction later. Here, we need only observe that the same experience — the Mofussil exhibition — gave rise to two quite different prose pieces: the first, a straightforward report in which the views and attitudes expressed may be taken as Rudyard Kipling's; the second, a farce in which the adventures of a fictional reporter are the product of a talented novice's still undeveloped imagination.

The publication of *Quartette*, then, marked both the culmination of Kipling's interest in the Gothic tale and the beginning of a new approach to fiction. He published scarcely any prose during the first four months of 1886, but when his next story appeared in the *Civil and Military* at the end of April, it showed how much he had learned from his prose experimentation of 1885. 'In the House of Suddhoo' is again told by the reporter, but told this time with striking success: the story represents both a liberation from the grotesque monologue and a new ability to come to grips with the real queerness of Indian life. At first, Kipling seems to be using the same ingredients as in 'The Phantom 'Rickshaw' and 'Morrowbie Jukes': the point of the story seems to be the weird display of *jadoo* — Indian sorcery — that the reporter is invited to witness. But when the *jadoo* turns out to be a sham, we realize that we are in a different world from the one we expected. The reporter has uncovered not another counterpart of Jukes's trap and Pansay's ghost but a network of greed, desire, and fraud that is, in its way, just as alien, just as menacing, as any of the sinister devices in the four monologues. Suddhoo, the victim of the seal-cutter's plots, instead of being sympathetic, is an 'old dotard', a miser and a fool who deserves his sordid fate. Although the seal-cutter is a rogue and a charlatan, he is skilful enough at his trickery to win the reporter's admiration. More complex than either of the men, Janoo the prostitute is 'a lady of a free-thinking turn of mind' and 'a woman of masculine intellect' — the reporter respects her, in other words, for seeing through the fakery — and yet her rage at the seal-cutter stems not from principle but from her frustration at being unable to cheat old Suddhoo herself, and we are told at the end that she will probably poison the seal-cutter unless he murders her first. Jukes and Pansay are faced by extreme and horrible situations; in the essentially Gothic world of those tales, we are asked to do little more than willingly suspend our disbelief. But 'Suddhoo's' world — inhabited only by the venal tenants of a decrepit and gullible landlord — is not Gothic but commonplace; since the *jadoo* is fake, the logic of the tale insists, then the wickedness must be real: we are asked not so much to suspend our disbelief as to believe.

It is likewise noteworthy that this shift in artistic intentions first brings to full flower Kipling's distinctive style. The reporter's transparent, conversational prose reinforces the reader's sense of the intrinsic plausibility of the action; verisimilitude is captured in the very texture of the language:

> Suddhoo sleeps on the roof generally, except when he sleeps in the street. He used to go to Peshawar in the cold weather to visit his son who sells curiosities near the Edwardes' Gate, and then he slept under a real mud roof. Suddhoo is a great friend of mine, because his cousin had a son who secured, thanks to my recommendation, the post of head-messenger to a big firm in the Station. Suddhoo says that God will make me a Lieutenant-Governor one of these days. I daresay his prophecy will come true.

Disarmingly simple, persuasive in their delicately controlled irony, these sentences tell us more about Kipling's development than pages of commentary. He no longer needs to apologize for 'blood-and-thunder magazine diction', for he has stripped his prose down to the merest essentials. He can use flat phrases like 'a real mud roof' or 'a great friend of mine' to yield precise meanings: we can reconstruct Suddhoo's circumstances, or guess how great a friend he is, without asking for further embellishment. Even the deliberate repetition of Suddhoo's name — it begins three of the five sentences — conveys the tone of the relationship between the reporter and the tiresome but pathetic old man. In two and a half years Kipling has come a long way from the 'interesting and popular manifestations' of 'The Dasera Festival'.

But the gap between 'In the House of Suddhoo' and 'The Dasera Festival' is not merely technical and stylistic. In the earlier piece, Indian life appeared as no more than a passing show to be judged and dismissed on its aesthetic merits by a superior — and very young — English spectator. In the 1886 story, however, Kipling has penetrated to the heart of the Anglo-Indians' historical dilemma with amazing swiftness and economy. On one level, Western technology, symbolized by the telegraph line between Peshawar and Lahore, has been perverted by the seal-cutter to the uses of fraud and superstition. On another, Western judicial institutions, embodied in the Indian Penal Code, have been made impotent by a conspiracy of custom, ignorance, and malice.

Kipling's next two stories, the last before he began the 'Plain Tales' series, show that 'In the House of Suddhoo' was no mere flash in the pan, because in them he uses the same device of the narrator-reporter to comment upon the same general theme: the inability of the British to cope with their Indian subjects.[1] In 'Naboth' (26 August 1886) a shrewd sweetmeat-seller appropriates more and

[1] Here and elsewhere I distinguish between the 'Plain Tales' (stories which appeared under that title in the *C. & M.G.*) and *Plain Tales* (the volume into which the original 'Plain Tales' and some other stories were first collected). See Chapter 5.

more of the reporter's garden, so that the reporter ends by driving the man from his property; peasant shrewdness forces the Englishman into a state of exasperation. 'The Story of Muhammad Din' (8 September 1886) is pathetic rather than sinister or comic, but like 'Suddhoo' and 'Naboth' it deals with frustration. In trying to make friends with his houseboy's son, the reporter attempts to approach and understand native India, for Kipling seems to make the child a representative of the Indian peoples. Not only is Muhammad Din precociously ceremonious in his manners, but his chief amusement is to project and construct elaborate palaces out of stale flowers, pebbles, bits of glass, and feathers, palaces that are as easily destroyed as they have been painstakingly built. When the child catches malaria, the reporter tries to save him with medical care, but he dies: '"They have no stamina, these brats"', says the doctor callously. The reporter is left conscious of the futility of his good intentions; he becomes symbolic of England's helplessness in the face of India's frailty, her triple curse of poverty, starvation, and disease.

'The Story of Muhammad Din' stands at the threshold of the next phase of Kipling's career — the 'Plain Tales', which require separate consideration. Looking back over his development as a prose writer, we can compare it in various respects to his development as a poet. Both instances are marked by significant changes of direction, changes that led Kipling to abandon traditional styles and modes in favour of a poetry and prose that were better suited to his own experience and to the audience for which he wrote. Just as the poetry of 'Departmental Ditties' can be seen as the expression of a single Anglo-Indian point of view, so the stories of 1886 become records of the experience of a typical Anglo-Indian trying to understand the conditions in which he lives and works. Viewed stylistically, Kipling's poetry and prose move from the formal to the colloquial, from self-conscious seriousness to irony and wit: in both cases he adjusted his rhetoric to the taste and expectations of his Anglo-Indian audience, the hard-working, tough-minded readers of the *Civil and Military Gazette*. But here the resemblance ends, for, although Kipling never became more than a vigorous and interesting poet, he developed into a master of the short story; and, as the period of his residence in India grew to an end, fiction rather than poetry absorbed his enormous energy and talent.

5. Plain Tales from the Hills

I

In the spring of 1886 Kipling was visited at Lahore by a young journalist who had recently been brought out from London to be assistant editor of the *Pioneer*.[1] Both men were interested in literature; both had published light verse in Anglo-Indian newspapers; Edward Kay Robinson was charmed by the brilliant Kipling family, and he and Rudyard quickly became friends. Later in the summer of 1886 Kipling came down from Simla to find that Robinson had replaced Stephen Wheeler as editor-in-chief of the *Civil and Military Gazette*; Kipling now had a cheerful and sympathetic friend as his immediate superior. At once his position at the office changed from that of grudging subordinate to enthusiastic collaborator. Robinson's first assignment from the proprietors was to enliven the *Civil and Military*: to put, as George Allen told him, 'some sparkle into it'.[2] The new editor and his assistant, who welcomed the change, plunged into their task; in his autobiography, Kipling recalled that the reorganization 'took up for a week or so all hours of the twenty-four and cost me a break-down due to lack of sleep. But we two were proud of the

[1] The visit is described by E. Kay Robinson in 'Kipling in India', *McClure's Magazine*, vii (1896), 99–109. The exact chronology of their early relationship is a trifle uncertain. Professor Carrington asserts that they published a poetic dispute about Christmas in India in 1885, but other bibliographers date the first appearance of Kipling's 'Christmas in India' as 24 December 1886. Cf. Charles Carrington, *Rudyard Kipling: His Life and Work* (London, 1955), p. 72.

[2] Carrington, op. cit., p. 77.

results.' In consequence of the renovation Kipling had to contribute far more original copy than he had written under Wheeler: 'One new feature', he tells us, 'was a daily "turnover" — same as the little pink *Globe* at Home — of one column and a quarter. Naturally, the "office" had to supply most of them and once more I was forced to "write short".'[1]

Although Kipling had made notable advances in the preceding year, he found that it was not easy to be witty and imaginative day after day. The ten pieces he published between the middle of August and the end of September show him casting about for subjects: he sketches native amusements, parodies Victor Hugo, satirizes the Theosophists, describes the torments of a sleepless night, and even descends to that Anglo-Indian standby, the exile's lament.[2] Only one piece — 'The Story of Muhammad Din' — has lasting value. Kipling published no prose at all during October; having exhausted for the time being his stock of subjects, he paused to take the measure of his problem.

The solution was near at hand: as Kipling wrote in *Something of Myself*, 'I forget who started the notion of my writing a series of Anglo-Indian tales, but I remember our [family] council over the naming of the series'.[3] The title chosen was of course 'Plain Tales from the Hills', and it appeared in connection with at least thirty-five stories published between 2 November 1886 and 10 June 1887. Later, twenty-nine of them were collected, along with three earlier stories and eight new ones, and published as *Plain Tales from the Hills* in January 1888. The title of the series and the general drift of Kipling's prose experimentation suggest the kind of stories he had in mind at the beginning. Plain in style, realistic in

[1] Rudyard Kipling, *Something of Myself*, 'Library Edition' (London, 1951), p. 66.

[2] See, respectively, '"A District at Play"', '"Les Misérables"', 'A Nightmare of Rule', 'From the Dusk to the Dawn', and 'Prisoners and Captives'.

[3] *Something of Myself*, p. 207.

intention, the tales were to be about people like the Kiplings and their friends — civil servants and officers who could afford to spend their holidays at Simla or another of the principal hill-stations. And, indeed, the Simla milieu, with its rituals of flirtation, courtship, and marriage, forms the substance and background of the earliest 'Plain Tales': for and about Anglo-Indians, the stories were evidently designed to hold a mirror up to their readers.

II

I have shown in the preceding chapter how Kipling moved away from the tradition of Poe and began to develop techniques that stemmed directly from his own newspaper reporting. Now that he had to supply fiction on demand, however, we might expect him to have depended heavily on older practitioners of the short story as models and sources. In fact, only two of Kipling's predecessors have been persistently advanced as influences upon him: I shall turn aside briefly from the 'Plain Tales' to consider their claims.

Although early critics considered Kipling a disciple of Bret Harte, the perspective of half a century has diminished the similarities and emphasized the differences between the two. We know that Kipling was an admirer of Harte; nevertheless, I find it difficult to believe that Kipling made any effort to imitate the famous Californian.[1] Where Harte is discursive, Kipling is concise; where Harte is sentimental, Kipling is detached and ironic. Harte wrote about mining camps and vagabonds for an audience predominantly metropolitan; it is doubtful whether the residents of Poker Flat would have recognized themselves from Harte's descriptions of them.

[1] The strongest case for Harte's influence is made by Walter Morris Hart, *Kipling the Story-Writer* (Berkeley, 1918), pp. 61–68. References to Bret Harte in Kipling's works are listed in Ann M. Weygandt, *Kipling's Reading and Its Influence on His Poetry* (Philadelphia, 1939), pp. 141–3.

Kipling, on the other hand, was a member of the social group he chiefly described. Londoners read the *Plain Tales* with avidity and enjoyed them, we may be sure, because the stories supplied a flavour of the remote land in which they were written. But seen in their proper environment, against the background of the Punjab Club and Peliti's, the 'Plain Tales' bear only the most broad and superficial resemblances to Harte's rambling pastorals.[1]

Early critics — and some later ones — likewise discerned an affinity between Kipling and Guy de Maupassant.[2] Both are masters of brevity and precision; both are notable for their cold and detached treatment of their characters; both appeared misogynistic and, in that reticent age, too interested in illicit sexual liaisons. But claims for the influence of Maupassant are frustrated by obstacles. In the first place, no case of borrowing has been discovered. The similarities between the two are neither specific nor striking: the work of one author could hardly be mistaken for that of the other. In the second place, there is no external evidence that Kipling was even aware of Maupassant during the eighties. Unlike most English writers, Kipling could have read the Frenchman's stories: of that much we can be certain. Translations of Maupassant's work did not appear in England until 1887, but numerous translations of French novels that could not be legally sold in England were available in India; moreover, Kipling read French easily and refers to Zola in his writings, so that neither official censorship nor a paucity of translations would necessarily

[1] Harte himself later parodied Kipling in *Condensed Novels: Second Series* (Boston, 1902), pp. 165–95. These 'Stories Three' are chiefly interesting as showing a wide acquaintance with Kipling's fiction.

[2] Perhaps the first to make the comparison in print was an anonymous *Times* reviewer writing in 1890: quoted by Carrington, *Rudyard Kipling*, p. 148. The debt to Maupassant is merely asserted by Edward Shanks, *Rudyard Kipling* (London, 1940), p. 64. It is suggested but not examined by Francis Léaud, *La Poétique de Rudyard Kipling* (Paris, 1958), p. 60.

have kept him from discovering Maupassant.[1] On the other hand, the one piece of external evidence we have, though indecisive, suggests that Kipling did not take advantage of his opportunities. In January 1890, Kipling, then in London, published in the *Civil and Military* a satiric sketch of some Wildean aesthetes for the amusement of his Indian readers. Asked repeatedly about certain French authors, 'I replied that all my French was confined to the Vie Parisienne and translations of Zola's novels with illustrations.' Finally, he decides to read them, and he reports: 'To this end I procured the whole Shibboleth from Guy de Maupassant even unto Pierre Loti by way of Bourget. Unwholesome was a mild term for some of these interesting books, which the young men assured me that they read for style.'[2] As evidence, the reference is dubious; the fact that Kipling does not do justice to his knowledge of French casts

[1] Of Lahore at night, Kipling wrote: 'Zola could describe it.' ('"The City of Dreadful Night"', 10 September 1885.) Describing his railway travels in Rajputana, he noted that 'There are many, and some very curious, methods of seeing India. One of these is buying English translations of the more Zolaistic of Zola's novels and reading them from breakfast to dinner-time in the verandah.' ('Letters of Marque', No. iv, 27 December 1887.) The existence of translations in India was pointed out by the 'Vigilance Association' that persecuted Vizetelly in 1888; see William C. Frierson, *L'Influence du naturalisme français sur les romanciers anglais de 1885 à 1900* (Paris, 1925), p. 256 n. It was reported in the *Week's News* that the Government intended to control the books sold at railway bookstalls, on account of 'the prominence with which cheap "unabridged" translations of dubious, or less than dubious, French novels are displayed at these establishments'. (*Week's News* [Allahabad], 9 February 1889, vol. ii, no. 6, 1.)

[2] Rudyard Kipling, 'The Three Young Men', in *Abaft the Funnel*, 'Authorized Edition' (New York, 1909), pp. 258–9. For Maupassant's English reputation, see Frierson, *L'Influence*, chap. v, and *The English Novel in Transition: 1885–1940* (Norman, 1942), p. 165. Some doubt is rightly cast on the existence of a 'Maupassant School' by George J. Worth, 'The English "Maupassant" School of the 1890's: Some Reservations', *MLN*, lxxii (1957), 337–40. But Worth does not deny that Maupassant had become well known in England by the nineties.

doubt over the trustworthiness of his other statements. But it is all the evidence there is, and it does not add to the plausibility of the case for Maupassant's influence.

Finally, Kipling's debt to earlier writers of Anglo-Indian fiction can be neither dismissed nor precisely ascertained. We have seen that he called attention to his general obligations to Anglo-Indian poetry, but in the case of fiction he left no such record. And the nature of Anglo-Indian fiction makes influence extraordinarily hard to demonstrate.[1] Little more than the English novel transplanted, the Anglo-Indian novel did not present Kipling with a strongly marked tradition to which he could attach himself.[2] With the exception of Meadows Taylor, British India produced no author with individual characteristics as striking, with a vision of India as personal and coherent, as Kipling's: it is hard to see what he could have learned from his predecessors. Setting Kipling's stories against novels like those of H. S. Cunningham or sketches like Aberigh-Mackay's *Twenty-One Days in India*, we can see that he writes about the same Anglo-Indian types — officials, mem-sahibs, flirtatious grass widows, and so forth.[3] Kipling probably read

[1] Anglo-Indian novels are as numerous as they are mediocre; I have had to depend on the following discussions of the subject: Edward Farley Oaten, *A Sketch of Anglo-Indian Literature* (London, 1908); Bhupal Singh, *A Survey of Anglo-Indian Fiction* (London, 1934); and Susanne Howe [Nobbe], *Novels of Empire* (New York, 1949).

[2] For the Englishness of Anglo-Indian literature, see Edward Farley Oaten, 'Anglo-Indian Literature', *CHEL*, xiv. 331. William Delafield Arnold's *Oakfield* rises above the prevailing mediocrity, but it differs from the norm in that it deals with British India from what might be called the point of view of a critical outsider: here India is primarily a background for Edward Oakfield's spiritual struggle, rather than the central fact of the book.

[3] Two novels by Henry Stewart Cunningham that show affinities to Kipling's work are *Chronicles of Dustypore*, new ed. (London, 1877); and *The Coeruleans*, 2 vols. (London, 1887). Sir George MacMunn traces possible sources in Aberigh-Mackay's *Twenty-One Days in India*; see his 'The Rough Ashlar: Some Kipling Affinities', *Kipling Journal*, no. 61 (April 1942), 5–6.

Cunningham and Aberigh-Mackay, but he need not have done so in order to have written about personages so typical of Anglo-Indian society. For these types were not merely available: in fact, they imposed themselves upon all Anglo-Indian writers whose aim was verisimilitude.

III

But is it fair to assume that Kipling's sole aim was verisimilitude, that he was attempting only to provide his readers with slices of Anglo-Indian life? The problem of 'realism' has haunted Kipling studies for so long that it demands at least a further effort at clarification.

Again and again we find that one of the 'Plain Tales' has an identifiable source in real persons and events.[1] Kipling's Anglo-Indian contemporaries were convinced that all the stories were *contes-à-clef*, so to speak, and wore away many a tiffin in disputes over the 'real' identity of Mrs. Hauksbee. Realism of one sort or another seems to have been characteristic of the Kipling family. Lockwood's art, as exemplified by the bas-relief illustrations to his son's work, has all the accuracy, the substance, the definiteness of outline that we find in Rudyard's stories. When Trix wrote the first of her two Anglo-Indian novels, *The Heart of a Maid*, she relied heavily upon the circumstances of her own marriage.[2] The autobiographical nature of *The Light That Failed* is well known, but more important is the aesthetic credo that the novel embodies. The whole merit of Dick Heldar's war painting is that it is photographically realistic, almost

[1] Professor Carrington identifies a number of sources in passing: *Rudyard Kipling*, pp. 91–112.

[2] Compare Beatrice Kipling [pseud. of Alice M. Fleming], *The Heart of a Maid* (New York, 1891), with the biographical material in Arthur Windham Baldwin, *The Macdonald Sisters* (London, 1960), pp. 124–6. In the first edition of her novel Trix's identity was further disguised under the pseudonym 'Beatrice Grange'.

trompe-l'œil. The measure of his success is displayed in the scene where two artillerymen admire one of Dick's battle pictures: '"They've chucked the off lead-'orse", said one to the other. "'E's tore up awful, but they're makin' good time with the others. That lead-driver drives better nor you, Tom. See 'ow cunnin' 'e's nursin' 'is 'orse."'[1]

In spite of a good deal of evidence of this kind, Kipling's claims to realism have been obscured by the history of fiction during his own lifetime. His English contemporaries realized in the eighties and nineties that the development of the novel was proceeding in two different directions. By and large, the classic mid-nineteenth-century English novelists, though predominantly realistic, were willing to include elements of the fortuitous and improbable for the sake of a good story. But with the demise of the three-decker and the growth of interest in French naturalism, readers began to demand a new realism in fiction and to manifest a new contempt for the improbable and romantic in novels that claimed to be 'serious'. This realism was matched, on the other hand, by a proliferation of romantic adventure stories, apparently in reaction to what was dull and sordid in novels of the other persuasion.[2] Later historians have allowed the categories to harden into a school of Zola-esque naturalism (Moore, Bennett, early Maugham) and a school of Stevensonian romance (Haggard, Doyle, Anthony Hope). The division is legitimate, but critics have tended to assign places to individual authors almost solely on the basis of subject matter, even of milieu: if a man writes of drab London streets, he is a Zolaist; if he writes about the Punjab or Pretoria, he is with Robert Louis Stevenson aboard the 'Hispaniola'.

[1] Rudyard Kipling, *The Light That Failed*, 'Library Edition' (London, 1951), p. 69.

[2] Frierson surveys the field and lists many articles of the period that recognize the existence of two fictional schools: see *The English Novel in Transition*, pp. 125–8.

The only exception normally made to this division is the case of Joseph Conrad. As Lionel Stevenson puts it in a recent book on the English novel, Conrad

> seems hard to classify because he wrote about exotic settings and perilous adventures that would be appropriate for Kipling, and yet he was a faithful adherent of Henry James. The explanation is that for Joseph Conrad the Malayan islands and the hardy life of seamen were not fascinating because they fulfilled daydreams that were beyond his actual scope; on the contrary, they had been the everyday reality of his life for so many years that they were as familiar to him as a London drawing room was to James or a Dorsetshire village to Hardy.[1]

Or, one is tempted to add, as the alleys of Lahore and the courts of minor maharajahs were to Rudyard Kipling. As Kenneth Burke puts it, 'One cannot awaken a sense of strangeness in the reader by talking of Xanadu, if the reader happens to be Kubla Khan.'[2] And, conversely, the most prosaic, naturalistic account of Indian life will seem strange and perhaps wonderful to an untravelled Englishman. In fact, the more detailed and circumstantial the account, the more alien will it seem: call a native butler a native butler and he will be more or less identifiable to all readers; call him a *khitmatgar* and he will be depressingly familiar to the Anglo-Indian, mysterious and exotic to the Liverpudlian. In many ways Kipling, with his notebook and spectacles, his ''satiable curtiosity' about technicians, soldiers, animals, and

[1] Lionel Stevenson, *The English Novel: A Panorama* (Boston, 1960), p. 431. By using the phrase 'daydreams that were beyond his actual scope', Professor Stevenson seems to credit the old theory that Kipling wrote about men of action because he wished he had been one himself. Such an allegation, of course, can neither be proven nor dismissed, but the more we learn about Kipling's dedication to the art of literature, the less tenable it becomes. For a full and sensitive treatment of the 'novels of adventure', including Kipling's, see Madeleine L. Cazamian, *Le Roman et les idées en Angleterre: 1860–1914*, 4 vols. (Paris, 1923–); esp. vol. iii, *Doctrines d'action et d'aventure: 1880–1914* (1955).

[2] Kenneth Burke, *Counter-Statement*, 2nd ed. (Chicago, 1957), p. 179.

machines, was closer to the *roman expérimental* of Zola, whom he admired, than to the *exotisme* of Loti, whom he depreciated.[1]

But to insist that Dick Heldar's photographic realism is Kipling's whole aesthetic transferred to another medium, or to suggest that he was a dogmatic Zolaist, would be to distort Kipling's intentions. The point is that he did not see himself as a romancer of the school of Stevenson: he needed to feel himself anchored in the facts of his own, or someone else's experience. 'A Germ-Destroyer', a minor 'Plain Tale', provides an instance that may be taken as characteristic of one of the ways his mind worked. The story concerns the officious private secretary of a Viceroy and his comic demise at the hands of a certain Mellish, the inventor of an infallible 'Fumigatory'. Wonder, the secretary, through mistaken zeal, allows Mellish to see the Viceroy, whereupon the inventor demonstrates the fumigatory, the powder makes a hideous smoke and stench, and Wonder is tactfully relieved of his secretarial job. As Professor Carrington reports, Wonder seems to have been modelled on a real person, Lord William Beresford, though no such discomfiture overtook Wonder's original.[2] The incident can probably be traced to an anecdote told by Sir J. H. Rivett Carnac in his memoirs. A certain Major Lucie-Smith discovered a vein of coal in the Chandah District. In his enthusiasm, he tried to demonstrate its qualities at Government House in Nagpore: 'and behold there was such a Fifth of November blaze that Government House, the public offices, and the new church nearly all perished in the conflagration'.[3] Rivett Carnac was a

[1] Kipling had this to say about French *exotisme* in general: 'I suppress here — though it was very beautiful — a denunciation of certain French writers who would represent their Colonial officers as mournfully devoured, beneath tropical moons, by a passion for drugs and fat black females.' *Souvenirs of France* (London, 1933), p. 48.

[2] Carrington, *Rudyard Kipling*, p. 65 n.

[3] John Harry Rivett Carnac, *Many Memories* (Edinburgh, 1910) p. 199.

friend of the Kipling family and an admirer of Rudyard's stories; he was, moreover, incurably anecdotal, as his memoirs testify. It seems likely that Kipling heard the story — if not from Rivett Carnac, then perhaps from his own parents — and constructed 'A Germ-Destroyer' from it. But in the process, of course, he made a tale out of it; he transformed the innocuous Lucie-Smith into the grotesque Mellish, added Lord William Beresford and a Viceroy who is not unlike Lord Dufferin, and finished by turning an amusing anecdote into a comedy of official manners. The result, to be sure, is not a distinguished short story, but neither is it a piece of *trompe-l'œil* realism, nor a groundless fantasy: it has just such plausibility as satiric comedy requires.

IV

If we were required to assign Kipling to either the realist or the romantic school, I think we could find plausible reasons on both sides. But in fact Kipling's achievement transcends such simple formulae. Like his great contemporaries Henry James, Conrad, and Stevenson, or like Zola himself, Kipling's traffic with the real world became a far more complex affair than the mere registry of sensory impressions. The 'Plain Tales from the Hills' hold the mirror up to their readers, but they do a lot more besides. It is this larger realm of accomplishment that we must now examine.

As the 'Plain Tales' series advanced through the autumn and winter of 1886, Kipling turned from the familiar banalities of Simla intrigue into the alleys of old Lahore and the all but unknown world of the military cantonments at Mian Mir; in so doing he had to come to an accommodation between the realistic mode he had so recently adopted and his growing sense of the strangeness of Indian life. For, though Kipling preferred Zola's naturalism to the exoticism of Loti, he never fully committed himself to the new realism of the eighties and nineties. He has periodically been accused of exploiting lush atmosphere and weird incidents so as to pander to the taste of his English readers, but even in the tales aimed specifically at the knowledgeable Anglo-Indian readers of the *Civil and Military Gazette*, Kipling often sought out instances of the startling, the supernatural, the bizarre. Strickland, we recall, 'was initiated into the *Sat Bhai* at Allahabad once' and knew the 'Lizzard Song' of the Sansis and *Halli-Hukk* dance; Trejago could decipher object-letters; Dumoise was haunted by his dead wife; the Bisara of Pooree had a way of turning up unexpectedly; and McIntosh Jellaludin was party to a variety of unspeakable secrets.

> A stone's throw out on either hand
> From that well-ordered road we tread,
> And all the world is wild and strange.[1]

But in Kipling's view, this wild, strange world could be made, had to be made, as much a part of contemporary India as tiffin at Peliti's or a ride round Jakko Hill. Because he was fascinated by it, he made an effort to learn all he could about the obscure underside of Indian life, an effort that few English writers, perhaps only Philip Meadows Taylor, had previously made. Thus, from a deliberate disparity between exotic subject and realistic treatment arises the most characteristic mode of the 'Plain Tales'. The reporter's conversational tone, understatement, and habitual irony maintain a constant pressure towards verisimilitude, even when the worlds he explores lie beyond the borders of his readers' normal experience.

This characteristic of the 'Plain Tales' can be clearly illustrated by a comparison of 'The Phantom 'Rickshaw' with 'By Word of Mouth', the last of the newspaper series and one of Kipling's best ghost stories. The

[1] Verse heading to 'In the House of Suddhoo'. It would be interesting to know whether it appeared with the tale in the *Civil and Military* or was added when the story was collected.

earliest version of 'The Phantom 'Rickshaw' consisted only of Pansay's narrative, beginning with the sentence: 'My doctor tells me that I need rest and change of air.' Thereafter we are in the mind of a man who either is mad or has seen a ghost; Kipling never fully commits himself to one side or the other, but in either case the effect of the story is decidedly Gothic: we accept the situation as being conventionally distant from everyday reality, nor do we need a narrator to reassure us of its verisimilitude. The atmosphere of plausibility in 'By Word of Mouth', however, is painstakingly established. In the first place, the reporter introduces himself at the outset in order to set a tone of tolerant scepticism: 'I have lived long enough in this India to know that it is best to know nothing, and can only write the story as it happened.' Next, this narrator surrounds himself with a shadowy but conventional society, the prosaic norm against which the strange drama will be played out: the hero, Dumoise, was 'our Civil Surgeon at Meridki, and we called him "Dormouse"'. From this point on, everything is as explicit and circumstantial as Kipling can make it. 'We had seven cases of typhoid in the Station that winter. . . . We wrestled with those typhoid cases for fifty-six days. . . . Chini is some twenty marches from Simla. . . . Bagi dâk-bungalow is open to all the winds and is bitterly cold.' The reporter could not know what Dumoise discovered at the dâk-bungalow, but Kipling anticipates the objection: 'In the evening Dumoise told his *locum tenens*, who was an old friend of his bachelor days, what had happened at Bagi.' Only by stripping both stories down to the bare bones can we see that 'By Word of Mouth' and 'The Phantom 'Rickshaw' are about the same thing — a man who encounters the ghost of a dead beloved and dies in anticipation of rejoining her. In all other respects, the stories take place in different worlds. Where the earlier is grotesque, the later is deliberately prosaic; where the one is feverish and exaggerated, the other is subtle, delicate, and understated. As Mr. Randall Jarrell puts it in one of the best recent discussions of the 'Plain Tales': 'The continual understatement, the continual contrast of form and content, the continual "writing short", all help to give the stories their particular force.' The contrast between these two stories not only indicates how much Kipling had learned from the discipline of writing turnovers; it also suggests the difficulty of isolating and defining Kipling's 'realism'.

But we should be doing Kipling an injustice if we were to treat *Plain Tales* solely through the analysis of his technique in isolated stories. To quote Mr. Jarrell again: 'Only six or eight of the forty *Plain Tales from the Hills* are very good stories, and yet somehow the whole book is better than the best of the stories, and gives the reader a surprisingly vivid and comprehensive feeling of the society that produced it.'[1] The whole is indeed greater than the sum of its parts, because in a sense all the stories sprang from the same impulse; they were written near enough together in time and circumstances to share many of their author's deepest and most pervasive concerns. Accordingly, we must now turn to the book as a whole. The stories will bear much closer scrutiny than I can give them here; I shall restrict my discussion to three interwoven themes: the author's relation to his narrator; the difficulty of distinguishing reality from false appearances in the world the stories describe; and the ambiguous vision of British India to which the author's discovery of reality ultimately gives rise.

V

Criticism of *Plain Tales from the Hills* sometimes begins with a division of the stories by subject-matter, a division that Kipling himself obliquely sanctioned by the way he treated his later *Pioneer* stories: soldier stories collected

[1] Randall Jarrell, Introduction to *In the Vernacular: The English in India: Short Stories by Rudyard Kipling* (New York, 1963), p. xiv.

in *Soldiers Three*, child stories in *Wee Willie Winkie*, and so forth.[1] But this is a mechanical division, for it suggests that each story can be categorized according to the colour, age, or occupation of its major characters. As it stands, *Plain Tales* reveals neither this arbitrary classification nor any chronological progression from early stories to later ones. The result is a considerable gain in the strength of the reader's total impression, for in fact *Plain Tales* is not 'about' ghosts or soldiers or natives or life at Simla; in so far as it has a subject, that subject is British India — as many aspects of British India as the young author's sensibility can encompass and control.

The nameless hero of *Plain Tales* is the narrator of the stories. Whether the reporter appears in a given story as 'I' or 'we' is unimportant; the fact is that all the stories are told by the same voice. No matter how much we may object to his brash or knowing tone, the speaker begins to take shape, and our interest is divided between the story he tells and the things he reveals about himself. Nor can we simply identify the reporter with Rudyard Kipling and go on to discuss the stories as if they were designed to expose their author's views, attitudes, and experiences. The narrator of *Plain Tales* is a created fictional character who exists in and through the stories he tells. Sometimes he takes on substance as an 'I' who has more or less of a role to play in the action; at other times, he is closer to what Wayne C. Booth calls the 'implied author', the person whose views, attitudes, sympathies, and moral standards we infer from the narrative itself.[2]

[1] It may be that the publisher, not Kipling himself, was responsible for this division; nevertheless, Kipling allowed it to be made.

[2] I use Professor Booth's phrase with some reservations, though I have found his study of fiction brilliant and convincing. If I understand him correctly, he would expect the 'implied author' to make the imperfections of the narrator clear to the reader, except in such cases of intentional ambiguity as 'The Turn of the Screw' and Joyce's *Portrait*. I think a case could be made for Kipling's deliberate use of an imperfect narrator,

I do not mean to insist that the reporter has nothing in common with the real, historical Rudyard Kipling; rather, their similarities are too obvious to require mention. It takes an effort of the imagination to separate the man from his fictional counterpart. One such effort was made by an early but sensitive student of Kipling's stories, Walter Morris Hart:

> On the whole, however, Kipling presents us, in the glimpses of himself, with material for a sufficiently flattering portrait — not the real Kipling, nor Kipling as the world saw him, but Kipling as Kipling, aged twenty-two, saw him. He is a member of the club, he moves in the best society; he is guide, philosopher, and friend to the best people in his stories, to Mrs. Hauksbee, the cleverest woman in India; to Strickland, who knew as much of the natives as the natives knew themselves.[1]

I doubt if the real Rudyard Kipling was nearly so blind to his own shortcomings, social and otherwise, as Hart makes him out to be, but the main point — that Kipling was not so widely acquainted as his reporter — needs to be made. Indeed, this is only one of several disparities between the real Kipling and his imaginary narrator. The latter seems to have none of Kipling's strong family ties, nor has he ever fallen in love; predominantly an idle listener, he rarely suggests that he is a journalist by profession.[2] On the other hand, the more we learn of the real Kipling, the more he appears to have been an earnest, friendly, susceptible young man who was not allowed by his family to take himself very seriously. He applied himself to learning such necessary social graces as riding and dancing, took pains with his dress, and fell

but the problem is too large and intricate for discussion here. See Wayne C. Booth, *The Rhetoric of Fiction* (Chicago, 1961), esp. pp. 70–77.

[1] *Kipling the Story-Writer*, p. 37.

[2] Except, of course, in 'The Man Who Would Be King', the exception that proves the rule, where the reporter is actually shown working at his desk.

mildly in love at frequent intervals.[1] If the reporter is a picture of Kipling himself, it is neither flattering nor accurate.

Approaching the problem from another angle and tracing possible autobiographical threads in the stories, we find several cases wherein events that did involve Kipling involve not the reporter but the characters whose experiences he relates. Dicky Hatt, of 'In the Pride of His Youth', may not be intended for a self-portrait, but his situation resembles Kipling's in certain respects: the story dramatizes what might have happened to Kipling if he had married Florence Garrard before leaving England. Again, a letter from Kipling to a Mrs. Maunsell identifies her implicitly as the original of Mrs. Landys-Haggert of 'On the Strength of a Likeness', with Kipling playing the role of the befuddled Hannasyde.[2] Wressley of the Foreign Office writes his great history for Tillie Venner, who doesn't appreciate it; we are reminded of a younger Kipling painstakingly copying out verses and stories and laying them at the feet of the elusive Florence. Finally, we discover that McIntosh Jellaludin, a drunken loafer, has written '"an account of the life and sins and death of Mother Maturin"', the

[1] This, at any rate, is the picture of Kipling that emerges from Professor Carrington's biography, and it is supported by the few reminiscences of the young Kipling that have appeared in print. See especially Edward Kay Robinson, 'Kipling in India'; and his 'Rudyard Kipling as Journalist', *Literature* (London), iv (18 March 1899), 284–86. See also Edmonia Hill, 'The Young Kipling: Personal Recollections', *Atlantic Monthly*, clvii (1936), 406–15. Carrington, Robinson, and Hill all mention Kipling's attraction for women and enjoyment of feminine company: 'He is the most susceptible person I ever knew', wrote Mrs. Hill (p. 410) — hardly an epithet one would apply to the personality of the reporter.

[2] A. L. S., Rudyard Kipling to Mrs. Maunsell, on *C. & M.G.* stationery, dated 10 June 1887. The letter contains the implication that Kipling was extremely disconcerted by Mrs. Maunsell's resemblance to Florence: he speaks of an uncanny facial likeness — he doesn't say to whom — and calls Mrs. Maunsell's attention to 'On the Strength of a Likeness' in the forthcoming *Plain Tales from the Hills*.

novel that Kipling hoped would make his reputation. *Plain Tales* is not an impersonal book. It shows forth many of Kipling's nearest concerns. But it doesn't do so by stating them overtly in the form of the reporter's breezy and cynical generalities. In fact, the situation may be quite the contrary. We have noted Kipling's urgent need to work in privacy, a need that led him to withhold his most personal poems from his readers. For all the external resemblances between Kipling and his supposed fictional counterpart, the reporter may well serve as a screen, a public version of the author that will distract attention from the real concerns of the stories.

One of the most important of these concerns — so important that it becomes one of the chief unifying themes of *Plain Tales* — is the difficulty of distinguishing reality from false appearances. While the reporter busily and tediously asserts that he knows everything there is to know, that he could tell you a hundred stories if he wanted to, Kipling returns again and again to the theme of deception and fraud. The theme takes on many forms. On the simplest and most frivolous level, it is embodied in the practical joke: the clever and sympathetic deceivers hoodwink the foolish villains, and we are expected merely to be amused by the discomfiture of the weaker party. 'His Wedded Wife' is about a masquerade; the White Hussars are panicked by a false ghost; the 'Three Musketeers' play an outrageous joke on Lord Benira Trig. 'Pig' and 'Watches of the Night' are more sinister versions of the same type. In the former, it is difficult to watch Nafferton gulling his victim without a growing sense of uneasiness; the story is an introduction to the tales of revenge discussed at length by Dr. J. M. S. Tompkins in her admirable book.[1] In 'Watches of the Night', the whole community joins in a conspiracy against the Colonel's wife: what begins as potential farce becomes a savage portrait of puritanical distrust in the process of destroying itself. At some remove from 'The

[1] *The Art of Rudyard Kipling* (London, 1959), chap. v.

Three Musketeers', yet still to be associated with it, is 'A Bank Fraud', wherein Reggie Burke's deception of Riley, his dying colleague, is not a joke at all: deception becomes an instrument of benevolence and links this tale to the theme of healing that Dr. Tompkins has discerned in Kipling's later writings.[1]

The foregoing stories have in common a deceiver and his victim, a deluder and a deluded. But an equally large group of stories deals with men who either delude themselves or are the chance victims of appearances. Central to this group is 'In Error'. Moriarty falls in love with Mrs. Reiver; thinking her to be noble and virtuous, he conquers his alcoholism in order to be worthy of her: 'Moriarty thought her something she never was, and in that belief saved himself; which was just as good as though she had been everything that he had imagined.' Wressley of the Foreign Office proves radically mistaken about the nature of Tillie Venner; Hannasyde falls in love with Mrs. Landys-Haggert 'on the strength of a likeness'; 'Very Young' Gayerson falls in love with the middle-aged Venus Annodomini, thinking her to be about twenty-five. These are gay stories, for the most part, but self-delusion can have terrible consequences. The Boy of 'Thrown Away' 'took all things seriously' and killed himself as a result; Dicky Hatt was 'kidnapped in his early, early youth . . . by a girl so nearly of his own caste that only a woman could have seen she was just the least little bit in the world below it', and the mistake cost him his career.

Normally, these self-deluders are blind to a state of affairs well-known to the community at large. Even when he feels sympathy for them, the reporter, as representative of the community's sophistication, patronizes them: hence the grotesque disparity between the beginning of 'Thrown Away', where the Boy is compared at length to an untrained puppy, and the end, where he is found a suicide in the jungle. But in some cases the

[1] *The Art of Rudyard Kipling* (London, 1959), chap. vi.

community itself is deluded. Everyone expects Saumarez in 'False Dawn' to propose to Maud Copleigh; in 'Cupid's Arrows' they expect Kitty to accept Barr-Saggott; in 'Tods' Amendment' the child has to tutor the Viceroy and Council as to the real needs of Indian peasants. Gradually the accumulation of instances drives home Kipling's meaning: no one in India is entirely free from the delusions caused by false appearances; on every hand pitfalls await the foolish or the over-confident.

In a world so full of delusion and disguise, one's clothing naturally takes on peculiar importance. Mrs. Cusack-Bremmil in 'Three and — an Extra' is on the point of losing her husband to Mrs. Hauksbee, until she recovers herself and dresses prettily; by changing her clothes, she changes herself into a new person. Lispeth symbolizes her disenchantment with English civilization by putting on native rags; Dunmaya, on the other hand, marries Phil Garron and presents a reasonable facsimile of a European wife: she 'dressed by preference in black and yellow, and looked well'. In caste-ridden India it can be dangerous or degrading to be taken for what you are not. Clothing is the badge of authority, separating not only the conquerors from the conquered but the upper ranks from the lower. 'The Arrest of Lieutenant Golightly', in most respects a trivial story, clearly exposes the connection between clothes and caste. 'If there was one thing on which Golightly prided himself more than another, it was looking like "an Officer and a Gentleman" ', the reporter tells us. But when Golightly is caught in a rainstorm, his servants desert him and his clothing disintegrates. Mistaken for a deserter, he is arrested, insulted, and beaten. Moreover, as Golightly's clothes go to pieces, so does his character. Instead of behaving like 'an Officer and a Gentleman', he rages and curses at the soldiers who have caught him: needless to say, his violent curses merely convince his captors that they have arrested the right man.

If Kipling were concerned only with delusion and

disguise, the *Plain Tales* would conform to a pattern that has often been ascribed to them by critics: that is, the narrator-author, a cocksure young cynic, is using the short story as a vehicle to persuade his readers that he has plucked out the heart of the Anglo-Indian mystery.[1] A number of the *Plain Tales*, especially the ones that deal with Mrs. Hauksbee and her circle, do fit this pattern. Kipling and his reporter take sides with the deluders in order to show how easily Anglo-Indian officialdom can be hoodwinked. From these stories in particular arises the knowingness that has so often offended Kipling's readers. But when we turn from Mrs. Hauksbee and her Simla friends to Strickland of the Police, we enter a somewhat different world, a world in which the reporter's self-confidence no longer strikes us as quite so unshakable; and it is this world, not Mrs. Hauksbee's, that gives *Plain Tales from the Hills* its special vitality and richness. In Strickland's hands, disguise becomes more than an instrument of delusion for the sake of knowledge and power; his ability to pass for an Indian also provides him with an avenue of escape. For if it is dangerous to be caught, like Golightly, with the wrong clothes on, it is intolerably constricting to be at all times a representative of law, order, and civilization. Strickland combines the public life of an energetic civil servant with a secret, anonymous life, a haven from what Kipling later called 'a land where every circumstance *and* relation of a man's life is public property'.[2]

Always capable of perceiving value in both modes of life, Kipling shows in *Plain Tales* an unusual sympathy for the anonymous and irresponsible. Though Miss Youghal and her family bring Strickland to heel, what counts in the Strickland stories is the delight Kipling makes us feel at the policeman's escapes from the world

[1] For an impressive statement of this view, see Lionel Trilling, 'Kipling', in *Kipling's Mind and Art*, ed. Andrew Rutherford (Edinburgh, 1964), pp. 86–87.

[2] *Something of Myself*, p. 52.

of conventional behaviour. Several of the more ambitious tales reveal the same conflict between prescribed duties and the impulse to flee, to disappear altogether from British India. In 'The Madness of Private Ortheris', homesickness of almost pathological intensity breaks through Ortheris's normal self-control, prompting him to exchange his uniform for anonymous civilian clothes and his soldier's disciplined life for the rich and chaotic disorder of the London slums. The fit wears off, and Ortheris is as horrified as Mulvaney at the idea of deserting, but Kipling has shown us the terrible strain that is required to keep up one's public role in India. We remember not Ortheris's repentance, but his desperate cry: ' "What must I do to get out o' this 'ere a-Hell?" ' Unlike Ortheris, McIntosh Jellaludin does not repent and recover his social position. He has disappeared once and for all into the Indian underworld, taken a native wife, become a convert to Islam. By every Anglo-Indian standard he has failed utterly. And yet he has captured Kipling's imagination: the conversations between McIntosh and the reporter suggest in a curious way that two conflicting impulses in Kipling himself are debating against one another; McIntosh embodies that part of Kipling's mind for which the restraints of Anglo-Indian life were intolerably burdensome. '"I am as the Gods, knowing good and evil, but untouched by either," ' McIntosh boasts. '"Is this enviable or is it not?" ' The reporter evades the question, but the story as a whole proposes a qualified affirmative. McIntosh is enviable to the extent that he has seen to the bottom of Indian life, and can therefore laugh at Strickland as an ignorant man. He is enviable as the author of 'Mother Maturin', the novel Kipling had begun but was never to complete.

Ortheris's madness is too arbitrary, his recovery too wholehearted, to gain our complete credence, and McIntosh's degradation too often becomes sentimental Byronism; but in 'Beyond the Pale' Kipling maintains a nearly perfect control of the contrary impulses towards conventionality on the one hand, and anonymity on the other. Like Strickland and McIntosh, Christopher Trejago seeks reality in the native world rather than the white, in 'the City where each man's house is as guarded and unknowable as the grave'. 'He knew too much in the first instance,' says the reporter's warning voice, 'and he saw too much in the second. He took too deep an interest in native life; but he will never do so again.' What Trejago finds in the City is love of a sort that British India cannot offer: the ultimate reward of this quest for India's hidden reality is not merely knowledge but Bisesa. To be sure, loving Bisesa is a dangerous adventure — Bisesa loses her hands in consequence of the affair, and Trejago nearly loses his life — but she is not hedged about with the dreary conventions of a Simla flirtation. Her passionate unworldliness is intensified by its contrast to the expedient courtship Trejago must pay to an Englishwoman he does not care for. 'Bisesa raged and stormed, and finally threatened to kill herself if Trejago did not at once drop the alien *Memsahib* who had come between them. Trejago tried to explain, and to show her that she did not understand these things from a Western standpoint. Bisesa drew herself up, and said simply — "I do not."' For the knowledge that enables Trejago to penetrate the depths of Amir Nath's Gully is an esoteric knowledge of object-letters and 'The Love Song of Har Dyal', not the commonplace knowledge of the laws of behaviour that the reporter has mastered.

'Beyond the Pale' suggests that a knowledge of public behaviour has a merely instrumental value: it will enable a man to survive, to avoid the most obvious traps that lie in the way of a socially ambitious young Anglo-Indian. But charting a course through an intricate pattern of delusion is a neutral achievement at best. You can expect to be rewarded with an engagement to Miss Youghal — who puts an end to Strickland's ventures into the underworld — or with the 'open-work jam-tart jewels in gold and enamel' that are the insignia of Barr-Saggott's high civilian rank. Bisesa, on the other hand, was to her Trejago 'an endless delight'. It was 'folly', the reporter cautiously tells us, but here the reporter is out of his depth; Kipling sees around his narrator and lets us know that the reporter is wrong, that we are not to accept his cautious warnings, that Bisesa and the world she represents are worth the terrible risks Trejago has run. 'Some one in the room grunted like a wild beast, and something sharp — knife, sword, or spear — thrust at Trejago in his *boorka*. The stroke missed his body, but cut into one of the muscles of the groin, and he limped slightly from the wound for the rest of his days.' The reminiscence of the punishment of Abelard is surely no accident; and the power of the old love story helps to commit us to Trejago in spite of all the warnings of embodied practical wisdom.

6. A Vision of India

THE publication of *Plain Tales from the Hills* might have constituted a turning point in Kipling's literary career. Now that he had a volume of stories in print, he could treat journalism as an unpleasant but necessary way to earn a living and reserve his energy for 'Mother Maturin', his manuscript novel. On the other hand, he could continue to treat the novel as an occasional diversion from his principal job, the enlightenment and entertainment of the Anglo-Indian newspaper public. Had he been living in London, he might have been persuaded by literary friends to finish the novel at all costs. Living in India, however, where there was not a single person who earned his living by writing fiction, he chose the latter course and threw himself into his journalistic work with extraordinary energy. During the eighteen months between Kipling's return from Simla in the late summer of 1887 and his departure from India in March 1889, his stories, poems, and sketches appeared at an average rate of three a week; nor is it unusual to find weeks wherein the rate of production reaches a piece a day.[1] In the autumn of 1887 he was transferred to the offices of the *Pioneer* in Allahabad, where he was given a variety of jobs: he edited the *Week's News*, a weekly supplement that was half newspaper, half magazine; he wrote a substantial story for the *News* every week for nine months; he contributed numerous turnovers to the *Civil and Military*, travelled widely in India so as to write travel sketches for the *Pioneer*, and turned out many occasional poems and satirical essays on con-

[1] For example, the week of 9–16 January 1888.

temporary Indian affairs. It was, as Kipling recalled, a 'furious spell of work', and it is a wonder that he did not resent the newspapers' demands.[1] But, like the overworked civil servants he portrayed, Kipling did not complain or rebel, for he took pride in being able to endure the strain.

Kipling's development kept on its steady course during his last two years in India. Not merely the life of Mother Maturin and her associates but India herself remained his great subject, for the bewildering profusion of his newspaper writings reflects the diversity of the land. But underneath this multiplicity may be found a single unifying consciousness: Kipling the artist cannot be divided from Kipling the journalist.[2] The young man's discovery of India proceeded at a continually accelerating rate, and he set down what he discovered in verse, fiction, and newspaper essay, making little effort to separate his various roles. As an artist, he continued to aim at verisimilitude, at the portrayal of a 'real' India free from the obscurities of ignorance, timidity, and sham romanticism; as a journalist, he saw India with the personal and discriminating vision that we associate with writers of fiction. And the roles overlap in other ways. For example, in travelling from Simla to Allahabad, Kipling is forced to halt at the flooded Gugger, and he passes the time in chatting with the old woman who tends the ford. On 28 July 1888 he reports the incident in the course of a bitter complaint about the state of the Umballa-Kalka

[1] Rudyard Kipling, *Something of Myself*, 'Library Edition' (London, 1951), p. 74.

[2] Such a division is suggested by Nelson S. Bushnell, 'Kipling's Ken of India', *University of Toronto Quarterly*, xxvii (1957), 65: 'In all but his latest treatments of India . . . the rapidly maturing professional was always at work as well as the marvellously endowed youngster; and the journalist tended to overshadow the artist.' The same split personality is detected by Humbert Wolfe, who symbolizes Kipling's two voices by the saxophone and the oboe: *Dialogues and Monologues* (New York, 1929), pp. 90–92.

road ('"In Forma Pauperis"'). Then, a fortnight later, he has transformed the incident into one of his most striking stories of Indian life — 'In Flood Time'. What began as an irksome delay has become part of his experience of India and her people.

And so the result of that furious spell of work is not a reporter's objective version of life and work in British India, nor is it an irresponsible storyteller's attempt to paint a false and glittering picture of the land. Out of thousands of observations he made, Kipling produced several hundred pieces of prose and verse; and these may be thought of as the various fragments of a single vision of India, a vision that strives for realism but is in fact personal, even idiosyncratic. Older readers of Kipling used to complain that such and such a fragment did not correspond with their Indian experiences: swayed by Kipling's claims to verisimilitude, they did not realize that they were asking from an author something that he never intended to give. Our task must rather be to reconstruct Kipling's vision of India from the fragments in which it lies — or, more properly, to sketch the outline of his vision, for Kipling tried never to repeat himself, and each fragment contributes something to the whole. If we have occasion to compare our outline with ascertainable historic facts, it is not because we feel a need to praise Kipling for his 'truth' or criticize him for his 'falsehood'; his vision remains autonomous, but the extent to which it corresponds to the experience of other observers is an important adjunct to any study of the development of Kipling's art.

I

The dominant theme of recent Anglo-Indian fiction has been the lack of understanding between Indians and Europeans: Forster's *A Passage to India* is the most notable example, but it is a subject that has fascinated such lesser writers as John Masters, John Berry, and many others.[1] In the late nineteenth century, however, for reasons I have explained in an earlier chapter, relations between the two races had broken down almost completely, so that in a sense the theme was not really available to novelists in Kipling's time. There was peace between the races and a degree of mutual respect, but there was little or no contact. As C. T. Buckland, one of Kipling's contemporaries, wrote, 'The more an Englishman sees of India, the less competent he feels to write about the natives of the country. They are a good and loveable people . . ., but we never seem to come to a true and thorough knowledge of them. The substance eludes our grasp, and we find ourselves contemplating an imaginary shadow.'[2] Artificial efforts to bring about understanding between the races had failed; those on both sides of the barrier were exceedingly awkward in one another's company. Wali Dad, Kipling's anglicized Moslem, bitterly remarks: '"I might wear an English coat and trousers. I might be a leading Mohammedan pleader [lawyer]. I might be received even at the Commissioner's tennis-parties where the English stand on one side and the natives on the other, in order to promote social intercourse throughout the Empire."'[3] He echoes Buckland, who reports that at such parties, whether given by native or English gentlemen, 'we fear that . . . there is very little real mutual enjoyment, and the hosts are usually very glad when the last of the guests has departed'.[4]

[1] The Anglo-Indian and Indo-British (written by Indians, but in English) novel has flourished since India's independence. In the Kipling tradition, though not of his stature, is John Masters, whose series of historical novels began in 1951 with *Nightrunners of Bengal* and have grown by almost a novel a year since then. Berry's interesting first novel, *Krishna Fluting* (New York, 1959), shows how far western writers have moved, since Kipling's time, towards an Indian view of Indian life.

[2] C. T. Buckland, *Sketches of Social Life in India* (London, 1884), p. 139.

[3] Wali Dad appears in 'On the City Wall', December 1888.

[4] Buckland, op. cit., p. 155.

Kipling's vision of India reflects his consciousness of this gap between the dark and the light. Although his 1887 stories explore the possibility of bridging it, Trejago's love for Bisesa ends in disaster, and Strickland's disguises come to an end with his marriage to Miss Youghal. Tentative efforts such as these serve only to emphasize the impossibility of real communication between the races. In *Plain Tales* he tests the social prohibitions that keep Englishmen and Indians apart, but he finds that — however artificial and constricting they may be — they are unyielding. The stories Kipling wrote in 1888 show him still trying to fathom the Indian mind, but he no longer tries to show the results of Anglo-Indian ventures into the life of the native Indians. He tells several fine stories from an Indian point of view, but these dramatic monologues do not concern Englishmen who are exploring India. He reports his own explorations in travel sketches, and newspaper essays and verses that deal with Indo-British social and administrative problems; but these sketches are dominated by the reporter, Kipling's public alter ego: they provide no opportunity for him to create fictional characters who doff their Englishness in order to move in freedom through the dark underworld of Indian cities. In 1888 Kipling looks across the gulf between the races instead of trying to bridge it.

As we might expect, what he sees on the other side is a partial and somewhat distorted version of the world of the native Indians. It is a version based on Kipling's own experience, to be sure, and as such it is true to the facts as he saw them; but his experience of India was sharply limited by his being a member of the conquering race. Moreover, his job as a reporter, though it required him to travel widely in India, showed him chiefly those classes of Indians whose lives were public property: the very rich and the very poor. For all Kipling's tact, curiosity, and linguistic skill, he could not gain access to a normal, middle-class Indian household.

As Buckland puts it, 'How can any Englishman venture to write about the real people of India? A civilian has no more true knowledge of the female portion of the native population than a native has of the members of the English peerage.'[1] Once again, Buckland's point is echoed in 'On the City Wall', where the reporter says to Wali Dad, in response to a question about Englishwomen, '"You never speak to us about your womenfolk and we never speak about ours to you. That is the bar between us."'

This general prohibition against contact on the domestic level — a prohibition that was Hindu in origin, rather than British — meant that no Englishman could see into the heart of Indian life, nor was Kipling an exception. Furthermore, the social groups that any conquering race sees the most of are servants and criminals; the prosperous and the law-abiding generally attend to their own affairs. Kipling had had, by 1888, plentiful experience in managing a household full of servants — very small wage demands and strict division of labour by caste and seniority meant that a large domestic staff was more practical than a small one. In a lull after the completion of the 'Plain Tales' Kipling wrote some turnovers based on his experiences with servants. They were collected as 'The Smith Administration' and may be read in *From Sea to Sea*; but they are jocular and condescending in tone and may be dismissed as exercises in a popular genre.[2] Since the British were largely responsible for the administration of justice, many of the men Kipling knew at the Club had apprehended criminals or heard their trials, so that Kipling's knowledge of Indian crime was fairly extensive. His general interest in the criminal mind was stimulated by his profession of newspaper reporter and editor, so that it is not surprising to

[1] Buckland, op. cit. p. 152.

[2] They may be compared with a popular collection of sketches of Indian servants: 'Eha' [pseud. of Edward Hamilton Aitken], *Behind the Bungalow*, 2nd ed. (Calcutta, 1889).

find a group of stories that deal with Indian criminals: 'Little Tobrah', 'Gemini', 'Through the Fire', and 'At Howli Thana' are good examples of the type.

It was as a reporter that Kipling became acquainted with the opposite end of the social scale — the Indian aristocracy. The activities of a prince become matters of public concern, as do the activities of a criminal. Carrington records some of Kipling's experiences with Indian aristocrats as early as 1884, when an Afghan *sirdar* tried to bribe him in order to win the *Civil and Military Gazette*'s favour.[1] His trip to Rawal Pindi in 1885, with its glimpse of the court of Abdurrahman, the Afghan Amir, resulted five years later in two grim poems, 'The Ballad of the King's Mercy' and 'The Ballad of the King's Jest'.[2] But it was not until the end of 1887 that Kipling was given his first real chance to form an opinion of the India of rajahs, elephants, and palaces. In November he was sent by the *Pioneer* on a railway journey through the native states of Rajputana in order to write up his impressions in a series of informal travel essays. The Native States, as they were generally called, give an example of the administrative complexity of the British raj. They had never been conquered and absorbed into British India; with few exceptions, the Rajput principalities were too weak to have offered the conquerors any military resistance, and so they had peacefully recognized British paramountcy. They were bound by separate treaties to submit their external affairs to the will of the Indian Government, but, so long as their rulers remained at peace with their neighbours and kept their own tyranny and corruption within limits, they were allowed to regulate their internal affairs as they pleased.

Here Kipling found a perplexing mixture of ancient

[1] Charles Carrington, *Rudyard Kipling* (London, 1955), pp. 56–57.

[2] 'The Ballad of the King's Mercy' owes something to a poem of Sir Alfred Lyall — 'The Amir's Message'. This source was first pointed out by Sir George MacMunn, 'Kipling and Alfred Lyall', *Kipling Journal*, no. 65 (April 1943), 4–6.

and modern. On the one hand, the land impressed him — perhaps for the first time in his life — with a sense of history, an interest that was to lie dormant until the writing of the 'Puck' stories many years later. Rajputana was filled with monuments of ancient wars. The abandoned citadels of Amber and Chitor recalled an age when feudal lords had fought savagely and put whole populations to the sword; the palace of Boondi, still inhabited by the court, appeared to be 'the work of goblins more than men' — a vast fortress carved out of the living rock.[1] The royal stables of Jodhpur, where the Maharaja hospitably displayed his treasures to the young reporter, proved to house more than four hundred superb horses in a luxury that took Kipling's breath away.[2] In Udaipur he fell into conversation with a maker of swords and found that 'Arms-venders in Udaipur are a sincere race, for they sell to people who really use their wares'.[3] He had with him a copy of Col. James Tod's *Annals and Antiquities of Rajasthan*, a classic history of the Rajput princes and their wars; he saw all around him cities and peoples that had, at first glance, changed little since the feudal age Tod described.

Fascinated though he was by these historical survivals, Kipling did not try to ignore signs that the old way of life was being undermined here and there by modern importations. If the first glance took in the dead city of Amber, the second glance fell upon the Maharaja's brand-new, steam-driven cotton-press, chugging away by the railway station and 'returning a profit of twenty-seven percent.', or upon the Jeypore Museum, financed by the Maharaja, that put to shame the impoverished Lahore Museum that Kipling, the curator's son, knew so well.[4] The cotton-press drove him to conclude that 'The modern side of Jeypore must not be mixed with the

[1] 'Letters of Marque', No. 17, 22 February 1888.

[2] 'Letters', No. 14, 4 February 1888.

[3] 'Letters', No. 7, 6 January 1888.

[4] 'Letters', Nos. 3 and 4, 24 and 27 December 1888.

ancient'; but, unlike many a traveller in search of the picturesque East, Kipling could write as enthusiastically about a clean water supply as about the awesome Tower of Victory, or the frightening sacred well called the Cow's Mouth.[1] Nor did the fact escape him that these almost absolute rulers, with enormous annual incomes, could, if they wished, outdo the Government of India in the construction of public works. They had but to command, and foreign experts were delighted to build them hospitals, canals, and railways. The Government, with its tangle of bureaux, appropriations, and red tape, seemed clumsy by comparison.[2]

Kipling's experience of Indian life led him to concern himself with opposite poles of Indian society, the very high and the very low, with a noticeable gap in the middle. But it was more than just experience that led him to polarize Indian society in this manner, for at both ends of the social scale he found ideals and values that he was predisposed to admire. He saw an India that was traditional in social structure, and the limitations of his vision were emphasized by the fact that he was prepared, by temperament and background, to appreciate the virtues of a quasi-feudal society. The Indian princes were autocrats and warriors; whatever their defects — and Kipling knew how backward and corrupt they could be, as *The Naulahka* testifies — they had about them the glamour of the European Middle Ages, a glamour that appealed to a young man who had once written Pre-

[1] The difference in spirit between Kipling and French *exotisme* is brought out vividly by a comparison of the 'Letters of Marque' with Pierre Loti's *India* (trans. George A. F. Inman, ed. R. H. Sherard, New York, n.d.). Loti's own title was *L'Inde* (*sans les Anglais*); he made every effort to avoid the signs of progress Kipling sought. Ironically, he fell into the hands of the Theosophists — whose creed was a product of the mixture of East and West — and took their doctrine for the genuine wisdom of the Mystic East.

[2] See especially 'Letters', No. 4. Not all the States were as progressive as Jeypore.

Raphaelite verses in his private notebook. These aristocrats do not play a large part in Kipling's poems and stories, if we except *The Naulahka*, but when they appear, they are found in heroic ballads like 'With Scindia to Delhi' and 'The Dove of Dacca', where their virtues are idealized. When Kipling writes the stirring lines,

> Four things greater than all things are,—
> Women and Horses and Power and War,[1]

one feels that the author is not merely giving his speaker values that are 'in character': he is somehow involved himself.

But the feudal virtues are not restricted to the aristocracy, and Kipling found something to admire among peasants and servants as well as among princes. In the first place, men of these classes could display remarkable ingenuity in hoodwinking the sahibs or one another. Mowgi the sweeper, hero of 'The Great Census', is a good example — he becomes rich merely by going from town to town posing as a tax-gatherer and recruiting agent: the inhabitants bribe him to go away. Eventually, the reporter meets him in a chain-gang; after hearing his story, he offers to make him his body-servant as soon as his jail term is over. In 'Gemini' the ingenuity of Ram Dass, the money-lender, results in a tale that, with suitable changes of names and places, could be a medieval *fabliau*; 'At Howli Thana' is of the same type, though here the ingenious Indians are defeated by an even more ingenious sahib. In the second place, it seemed to Kipling that these men of the lower classes were in close touch with substantial reality, with starvation and disease, passion and death. 'Little Tobrah', a brilliant sketch of the horrors of famine, is a story cut down to the bare bones of narrative, yet the hero, a little boy who kills his blind sister to save her from starving to death, emerges as a person of dignity and courage. The

[1] 'The Ballad of the King's Jest', first published in *Macmillan's Magazine*, February 1890.

dramatic monologue 'Dray Wara Yow Dee', whose savagery has disturbed Indian critics, is a pure distillation of the passion of jealousy, an uncivilized, even primordial response to the betrayal of love. And to counter its effect we find 'In Flood Time', a reworking of the legend of Hero and Leander, where love is expressed not through morbid jealousy but by heroic endurance in a flooded river.

Like many of his contemporaries, therefore, Kipling admired the virtues of an India that had perished in the Mutiny of 1857, an India of memory and tradition. It follows that he was not receptive to the values of what was to be the most important segment of a new Indian society — the rising middle class.[1] In 1882 Ripon's attempts at reform had antagonized Kipling, as well as nearly all his acquaintances; and the principles Ripon stood for had been acting like yeast ever since among the Indian clerisy, the educated spokesmen of the middle class. The members of this group were held together not only by the fact of their superior education, but also by their common reliance on words as a mode of action. They were lawyers, schoolteachers, and journalists, for the most part, or men in the service of the Government. Their training in English-language schools had exposed them to British constitutional history, where principle after principle had won out over the opposition of an armed and wealthy conservatism. In the English past they read the future history of India; it is not surprising that they developed an exaggerated faith in abstract principles and in the power of words to turn them into political facts.

After the Ilbert Bill controversy subsided, Kipling concerned himself little with the new Indian middle class; Lahore was not a favourable place to observe their

[1] A fine discussion of the rise and character of this new middle class may be found in T. G. Percival Spear's new and authoritative *India: A Modern History*, The University of Michigan History of the Modern World (Ann Arbor, 1961), especially chaps. xxvi and xxvii.

activities, for they were chiefly to be found in Bengal. But in the early months of 1888 Kipling was sent on another journey for the *Pioneer*, this time to Calcutta, where he was forced to take notice of the clerisy. His first response to the Indian metropolis reminds us of his provinciality. He expected to find 'a real live city', an Indian counterpart to London, but all he could think of at first was the stench that permeated every corner of the town. It seemed to him that an efficient English municipal government would have made short work of the sanitary problem; but Calcutta was experimenting with local self-government, so that Kipling readily found an excuse for attacking the clerisy: 'In spite of that stink, they allow, even encourage, natives to look after the place! The damp, drainage-soaked soil is sick with the teeming life of a hundred years, and the Municipal Board list is choked with the names of natives — men of the breed born in and raised off this surfeited muckheap!' [1] His animus was increased by a visit to a meeting of the Bengal Legislative Council. Traces of the 'Big Calcutta Stink' drifted into Writers' Buildings, and yet the Indians who sat there debating municipal business seemed to take no notice of it. They talked at length about matters Kipling does not appear to have understood. All he could think of was cleaning up the city: 'Where is the criminal, and what is all this talk about abstractions? They want shovels, not sentiments, in this part of the world.' [2]

'Shovels, not sentiments' adequately sums up Kipling's rejection of the Indian middle class and its ideals. He was not a racial bigot: though he was susceptible to theories of race characteristics that were in the air at the time, he recognized merit where he found it. But for orators who relied on 'principles' and 'precedents' he had nothing but contempt. He did not spend much time attacking the clerisy during the remainder of 1888, and

[1] 'A Real Live City', 2 March 1888.

[2] 'The Council of the Gods', 18 February 1888.

he wisely suppressed his newspaper essays on the subject. Two such sketches — 'The Tracking of Chuckerbutti' (1 March 1888) and 'A Free Gift' (19 March) — ridicule the pretensions of an inflammatory Indian journalist; in other pieces he satirizes, in passing, the British and Anglo-Indian liberals who were in sympathy with Chuckerbutti and his fellows. But a long essay on the 1888 meeting of the Indian National Congress, then in its third year, leaves no doubt about his point of view.[1] It is perhaps significant that Kipling's critique of Congress is so outspoken that one of the persons he refers to assaulted the editor of the *Pioneer*.[2] But the essay itself need not concern us at length, for Kipling merely rehearses arguments that were current in Anglo-Indian circles: that Congress did not represent the Indian masses; that the delegates had no clear purpose; that they were incapable of conducting an orderly meeting, let alone the affairs of a subcontinent. In fact, it is hard to conceive that any group made up of members of the Indian clerisy could have won Kipling's approval. The avowed aim of Congress was discussion, not action — the group was in no position to transform theories and principles into concrete political facts. Had they been plotting an armed mutiny, I think Kipling could have understood them and perhaps even admired them. As it was, he found no place in his vision of India for these seemingly ineffectual orators; he would have found it hard to believe that their 'principles' and 'precedents' would some day induce England to relinquish her Indian Empire.

Kipling achieves his most complex portrayal of native India in a story that has not been much discussed by critics — 'On the City Wall', first published as part of *In Black and White* in December 1888. It is a story that takes little account of the conventions of the narrative art: the ostensible climax, for instance, where the reporter

[1] 'A Study of the Congress: By an Eye Witness', 1 January 1889.

[2] Carrington, *Rudyard Kipling*, p. 114.

discovers that he has unwittingly helped a revolutionary to escape from the police, is too minor an incident, placed too close to the end of the tale, to seem in proportion with the rest of the story. But 'On the City Wall' is more than the account of an exciting night of religious riot in the alleys of Lahore. In its pages the forces that were to shape modern India confront one another and struggle towards a partial and ironic resolution. At the centre of the story, involved in the action and yet apart from it, is the figure of Lalun, the courtesan.[1] India as a sinister, desirable woman is an old symbol, but for Kipling it still kept part of its validity.[2] He had seen Lalun's counterpart standing at the door of a decayed house in Calcutta, caught in the glare of a policeman's lantern, 'blazing — literally blazing — with jewellery from head to foot'.[3] But Lalun herself — with her barbaric wealth, her ancient songs, her beauty, her uncanny knowledge of worldly affairs, her inaccessibility — becomes less a real prostitute than a representative figure of India; she will take part in the scheme to liberate Khem Singh, but in the end she will be unchanged, unaffected by its outcome.

The actual conspirators are shadowy figures, though led, it seems, by a member of the Indian clerisy: 'a fat person in black, with gold pince-nez'. Khem Singh, the old soldier, is merely their tool. He is, of course, a symbol of the warrior class of traditional India, the men who fought the British in 1857 but who, in 1888, no

[1] By means of some patient detective work, Mr. Charles L. Ames has identified Lalun's name and song as coming from the mysterious book by Mirza Murad Ali Beg, referred to by the reporter in 'To Be Filed for Reference'; the book is a novel, now very rare, called *Lalun, the Baragun*. See Ames, 'Lalun, the Baragun', *Kipling Journal*, xxii, no. 114 (July 1955), 6–8.

[2] Cf., for example, the sketch called 'The Burden of Nineveh' (6 June 1888), where the 'Patient East' appears as a confused but seductive *femme fatale*, who terrifies a visiting British M.P.

[3] 'The City of Dreadful Night', 22 March 1888.

longer seemed a force to reckon with; it is characteristic of Kipling's blindness to the real aims of the clerisy that he should have imagined their employing so blunted a weapon. Their antagonist, the Supreme Government, also stands in the shadows, but its concrete manifestation is the guns of Fort Amara, 'the line of guns that could pound the City to powder in half an hour'. But this is a last resort: the guns will not be turned on the City, nor will the soldiers fire their rifles into the thronging rioters.

For the central struggle of 'On the City Wall' is more complex than a mere play of force against force, and its protagonist is the bitter young Moslem, Wali Dad. Educated at an English Mission-school, Wali Dad is trapped between two Indias, the traditional and the new. He has lost his faith in Islam, but he can see no future in collaborating with the English conquerors. Though he wastes his time courting Lalun and dabbling ineffectually in the conspiracy, he nevertheless has a clearer insight into modern India than the conspirators themselves. Wali Dad correctly estimates old Khem Singh as an 'Interesting Survival': '"He returns to a country now full of educational and political reform, but, as the Pearl says, there are many who remember him. He was once a great man. There will never be any more great men in India. They will all, when they are boys, go whoring after strange gods, and they will become citizens — 'fellow-citizens' — 'illustrious fellow-citizens'. What is it that the native papers call them?"' The irony here is sustained and complex: Wali Dad is describing himself, yet he has committed himself to this lost cause; he will prove right in his evaluation of Khem Singh, yet the strange gods after whom he will go whoring are the old familiar gods of Islam; in reverting to the old religion, he will throw himself back on traditional India, but he will render himself useless to the conspiracy in doing so. In the end, of course, it is the reporter who guides Khem Singh through the rioting city: appropriately, for the reporter himself is enchanted with Lalun and to some extent has come to share Wali Dad's ambivalent position, though he has approached it from the other direction. And in the end, the ironic circle is complete. The conspiracy succeeds in spite of Wali Dad's reversion to Moslem fanaticism, but final victory lies with the Supreme Government after all, and for the reasons advanced by Wali Dad. Khem Singh 'went to the young men, but the glamour of his name had passed away, and they were entering native regiments or Government offices, and Khem Singh could give them neither pension, decorations, nor influence — nothing but a glorious death with their back to the mouth of a gun'. And so Khem Singh gives himself up and returns to prison, and Wali Dad presumably remains as impotent as ever. In so far as 'On the City Wall' is a prediction of the future of Indian nationalism, Kipling made a plausible guess. He could not know that India would belong to young men who would cross the line Wali Dad was unable to cross, and who would not revert to what they once had been.

II

The gulf that divided dark India from white, though it obscured much, gave Kipling a certain perspective. In writing about Indians, Kipling was dealing with facts and attitudes that have since become history and practical politics. We can examine his work and point with some confidence to areas where his vision was distorted or weak. But Kipling himself is very nearly the sole historian of the day-to-day life of British India. Was the social life of Simla really based upon not-quite-adulterous friendships between young men and older married women, or is this aspect of Kipling's world a distortion of reality? I have been unable to find evidence that either confirms or denies Kipling's version of this society; but one cannot eliminate the possibility that other writers of fiction either ignored or chose to suppress what was a widespread and disturbing state of affairs. Kipling's treatment of other aspects of Anglo-Indian life presents a slightly different problem. It has often been claimed that Kipling was the first to deal realistically with civil engineers, or the Indian Army, or a polo match; but can we trust the testimony of inexperienced readers who were delighted to find their special interests taken note of in readable, exciting stories? Amidst the chorus of praise from technical men, enthusiastically claiming Kipling's verisimilitude, it is well to listen to an occasional dissenting voice, like that of the social historian Dennis Kincaid: 'Simla remained cold. The fellow [Kipling] was clearly a bounder; his stories of life in the Hills were informed by the natural envy of a cad who had sought and been refused an entrée into Simla society.' [1] No doubt Kincaid exaggerates, but the existence of such an anti-Kipling sentiment in India may find corroboration in the fact that, after the appearance of *Echoes*, neither the *Calcutta Review* nor the *Asiatic Quarterly Review* — the chief spokesmen for Anglo-Indian culture — reviewed his books, even after his recognition in England as the greatest writer British India had produced. Until the appearance of an exhaustive, unbiased study of Anglo-Indian society and the Anglo-Indian mind, we have no way of deciding to what degree Kipling's vision of British India corresponds with the vision of other observers.

If any pattern fits the majority of Kipling's Anglo-Indian stories, it is that they deal with the problem of how to behave in situations of extreme physical and emotional stress — a problem that recurs throughout Kipling's writings. Many of Kipling's stories take on the nature of moral experiments: characters and the values they live by are tested against circumstances; they may win, suffer defeat, or achieve no more than a stalemate. But in fiction, as in the laboratory, some experiments are more illuminating than others. If the experimenter's prejudices

[1] Dennis Kincaid, *British Social Life in India, 1608–1937* (London, 1939), p. 230.

lead him to set up conditions that favour one result over another, the test will be worthless: the only way to determine the strength of a material is to break it. Thus, Kipling's least interesting Anglo-Indian stories are the ones in which his predispositions in favour of a particular set of values lead him to moderate the stresses to which the values are subjected. In his weakest stories, he allows his characters and their way of life too easy a triumph.

Kipling's failures are usually the result of his uncritical acceptance of moral values that are, in themselves, quite admirable. The conditions of life in India were constantly testing the physical and emotional stamina of Europeans — the soldier had to resist boredom, discomfort, and disease, enemies more subtle and dangerous than the armed tribesmen of the Border; the civilian had to face the same enemies as well as constant hard work and an even more exhausting load of responsibility. Short of attacking the whole system or abandoning the Indian Empire, there was little one could do but exalt courage and strength. 'Only a Subaltern' provides an example of a case where Kipling allows his admiration for these virtues to get the better of him. Bobby Wick, the subaltern of the title, is not so much a character as an article carefully manufactured to meet prior specifications. The specifications are not bad, for a human being with Wick's qualities would probably be an effective subaltern and a loyal and generous friend. But as a moral experiment the story is of no value: Wick's courage and devotion never flag, for he has been designed by his creator to triumph over just such strain as he is subjected to. 'Only a Subaltern', in other words, is sentimental, for the author has set out to control all his reader's responses, to draw upon the reader's easily accessible stores of admiration and pity. Bobby Wick's victory is too easy.

Kipling knew better than to fill a gallery with portraits of Bobby Wick, but similar motives can be detected in other stories that risk the charge of sentimentality. In

'His Majesty the King' the facile victory is won by childish innocence; in 'Wee Willie Winkie' innocence and courage rather awkwardly combine in order to prove that even a six-year-old sahib can be a match for Border tribesmen: in each case the reader's stock responses to the idea of childhood are drawn out and manipulated. 'The Story of the Gadsbys' is nothing but a series of ordeals, some facetious and some serious. The whole was intended to be 'an Anglo-Indian *Autour du mariage*', and it might have turned out well, for the Gadsbys' marriage has to outlast nearly every strain to which an Anglo-Indian marriage can be subject.[1] But something went wrong, as Kipling realized later. The innocence and good intentions of old Gaddy and his Minnie win victories that seem contrived, and the story keeps descending into troughs of the commonplace: the nervous bridegroom, the compromising letter from an old flame, the tender announcement of pregnancy. Only at the end does Gadsby face a real dilemma and the story take on substance. The carefully built structure of domestic happiness is finally confronted by a moral imperative, the Captain's duty to his regiment; Gadsby's weakness is exposed, and for a moment he becomes real.

In writing of barracks life, Kipling is less apt to fall into clichés than he is when dealing with men and women of his own class, nor does he stack the cards quite so decisively in favour of a given system of values: apart from the fact that courage and cleanliness are good, dirt and cowardice bad, the author's own predilections are never as apparent as in 'Only a Subaltern' or 'His Majesty the King'. Mulvaney, the central figure of the barracks stories, most often rescues them from sentimentality. As long as Kipling can maintain his own poise, the reader has in mind that Mulvaney is not always a lovable rogue but at times a thief, and even, as 'The Solid Muldoon' shows, a fairly cold-blooded adulterer.

[1] Kipling discusses the story and its debt to 'Gyp' in *Something of Myself*, pp. 71–72.

As the reporter's voice dies away and Mulvaney's voice takes over, we move into a new realm of values. It is possible for us to suspend judgment while Mulvaney saunters through the married quarters, for his behaviour is, in a sense, wrapped in the insulation of his nostalgic pride in being 'the Imperor av the Earth in me own mind'. 'With the Main Guard' succeeds almost perfectly in what it sets out to do, for it explores the savagery of hand-to-hand fighting in such a way that the reader's presumable dislike of the actuality of violence is never brought into play. The stifling inactivity of the hot night in Fort Amara prepares the reader to accept Mulvaney's version of the battle in Silver's Theatre, not as a ghastly and irresponsible attempt to make the reader lust for blood, but as a work of art; Mulvaney's imagination has sustained his companions in an hour of need.

> 'Oh, Terence!' I said . . ., 'it's you that have the Tongue!'
>
> He looked at me wearily; his eyes were sunk in his head, and his face was drawn and white. 'Eyah!' said he; 'I've blandandhered thim through the night somehow, but can thim that helps others help thimselves? Answer me that, sorr!'

In stories like these the conditions of barracks life in India set up searching tests of the values a soldier lives by. Mulvaney normally resolves these dilemmas by means of his courage and strength — 'Black Jack' is a good example — but his victories are not easy, and, in the long run, the last victory always eludes him. For he is not the pattern of a successful private soldier, as Bobby Wick is of the perfect subaltern; Mulvaney's courage and strength are not adequate to overcome his own weaknesses and lusts; we do not feel that the author is manipulating our responses in such a way as to foist upon us a conventional system of values.

At his best, Mulvaney becomes larger than life. Tougher, stronger, more imaginative than any man could be, he takes on heroic size and enters a realm that is outside normal human experience; part of the greatness of 'The Incarnation of Krishna Mulvaney' lies in the fact that he becomes, in some mysterious way, equivalent to Krishna, the legendary hero whom he impersonates. The trouble with Mrs. Hauksbee, on the other hand, is that Kipling tries too hard to reveal her 'character'. When she first makes her appearance in the 'Plain Tales', she comes before us as a brilliant creation: mischievous, intelligent, fascinating, she is the embodiment of the spell that Simla cast over the young Kipling. But in the later stories, especially the overlong 'Education of Otis Yeere', a good deal of the life goes out of her. Splendid to watch in action, she is less amusing to listen to. Worse still, Kipling sentimentalizes her. As an admirer of the early Mrs. Hauksbee, I find the 'many sobs and much promiscuous kissing' of 'A Second-Rate Woman' awkward and embarrassing; for Kipling's vision of Anglo-Indian social life is basically anti-heroic, so that in trying to make Mrs. Hauksbee into a heroine — a representative, that is, of the values he stands for — Kipling defeats his own purposes. It is significant that he had to invent a cardboard villainess, Mrs. Reiver, in order to set off Mrs. Hauksbee's virtues.

In his stronger Simla stories, Kipling reveals a moral bias, as it were, by default; he no longer tries to provide a hero. Simplest in conception of this group is 'At the Pit's Mouth', where two nameless and unpleasant people cross the narrow line from flirtation into adultery: there is no doubt that the narrator strongly disapproves of them, but his obvious hostility gives them more autonomy than they would have if he had indulged in any sort of special pleading. The contrived dénouement — a particularly ghastly riding accident — is so vividly presented that we can forget that the 'fate' that overtakes the Tertium Quid is merely the caprice of the author, at pains to dispose of an evil character by appropriately horrible means. In 'The Hill of Illusion', however, Kipling scorns such a mechanical punishment; instead, he allows his characters to expose one another for what they are. He is not at his best in this artificial form — a story entirely in dialogue — but I doubt whether any other Englishman writing in 1888 could have exposed so coldly and neatly the itch of mutual distrust that afflicts a couple on the eve of an adulterous elopement.

'The Hill of Illusion' is an impressive attempt, but it is overshadowed by 'A Wayside Comedy'. The former could take place anywhere, but the latter is peculiarly Anglo-Indian in the moral ordeal its characters must suffer. Like Morrowbie Jukes, they are trapped, but without any of the paraphernalia of Gothic melodrama: 'Kashima is bounded on all sides by the rock-tipped circle of the Dosehri hills', and that circle, by the laws that govern the lives of Anglo-Indian civil servants, cannot be broken. The experimenter has achieved the fictional equivalent of a controlled laboratory environment: 'Sorrow in Kashima is as fortunate as Love because there is nothing to weaken it save the flight of Time.' Kurrell and Mrs. Boulte, having nothing else to do, fall into a safe and static adultery. But external conditions change: Mrs. Vansuythen comes to the Station; Boulte and Kurrell both fall in love with her; in anguish at her loss, Mrs. Boulte forces an exposure of their tangled relationships. Their ordeal is simply to live with one another, to solve the problem of how to behave in these circumstances of intolerable stress. And there is no solution. Being what they are, these people behave as they must, without any of the obvious virtues — courage, strength, wit, honour — with which Kipling has endowed his characters elsewhere. The isolation so characteristic of life in British India has forced them into a moral dilemma, but the best resolution they can achieve is a stalemate: they must wait until chance releases them from one another's intolerable proximity.

'The Man Who Would Be King', the best of the stories Kipling wrote in India, must conclude any study of his apprenticeship, not only because of its brilliance, but because in a sense it embodies and sums up Kipling's attitude to India and the role of the British in the land they had conquered. The story is susceptible of innumerable interpretations: in its mysterious way it is concerned with issues larger than the adventures of a pair of English ne'er-do-wells in the unexplored hills of Kafiristan.[1] Nevertheless, the form of the tale is straightforward. Dravot and Carnehan are tragic figures, conquerors who, like Tamburlaine, conceive the ambition of becoming emperors. They are above the common run of mankind; they are as strong and vigorous as Mulvaney, as subtle at disguise as Strickland, as worldly and cynical as McIntosh Jellaludin. With courage and luck they pile success upon success until they become gods in the eyes of their primitive subjects. But in the end they violate the conditions of their success. Dravot overreaches himself in wanting to take a wife from among their subjects, and his failure of judgment causes him to pull down upon his own head the frail structure his courage and ambition have reared.

Like 'A Wayside Comedy', 'The Man Who Would Be King' is peculiarly Indian in the moral experiment to which its heroes are subjected. 'A Wayside Comedy', however, displays Anglo-Indians in a state of paralysis. Isolated in the remote valley of Kashima, the heirs of the conquerors are unable to enjoy the fruits of conquest. They are a far-flung patrol of an army of occupation, but they lack the inner strength to survive the rigours of such a calling; India is too much for them. In a sense, 'The Man Who Would Be King' looks back to an earlier generation, a generation less troubled by boredom, isola-

[1] The most complex and suggestive analysis of the story is by Paul Fussell, Jr.: 'Irony, Freemasonry, and Humane Ethics in Kipling's "The Man Who Would Be King"', *ELH*, xxv (1958), 216–33. Prof. Fussell elucidates many of Kipling's Biblical and Masonic allusions and does a thorough and illuminating job of close reading. He is not concerned with the social and historical backgrounds that seem to me of importance to a full understanding of the story.

tion, and responsibility. Dravot and Carnehan recapitulate the British conquest.[1] Like Clive and the great generals who followed him, they prove that a disciplined native army, provided with effective weapons, is a match for a much larger force of untrained tribesmen. Like the great Anglo-Indian administrators, they find the land divided by petty rulers: they put an end to internecine war, establish the pax Britannica, and win the support of tribesmen who prefer subjection to anarchy. Even their motives show the odd mixture of patriotism and personal ambition that characterized the men who conquered the world for England: '". . . we'd be an Empire. When everything was shipshape, I'd hand over the crown — this crown I'm wearing now — to Queen Victoria on my knees, and she'd say : 'Rise up, Sir Daniel Dravot.'"'

Why, then, does this simulacrum of the Indian Empire fall and crush its makers? The meaning of Dravot's and Carnehan's failure is complex. On the one hand, they have effected their conquest under false pretences. They have concealed from their people the real significance of the Masonic Mark; '"'Only the Gods know that,'"' says Billy Fish; '"'We thought you were men till you showed the Sign of the Master.'"' In Kipling's stories deceit is often a risky business: the truth that underlies situations and men has a powerful tendency to manifest itself. Kafiristan, like India, is a place of extremes; circumstances corrode and destroy false appearances. On the other hand, Dravot and Carnehan succeed as gods and

[1] The view of 'The Man Who Would Be King' as a myth of imperialism was brought forward many years ago by Eugène Marie Melchior, Vicomte de Vogüé, 'Les Pères de l'impérialisme anglais', in *Pages d'histoire* (Paris, 1902), pp. 121–34. The references in the story to Rajah Brooke of Sarawak make it plain that Kipling also had recent events in mind and that Dravot and Carnehan are explicitly intended to represent a phase of British imperialism. In this connection, it should be noted that the crucifixion of Carnehan, whatever its symbolic role in the story, probably first made contemporary readers think of the rumours that British captives were being crucified by the Burmese in the wars of the late eighties.

fail only when their manhood is revealed. One of the many ironies of the story is provided by Carnehan's perpetual awareness of his rough-and-tumble background, his continual reduction of their royal acts to the terms he best understands. And so, when Dravot proposes to take a wife — '" 'A Queen out of the strongest tribe, that'll make them your blood-brothers, and that'll lie by your side and tell you all the people thinks about you and their own affairs' "' — Carnehan can see it only in terms of a casual liaison with a native girl: '" 'Do you remember that Bengali woman I kept at Mogul Serai when I was a platelayer?' says I. 'A fat lot o' good she was to me.' "' Dravot is justifiably angered by the comparison; and yet Peachey is not entirely wrong about Dravot's motives: rather, he is oversimplifying them. Dravot's desire for a queen is more than lust and more than political strategy; in a sense, it is one of those gestures towards a real contact with the conquered land that occur in *Plain Tales* and always come to nothing. Like the British in India, Dravot and Carnehan can move just so far in the direction of acclimatizing themselves to Kafiristan before they are forcibly reminded that an immense gulf lies between them and their subjects. Reducing the problem to his own simple terms, Carnehan sums it up thus: '" 'There's no accounting for natives. This business is our 'Fifty-Seven.' "' It is appropriate that Dravot, the unsuccessful builder of a bridge between races, should die as he does, hurled into a chasm from a broken bridge, a bridge that has been destroyed by the tribesmen he has tried to civilize and enlighten.

The twenty-two-year-old newspaper reporter who wrote 'The Man Who Would Be King' was no longer an apprentice. For six years he had had to write prose and verse on demand; each year his output had grown more copious, his style more individual and assured. India had provided a strange environment for a young writer, but on the whole Kipling could — and did — count himself fortunate in having lived there. Conventional modes of literary development were closed to him: he knew nothing of the University, the ephemeral little magazines, the awkward attempt at a first novel, the struggle for acceptance by the established literati. On the contrary, he had no rules to follow; his imagination could be fertilized by direct exposure to an enigmatic land that lay outside the borders of English literary tradition; he had to forge a style that would capture the interest of an audience quite unlike the English literary public. Kipling sailed from India in March 1889, but in a sense he never left it behind him. Not only was his great reputation based on his Indian stories; not only did he return to the land in his imagination, in London, Sussex, and even far-away Vermont. For the rest of his life he would remain, to some extent, a 'returned Anglo-Indian': a homeless man who had left a vital part of himself in the East; a writer whose view of the world was inexorably conditioned by the land and the people amongst whom he had grown to maturity.

Appendix I

A CHRONOLOGICAL LIST OF KIPLING'S WRITINGS FROM OCTOBER 1882 TO MARCH 1889

APPENDIX I lists in order of published appearance the nearly four hundred Kipling items that appeared in print between October 1882 and March 1889. I have dealt with the problem of authenticity in another appendix; let it suffice to say here that I have seen texts — of varying authority — of all but a very few of the items listed. The appendix represents not only a convenient device for bringing home the variety and fecundity of Kipling's production, but also a modest step in the direction of establishing a Kipling canon for the years 1882–8. Each date supplies a *terminus ad quem* for the composition of the piece associated with it, and in most cases we can be fairly certain that the item was written not much more than a week before publication. In addition to the date and place of first appearance I have listed the published collection, if any, wherein it may conveniently be read. The following are titles of authorized collections and may be found in any collected edition of Kipling's works: *Plain Tales from the Hills*, *Soldiers Three*, *Wee Willie Winkie*, *Under the Deodars*, *In Black and White*, *The Phantom 'Rickshaw*, *The Story of the Gadsbys*, *Life's Handicap*, and *From Sea to Sea*. *Schoolboy Lyrics*, *Echoes*, and *Quartette* are discussed fully in the text. The following notes will explain other references in the list.

1. *Typographical Convention.* I follow the Chandler *Summary* in using all capitals for PROSE TITLES, upper and lower case, without quotation marks, for the titles of poems. Quotation marks are used only where they form an integral part of the

original title. Titles of *published books* are italicized; titles of periodicals are not.

2. *Abbreviations* are avoided as much as possible, but the following are commonly used: 'U.S.C.C.' for United Services College Chronicle; 'C. & M.G.' for Civil and Military Gazette; '*Def. Ed.*' for *The Definitive Edition of Rudyard Kipling's Verse*; 'D.D.' for *Departmental Ditties*; 'B.-R.B.' for *Barrack-Room Ballads*. The last two are supplied only as supplementary information, not to indicate where poems may be found; hence, they are not italicized. The asterisk (*) at the end of some of the entries for 1886 and 1887 indicates that they appeared in the C. & M.G. under the series title 'Plain Tales from the Hills'.

3. *Sussex Ed., Outward Bound Ed., and Ed. De Luxe.* These relatively expensive collected editions include a few stories and poems not collected anywhere else.

4. *Early Verse.* A collection of such verse that appears in some collections of Kipling's complete works. It is most readily available to American readers as volume xvii of the *Outward Bound Edition*.

5. *The City of Dreadful Night.* Kipling borrowed James Thomson's title and used it to head four different entities: (*a*) A sketch of Lahore that appeared in the C. & M.G. on 10 September 1885. (*b*) A collection of travel sketches and miscellaneous pieces that was published without Kipling's permission and immediately suppressed (referred to in the list as 'suppressed *City of Dreadful Night*'). (*c*) A series of travel sketches describing Calcutta: hence, 'City' becomes one of the subtitles of *From Sea to Sea*, along with 'Letters of Marque', 'The Smith Administration', 'Among the Railway Folk', and 'The Giridih Coal Fields'. (*d*) A sketch of Calcutta (22 March 1888) from which the series took its name.

6. *Turnovers I–III.* The so-called 'turnovers', instituted by Kay Robinson in the C. & M.G., were popular enough to warrant the publication of collections in book form. Although these little books are now rare, there are several copies in American libraries; they provide texts of certain pieces that would otherwise be nearly inaccessible.

7. *Abaft the Funnel.* An unauthorized collection published in America in 1909. By no means a rare item, *Abaft* gives access to several interesting stories that would otherwise have remained uncollected.

CHRONOLOGY OF KIPLING'S WRITINGS

1882

18 October, Kipling arrives at Bombay
8 November, Two Lives, The World, Sussex Ed., vol. 35
11 December, The Song of the Sufferer, U.S.C.C., *Early Verse*

1883

9 August, LORD TRURO AND INDIAN CRIME, C. & M.G., uncollected
2 October, THE DASERA FESTIVAL, C. & M.G., uncollected
2 October, THE VOLCANIC EXPLOSION IN JAVA, C. & M.G., uncollected
15 October, The Song of the Exiles, U.S.C.C., *Early Verse*
16 October, THE VICEREGAL TOUR IN CASHMERE, C. & M.G., uncollected
7 November, WILLIAM MORRIS'S POEM 'THE DAY IS COMING', C. & M.G., uncollected

1884

28 March, On Fort Duty, U.S.C.C., *Early Verse*
23 May, 'The May Voyage', C. & M.G., uncollected
15 September, Lord Ripon's Reverie, C. & M.G., uncollected
26 September, THE GATE OF THE HUNDRED SORROWS, C. & M.G., *Plain Tales*
29 September, The Story of Tommy, C. & M.G., uncollected
10 October, The Descent of the Punkah, C. & M.G., uncollected
30 October, The Boar of the Year, U.S.C.C., *Early Verse*
20 November, 'Laid Low', C. & M.G., uncollected
November, *Echoes*, including first publication of:
A Vision of India (Tennyson)

The City of the Heart (Longfellow)
The Indian Farmer at Home (Burns)
The Flight of the Bucket (Browning)
Laocoon (Arnold)
Nursery Rhymes for Little Anglo-Indians
Tobacco (Keats)
Appropriate Verses on an Elegant Landscape (Cowper)
His Consolation (Browning)
The Cursing of Stephen (Tennyson)
Nursery Idyls (C. Rossetti's *Sing-Song*)
Sonnet (Blunt)
Kopra Brahm (Emerson)
The Sudder Bazar
Commonplaces (Heine)
Quaeritur (Swinburne)
London Town (Impressionist School)
Himalayan (Joaquin Miller)
Our Lady of Many Dreams
A Murder in the Compound
Way Down the Ravee River
Amour de Voyage (Praed)
Failure
How the Day Broke
A Locked Way
Land Bound
The Ballad of the King's Daughter
How the Goddess Awakened
The Maid of the Meerschaum (Swinburne or Austin Dobson)
Estunt the Griff (Morris)
Cavaliere Servente (D. G. Rossetti)

16 December, The Moon of Other Days, Pioneer, *Def. Ed.* (D.D.)
25 December, THE DREAM OF DUNCAN PARRENNESS, C. & M.G., *Life's Handicap*

1885

3 January, PROCLAMATION DAY AT LAHORE, C. & M.G., uncollected

7 January, A MOFUSSIL EXHIBITION, C. & M.G., uncollected
9 January, TWENTY YEARS AFTER, C. & M.G., uncollected
27 January, To the Unknown Goddess, Pioneer, *Def. Ed.* (D.D.)
6 March, Lord D–ff–r–n's Clôture, C. & M.G., uncollected
20 March, In Springtime, Pioneer, *Def. Ed.* (D.D.)
22 June, After the Fever or Natural Theology in a Doolie, Pioneer, uncollected
4 July, 'DIS ALITER VISUM', Pioneer, uncollected
8 July, My Rival, Pioneer, *Def. Ed.* (D.D.)
13 July, Possibilities, Pioneer, *Def. Ed.* (D.D.)
15 August, The Tale of Two Suits, Pioneer, uncollected
19 August, Divided Destinies, Pioneer, *Def. Ed.* (D.D.)
22 August, The Mare's Nest, Pioneer, *Def. Ed.* (D.D.)
27 August, A Tale of Yesterday's 10,000 Years, Pioneer, uncollected
31 August, A Lost Leader, C. & M.G., uncollected
31 August, Revenge: A Ballad of the Fleeter, Pioneer, uncollected
4 September, An Indignant Protest, C. & M.G., uncollected
5 September, The Legend of the Pill, Pioneer, uncollected
10 September, 'THE CITY OF DREADFUL NIGHT', C. & M.G., *Life's Handicap*
16 September, Trial by Judge, C. & M.G., uncollected
8 October, HIS EXCELLENCY, C. & M.G., uncollected
8 October, The Undertaker's Horse, C. & M.G., *Def. Ed.* (D.D.)
19 October, THE CITY OF TWO CREEDS (1), C. & M.G., uncollected
20 October, THE CITY OF TWO CREEDS (2), C. & M.G., uncollected
20 October, Carmen Simlaense, C. & M.G., *Early Verse*
October, The Vision of Hamid Ali, Calcutta Review, *Sussex Ed.*, vol. 35
14 November, EAST AND WEST, C. & M.G., uncollected
21 November, The Indian Delegates, C. & M.G., uncollected
18 December, Exchange, C. & M.G., uncollected
25 December, *Quartette*, including first publication of:
Divided Allegiance, uncollected

At the Distance, uncollected

THE UNLIMITED 'DRAW' OF 'TICK' BOILEAU, uncollected

A Tragedy of Teeth, uncollected

The Second Wooing, uncollected

THE STRANGE RIDE OF MORROWBIE JUKES, *Phantom 'Rickshaw*

MY CHRISTMAS AT THE AJAIBGAUM EXHIBITION, uncollected

THE PHANTOM 'RICKSHAW, *Phantom 'Rickshaw*

From the Hills, uncollected

Various dates, THE WEEK IN LAHORE, C. & M.G., uncollected

1886

16 January, The Quid Pro Quo, C. & M.G., uncollected

30 January, The Rupaiyat of Omar Kal'vin, C. & M.G., *Def. Ed.* (D.D.)

5 February, THE HISTORY OF A CRIME, Pioneer, uncollected

5 February, PROVERBS OF SILLYMAN, Pioneer, uncollected

9 February, Army Headquarters, C. & M.G., *Def. Ed.* (D.D.)

16 February, Study of an Elevation, in Indian Ink, C. & M.G., *Def. Ed.* (D.D.)

23 February, A Legend of the Foreign Office, C. & M.G., *Def. Ed.* (D.D.)

3 March, The Story of Uriah, C. & M.G., *Def. Ed.* (D.D.)

9 March, Public Waste, C. & M.G., *Def. Ed.* (D.D.)

16 March, The Post That Fitted, C. & M.G., *Def. Ed.* (D.D.)

23 March, The Man Who Could Write, C. & M.G., *Def. Ed.* (D.D.)

30 March, Pink Dominoes, C. & M.G., *Def. Ed.* (D.D.)

6 April, A Code of Morals, C. & M.G., *Def. Ed.* (D.D.)

? 12 April, 'The City of Delhi Is Hushed and Still', U.S.C.C., uncollected

13 April, The Last Department, C. & M.G., *Def. Ed.* (D.D.)

16 April, The Plea of the Simla Dancers, C. & M.G., *Def. Ed.* (D.D.)

1886 *1886*

26 April, Parturiunt Montes, C. & M.G., uncollected

30 April, IN THE HOUSE OF SUDDHOO, C. & M.G., *Plain Tales*

April, The Seven Nights of Creation [complete], Calcutta Review, uncollected, though the incomplete version appears in *Early Verse*, collected from *Schoolboy Lyrics* (1881)

13 May, THE INSTALLATION AT JUMMU (1), C. & M.G., uncollected

14 May, THE INSTALLATION AT JUMMU (2), C. & M.G., uncollected

14 May, Fair Play, C. & M.G., uncollected

21 May, Distress in the Himalayas, C. & M.G., uncollected

26 May, A Levee in the Plains, C. & M.G., *Early Verse*

? 3 June, THE BURNS MANUSCRIPTS, C. & M.G., uncollected

15 June, Our Lady of Rest, C. & M.G., *Early Verse*

16 June, Pagett, M.P., Pioneer, *Def. Ed.* (D.D.)

June, *Departmental Ditties*, including first publication of:
A General Summary
The Lovers' Litany
Certain Maxims of Hafiz
Arithmetic on the Frontier
Giffen's Debt — all collected in *Def. Ed.*

2 July, The Battle of Assye, U.S.C.C., *Early Verse*

20 July, Cupid's Department, Pioneer, uncollected

July, The Explanation, Calcutta Review, *Def. Ed.* (B.-R.B.)

July, King Solomon's Horses, Calcutta Review, uncollected

12 August, 'FROM OLYMPUS TO HADES', C. & M.G., uncollected

26 August, NABOTH, C. & M.G., *Life's Handicap*

27 August, 'A DISTRICT AT PLAY', C. & M.G., *From Sea to Sea* (Smith Administration)

28 August, 'LES MISÉRABLES': A TALE OF 1998, C. & M.G., uncollected

3 September, A NIGHTMARE OF RULE, C. & M.G., uncollected

8 September, THE STORY OF MUHAMMAD DIN, C. & M.G., *Plain Tales*

10 September, A LETTER FROM GOLAM SINGH,

C. & M.G., *From Sea to Sea* (Smith Administration)

14 September, FROM THE DUSK TO THE DAWN, C. & M.G., uncollected

15 September, Two Months (1), C. & M.G., *Def. Ed.* (D.D.)

17 September, WHAT CAME OF IT, C. & M.G., uncollected

29 September, PRISONERS AND CAPTIVES, C. & M.G., uncollected

4 October, On a Recent Appointment, C. & M.G., uncollected

9 October, At the Bar, C. & M.G., uncollected

11 October, Delilah, C. & M.G., *Def. Ed.* (D.D.)

? 2 November, LOVE-IN-A-MIST, C. & M.G., uncollected * (Items so designated * appeared in the C. & M.G. under the series title 'Plain Tales from the Hills.')

10 November, The Fall of Jock Gillespie, C. & M.G., *Def. Ed.* (D.D.)

? 11 November, HOW IT HAPPENED, C. & M.G., uncollected *

13 November, THE OTHER MAN, C. & M.G., *Plain Tales* *

15 November, LE ROI EN EXIL, C. & M.G., uncollected

17 November, THREE AND — AN EXTRA, C. & M.G., *Plain Tales* *

23 November, Alnaschar, C. & M.G., uncollected

23 November, THE ARREST OF LIEUTENANT GOLIGHTLY, C. & M.G., *Plain Tales* *

29 November, LISPETH, C. & M.G., *Plain Tales* *

1 December, A STRAIGHT FLUSH, C. & M.G., uncollected *

4 December, VENUS ANNODOMINI, C. & M.G., *Plain Tales* *

7 December, 'YOKED WITH AN UNBELIEVER', C. & M.G., *Plain Tales* *

9 December, CONSEQUENCES, C. & M.G., *Plain Tales* *

10 December, A Nightmare of Names, C. & M.G., uncollected

13 December, A SCRAP OF PAPER, C. & M.G., uncollected *

24 December, Christmas in India, Pioneer, *Def. Ed.* (D.D.)

25 December, Ichabod, C. & M.G., uncollected

25 December, THE MYSTIFICATION OF SANTA CLAUS, C. & M.G., uncollected

1886 *1886–7*

Winter, *Departmental Ditties*, 2nd ed., including first publication of:
Lucifer
A Ballade of Burial
A Ballade of Jakko Hill
The Overland Mail
L'Envoi — all but 'Lucifer' collected in *Def. Ed.*

? The Ballad of Ahmed Shah, Indian Planter's Gazette, uncollected

1887

1 January, New Year Resolutions, C. & M.G., uncollected
7 January, The Plaint of a Junior Civilian, C. & M.G., *Early Verse*
10 January, ON THE STRENGTH OF A LIKENESS, C. & M.G., *Plain Tales* *
24 January, IN ERROR, C. & M.G., *Plain Tales* *
14 February, A LITTLE LEARNING, C. & M.G., uncollected *
18 February, For the Women, C. & M.G., *Early Verse*
25 February, HIS WEDDED WIFE, C. & M.G., *Plain Tales* *
? 2 March, TRANSPORT SHORTCOMINGS, Pioneer, uncollected
4 March, THE BISARA OF POOREE, C. & M.G., *Plain Tales* *
11 March, THE THREE MUSKETEERS, C. & M.G., *Plain Tales* *
21 March, KIDNAPPED, C. & M.G., *Plain Tales* *
25 March, WATCHES OF THE NIGHT, C. & M.G., *Plain Tales* *
2 April, HIS CHANCE IN LIFE, C. & M.G., *Plain Tales* *
6 April, THE BROKEN-LINK HANDICAP, C. & M.G., *Plain Tales* *
11 April, THE TAKING OF LUNGTUNGPEN, C. & M.G., *Plain Tales* *
14 April, A BANK FRAUD, C. & M.G., *Plain Tales* *
16 April, TODS' AMENDMENT, C. & M.G., *Plain Tales* *
19 April, BITTERS NEAT, C. & M.G., *Plain Tales* * (*Outward Bound Ed.*)
21 April, 'As the Bell Clinks', C. & M.G., *Def. Ed.* (D.D.)

1887 *1887*

25 April, MISS YOUGHAL'S SAIS, C. & M.G., *Plain Tales* *
28 April, THE CONVERSION OF AURELIAN MCGOGGIN, C. & M.G., *Plain Tales* *
2 May, A FRIEND'S FRIEND, C. & M.G., *Plain Tales* *
4 May, What the People Said, C. & M.G., *Def. Ed.* (D.D.)
5 May, IN THE PRIDE OF HIS YOUTH, C. & M.G., *Plain Tales* *
9 May, Municipal, C. & M.G., *Def. Ed.* (D.D.)
11 May, THE DAUGHTER OF THE REGIMENT, C. & M.G., *Plain Tales* *
17 May, A GERM-DESTROYER, C. & M.G., *Plain Tales* *
20 May, WRESSLEY OF THE FOREIGN OFFICE, C. & M.G., *Plain Tales* *
? 23 May, An Excellent Reason, Pioneer, uncollected
27 May, HAUNTED SUBALTERNS, C. & M.G., *Plain Tales* * (*Outward Bound Ed.*)
2 June, A Tale of Two Cities, C. & M.G., *Def. Ed.* (D.D.)
3 June, PIG, C. & M.G., *Plain Tales* *
7 June, La Nuit Blanche, C. & M.G., *Def. Ed.* (D.D.)
10 June, BY WORD OF MOUTH, C. & M.G., *Plain Tales* *
6 July, THE CASE OF ADAMAH, C. & M.G., uncollected
15 July, THE HANDS OF JUSTICE, C. & M.G., *From Sea to Sea* (Smith Administration)
1 August, Prologue for a Theatrical Performance, Pioneer, uncollected
8 August, THE SERAI CABAL, C. & M.G., *From Sea to Sea* (Smith Administration)
12 August, THE JUDGMENT OF PARIS, C. & M.G., collected only in suppressed *City of Dreadful Night* (1890)
13 August, Blue Roses, C. & M.G., *Def. Ed.*
15 August, An Old Song, C. & M.G., *Def. Ed.* (D.D.)
15 September, OUR CAT HUNT, C. & M.G., uncollected
28 September, THE HILL OF ILLUSION, C. & M.G., *Under the Deodars*
4 October, JEWS IN SHUSHAN, C. & M.G., *Life's Handicap*
7 October, THE OPINIONS OF GUNNER BARNABAS, C. & M.G., *From Sea to Sea* (Smith Administration)
10 October, HUNTING A MIRACLE, C. & M.G., *From Sea to Sea* (Smith Administration)

13 October, THE RECURRING SMASH, C. & M.G., uncollected

17 October, THE STORY OF A KING, C. & M.G., *From Sea to Sea* (Smith Administration)

22 October, THE DREITARBUND, C. & M.G., collected only in suppressed *City of Dreadful Night*

3 November, THE VENGEANCE OF LAL BEG, C. & M.G., *From Sea to Sea* (Smith Administration)

4 November, THE COW-HOUSE JIRGA, C. & M.G., *From Sea to Sea* (Smith Administration)

21 November, A BAZAAR DHULIP, C. & M.G., *From Sea to Sea* (Smith Administration)

14 December, LETTERS OF MARQUE, NO. 1, Pioneer, *From Sea to Sea*

23 December, LETTERS OF MARQUE, NO. 2, Pioneer, *From Sea to Sea*

24 December, LETTERS OF MARQUE, NO. 3, Pioneer, *From Sea to Sea*

27 December, LETTERS OF MARQUE, NO. 4, Pioneer, *From Sea to Sea*

30 December, A KING'S ASHES, Pioneer, *From Sea to Sea* (Smith Administration)

31 December, A MERRY XMAS, C. & M.G., uncollected

31 December, LETTERS OF MARQUE, NO. 5, Pioneer, *From Sea to Sea*

1888

January, *Plain Tales from the Hills*, including first publication of:

THROWN AWAY
FALSE DAWN
CUPID'S ARROWS
BEYOND THE PALE
THE ROUT OF THE WHITE HUSSARS
THE MADNESS OF PRIVATE ORTHERIS
TO BE FILED FOR REFERENCE
THE BRONCKHORST DIVORCE-CASE

1 January, THE NEW YEAR'S SERMON, C. & M.G., uncollected

1888 *1888*

2 January, What Happened, Pioneer, *Def. Ed.* (D.D.)

3 January, LETTERS OF MARQUE, NO. 6, Pioneer, *From Sea to Sea*

6 January, LETTERS OF MARQUE, NO. 7, Pioneer, *From Sea to Sea*

7 January, THE GOD FROM THE MACHINE, Week's News, *Soldiers Three*

7 January, The Grave of the Hundred Head, Week's News, *Def. Ed.* (D.D.)

9 January, THE GREAT CENSUS, C. & M.G., *From Sea to Sea* (Smith Administration)

10 January, LETTERS OF MARQUE, NO. 8, Pioneer, *From Sea to Sea*

11 January, A LITTLE MORALITY, C. & M.G., uncollected

11 January, MISTER ANTHONY DAWKING, C. & M.G., coll. only in suppressed *City of Dreadful Night* and *Turnovers I*

12 January, LETTERS OF MARQUE, NO. 9, Pioneer, *From Sea to Sea*

14 January, LETTERS OF MARQUE, NO. 10, Pioneer, *From Sea to Sea*

14 January, GEMINI, Week's News, *In Black and White*

17 January, 'THE LUCK OF ROARING CAMP', C. & M.G., coll. only in suppressed *City of Dreadful Night* and *Turnovers I*

17 January, LETTERS OF MARQUE, NO. 11, Pioneer, *From Sea to Sea*

18 January, BUBBLING WELL ROAD, C. & M.G., *Life's Handicap*

18 January, THE WRITING OF YAKUB KHAN, Pioneer, *From Sea to Sea* (Smith Administration)

21 January, The Lament of the Border Cattle Thief, Week's News, *Def. Ed.* (B.-R.B.)

21 January, A WAYSIDE COMEDY, Week's News, *Under the Deodars*

24 January, LETTERS OF MARQUE, NO. 12, Pioneer, *From Sea to Sea*

27 January, LETTERS OF MARQUE, NO. 13. Pioneer, *From Sea to Sea*

28 January, WEE WILLIE WINKIE, Week's News, *Wee Willie Winkie*

30 January, LANDMARKS IN THE WILDERNESS, C. & M.G., coll. only in *Turnovers I*

3 February, VERBATIM ET LITERATIM, C. & M.G., uncollected

4 February, LETTERS OF MARQUE, NO. 14, Pioneer, *From Sea to Sea*

4 February, THE LIKES O' US, Week's News, *Abaft the Funnel*

4 February, The Man and the Shadow, Week's News, *Early Verse*

4 February, 'Struck Ile', Pioneer, uncollected

8 February, THE BRIDE'S PROGRESS, Pioneer Mail, *From Sea to Sea* (Smith Administration)

10 February, LETTERS OF MARQUE, NO. 15, Pioneer, *From Sea to Sea*

11 February, A Ballad of Bad Entertainment, Week's News, *Early Verse*

11 February, THE SENDING OF DANA DA, Week's News, *In Black and White*

16 February, THE WEDDING GUEST, C. & M.G., coll. only in *Turnovers I*

17 February, LETTERS OF MARQUE, NO. 16, Pioneer, *From Sea to Sea*

18 February, AT TWENTY-TWO, Week's News, *In Black and White*

18 February, THE COUNCIL OF THE GODS, Pioneer, *From Sea to Sea* (The City of Dreadful Night)

22 February, LETTERS OF MARQUE, NO. 17, Pioneer, *From Sea to Sea*

24 February, THE LITTLE HOUSE AT ARRAH, Pioneer, coll. only in suppressed *City of Dreadful Night*

25 February, LETTERS OF MARQUE, NO. 18, Pioneer, *From Sea to Sea*

25 February, MY OWN TRUE GHOST STORY, Week's News, *Phantom 'Rickshaw*

28 February, LETTERS OF MARQUE, NO. 19, Pioneer, *From Sea to Sea*

1 March, THE TRACKING OF CHUCKERBUTTI, Pioneer, coll. only in suppressed *Smith Administration*

1888 *1888*

2 March, A REAL LIVE CITY, Pioneer, *From Sea to Sea* (The City of Dreadful Night)

3 March, The Ballad of Fisher's Boarding House, Week's News, *Def. Ed.* (D.D.)

3 March, GEORGIE PORGIE, Week's News, *Life's Handicap*

5 March, THE REFLECTIONS OF A SAVAGE, Pioneer, *From Sea to Sea* (The City of Dreadful Night)

9 March, ON THE BANKS OF THE HOOGHLY, Pioneer, *From Sea to Sea* (The City of Dreadful Night)

10 March, THE EDUCATION OF OTIS YEERE (1), Week's News, *Under the Deodars*

14 March, WITH THE CALCUTTA POLICE, Pioneer, *From Sea to Sea* (The City of Dreadful Night)

14 March, BREAD UPON THE WATERS, C. & M.G., coll. only in suppressed *City of Dreadful Night* and suppressed *Smith Administration*

16 March, A FALLEN IDOL, C. & M.G., *Abaft the Funnel*

17 March, THE EDUCATION OF OTIS YEERE (2), Week's News, *Under the Deodars*

19 March, A FREE GIFT, Pioneer, uncollected

22 March, PLEADERS AND MUNSIFS, Pioneer, uncollected

22 March, THE CITY OF DREADFUL NIGHT, Pioneer, *From Sea to Sea* (The City of Dreadful Night)

24 March, THE BIG DRUNK DRAF', Week's News, *Soldiers Three*

27 March, THE MINSTREL, C. & M.G., coll. only in *Turnovers I*

30 March, A HILL HOMILY, Pioneer, uncollected

31 March, AT HOWLI THANA, Week's News, *In Black and White*

5 April, DEEPER AND DEEPER STILL, Pioneer, *From Sea to Sea* (The City of Dreadful Night)

7 April, HIS BROTHER'S KEEPER, Week's News, *Abaft the Funnel*

9 April, CONCERNING LUCIA, Pioneer, *From Sea to Sea* (The City of Dreadful Night)

10 April, THE 'KINGDOM' OF BOMBAY, Pioneer, uncollected

14 April, IN THE MATTER OF A PRIVATE, Week's News, *Soldiers Three*

16 April, BOMBAYSTES FURIOSO, Pioneer, uncollected

16 April, THE STRANGE ADVENTURES OF A HOUSE-BOAT, C. & M.G., coll. only in *Turnovers II*

17 April, The Song of the Women, Pioneer, *Def. Ed.* (D.D.)

25 April, THE REFORM CLUB, Pioneer, uncollected

28 April, DRAY WARA YOW DEE, Week's News, *In Black and White*

30 April, NEW SONGS AND OLD, Pioneer, uncollected

4 May, A DAY OFF, C. & M.G., coll. only in *Turnovers II*

5 May, HIS MAJESTY THE KING, Week's News, *Wee Willie Winkie*

10 May, A SELF-MADE MAN, C. & M.G., *From Sea to Sea* (Smith Administration)

12 May, THE KILLING OF HATIM TAI, C. & M.G., *From Sea to Sea*

12 May, 'SLEIPNER', LATE 'THURINDA', Week's News, *Abaft the Funnel*

15 May, AN UNPUNISHABLE CHERUB, C. & M.G., coll. only in *Turnovers II*

17 May, HOT WEATHER COUNSELS, C. & M.G., coll. only in *Turnovers II*

18 May, IN GILDED HALLS, C. & M.G., coll. only in *Turnovers II*

19 May, A SUPPLEMENTARY CHAPTER, Week's News, *Abaft the Funnel*

26 May, POOR DEAR MAMMA, Week's News, *Story of the Gadsbys*

? 26 May, 'IN THE DAYS OF ALEXANDER', C. & M.G., coll. only in *Turnovers II*

28 May, THROUGH THE FIRE, C. & M.G., *Life's Handicap*

31 May, HIMALAYAN COUNCILS, C. & M.G., coll. only in *Turnovers II*

1 June, THE EXPLANATION OF MIR BAKSH, C. & M.G., *From Sea to Sea* (Smith Administration)

1 June, To the Address of W. W. H., Pioneer, uncollected

4 June, THE FOUNTAIN OF HONOUR, C. & M.G., uncollected

1888 *1888*

6 June, THE BURDEN OF NINEVEH, C. & M.G., coll. only in *Turnovers II*

9 June, THE SOLID MULDOON, Week's News, *Soldiers Three*

9 June, WITH ANY AMAZEMENT, Week's News, *Story of the Gadsbys*

16 June, THE GARDEN OF EDEN, Week's News, *Story of the Gadsbys*

23 June, THE VALLEY OF THE SHADOW, Week's News, *Story of the Gadsbys*

30 June, THE SWELLING OF JORDAN, Week's News, *Story of the Gadsbys*

8 July, SPECIAL CORRESPONDENCE: SIMLA, Pioneer Mail, uncollected

10 July, THAT DISTRICT LOG BOOK, C. & M.G., coll. only in suppressed *City of Dreadful Night* and *Turnovers III*

10 July, HIS NATURAL DESTINY, Pioneer, uncollected

11 July, 'AN UNEQUAL MATCH', Pioneer, uncollected

12 July, THE TRACK OF A LIE, C. & M.G., *Ed. De Luxe*, vol. v

14 July, PRIVATE LEAROYD'S STORY, Week's News, *Soldiers Three*

15 July, SPECIAL CORRESPONDENCE: SIMLA, Pioneer Mail, uncollected

17 July, LITTLE TOBRAH, C. & M.G., *Life's Handicap*

19 July, 'O Baal, Hear Us!', Pioneer, *Early Verse*

22 July, SPECIAL CORRESPONDENCE: SIMLA, Pioneer Mail, uncollected

24 July, A HORRIBLE SCANDAL, C. & M.G., uncollected

24 July, A RAILWAY SETTLEMENT, Pioneer, *From Sea to Sea* (Among the Railway Folk)

28 July, THE JUDGMENT OF DUNGARA, Week's News, *In Black and White*

28 July, 'IN FORMA PAUPERIS', Pioneer, uncollected

29 July, SPECIAL CORRESPONDENCE: SIMLA, Pioneer Mail, uncollected

3 August, NEW BROOMS, C. & M.G., *Abaft the Funnel*

4 August, WITH THE MAIN GUARD, Week's News, *Soldiers Three*

1888 *1888*

4 August, THE SHOPS, Pioneer, *From Sea to Sea* (Among the Railway Folk)

? 6 August, HONORARY MAGISTRATES, C. & M.G., uncollected

8 August, VULCAN'S FORGE, Pioneer, *From Sea to Sea* (Among the Railway Folk)

11 August, IN FLOOD TIME, Week's News, *In Black and White*

13 August, Virginibus Puerisque, Pioneer, uncollected

14 August, AN EXERCISE IN ADMINISTRATION, C. & M.G., collected only in *Turnovers III*

18 August, THE TENTS OF KEDAR, Week's News, *Story of the Gadsbys*

24 August, ON THE SURFACE, Pioneer, *From Sea to Sea* (Giridih Coal Fields)

25 August, ONLY A SUBALTERN, Week's News, *Under the Deodars*

? 26 August, REFLECTIONS ON THE NATIONAL CONGRESS, Pioneer Mail, uncollected

1 September, The Ballad of Boh Da Thone, Week's News, *Def. Ed.* (B.-R.B.)

1 September, A Job Lot, Pioneer, uncollected

4 September, A POINTSMAN'S ERROR, C. & M.G., uncollected

6 September, IN THE DEEPS, Pioneer, *From Sea to Sea* (Giridih Coal Fields)

8 September, A SECOND-RATE WOMAN, Week's News, *Under the Deodars*

15 September, Hans Breitmann as an Administrator, Pioneer, uncollected

15 September, THE LAST OF THE STORIES, Week's News, *Abaft the Funnel*

20 September, THE PERILS OF THE PITS, Pioneer, *From Sea to Sea* (Giridih Coal Fields)

29 September, The Supplication of Kerr Cross, Missionary, Pioneer, uncollected

? 6 October, THE DIGNITY OF IT, Pioneer, uncollected

8 October, 'The Way av Ut', Pioneer, uncollected

? 18 October, 'To Save Trouble', Pioneer, uncollected

20 October, IN WONDERLAND, Pioneer, uncollected

1888 *1888*

23 October, A CAMPAIGNING PHRASE BOOK, Pioneer, uncollected

26 October, The Masque of Plenty, Pioneer, *Def. Ed.* (D.D.)

26 October, TIGLATH PILESER, C. & M.G., *Abaft the Funnel*

5 November, WHAT IT COMES TO, C. & M.G., *From Sea to Sea* (Smith Administration)

10 November, 'A FREE HAND', Pioneer, uncollected

14 November, SUSANNAH AND THE ELDER, Pioneer Mail, uncollected

21 November, The Betrothed, Pioneer, *Def. Ed.* (D.D.)

? 22 November, ADDISON AND GINWALLA, Pioneer, uncollected

December, BLACK JACK, *Soldiers Three*

December, A Dedication (To 'Soldiers Three'), *Def. Ed.*

December, THE WORLD WITHOUT, *Story of the Gadsbys*

December, FATIMA, *Story of the Gadsbys*

December, L'Envoi, *Story of the Gadsbys*

December, ON THE CITY WALL, *In Black and White*

December, AT THE PIT'S MOUTH, *Under the Deodars*

December, THE MAN WHO WOULD BE KING, *The Phantom 'Rickshaw*

December, THE DRUMS OF THE FORE AND AFT, *Wee Willie Winkie*

December, BAA BAA, BLACK SHEEP, *Wee Willie Winkie*

? 4 December, WHAT THE WORLD SAID, Pioneer, uncollected

7 December, One Viceroy Resigns, *Def. Ed.* (D.D.)

20 December, AN INTERESTING CONDITION, Pioneer, uncollected

22 December, The Law of Libel, Pioneer, uncollected

1889

? 1 January, 'THE JOKER', Pioneer, uncollected

1 January, New Lamps for Old, Pioneer, *Early Verse*

1 January, A STUDY OF THE CONGRESS, Pioneer, uncollected

? 18 January, The Question of Givens, Pioneer, uncollected

? 24 January, The Rhyme of Lord Lansdowne, Pioneer, uncollected

18 February, The Irish Conspiracy, Pioneer, uncollected

9 March, Kipling leaves India

Appendix II

THE GARRARD NOTEBOOKS

THE Berg Collection in the New York Public Library contains several items in Kipling's autograph which I shall call, for the sake of convenience, the Garrard Notebooks, though some of the items are sheets torn from notebooks rather than complete books. These Notebooks raise a number of unanswerable questions; at the same time, however, they cast a dim light on one of the most perplexing problems of Kipling's biography — his relationship with his childhood sweetheart, Florence Garrard. I have dealt at some length with SUNDRY PHANSIES, the earliest and most interesting of the Notebooks, in Chapter I, above. I shall here present their hypothetical provenance and a brief description of the Notebooks themselves, followed by my conclusions — and guesses — as to their significance.

All the Notebooks came to the Berg Collection from the library of the late Owen D. Young. Dr. John Gordan, curator of the Berg Collection, has told me that he was informed by his predecessors that Young had purchased all the Notebooks from Florence Garrard, but unfortunately there appear to be no written records of where and how Young came by the manuscripts. The only extant record concerns SUNDRY PHANSIES. It is in the form of a letter, laid into the Notebook, from the London firm of Robert Rivière & Sons to the New York bookseller Gabriel Wells. Dated 12 February 1926, the letter merely reports that Ernest W. Martindell examined the manuscript and attested its authenticity. (Martindell's supporting letter is also laid in the Notebook.) No mention is made of Miss Garrard or of the manner in which the Notebook came to the hands of Rivière. The internal evidence — the contents of SUNDRY PHANSIES — very strongly suggests that it could only have been written for Florence. Although the association of the other Notebooks with Miss Garrard is not so definitely confirmed by the evidence of their contents, it seems likely that all were prepared in order to be sent to her. The flyleaf of WORDS WISE AND OTHERWISE is inscribed as follows: 'To you my dear Boy with all good wishes for Xmas and New Year / Florence 1888.' Nearly all the poems in WORDS postdate 1888; thus, Miss Garrard would seem to have sent Kipling the blank manuscript book as a Christmas gift, knowing that he habitually used bound notebooks of this kind for his poems; Kipling then copied into the gift-book poems and prose over the course of a number of years (see the description of WORDS below).

On the other hand, there is room left for the possibility that all the Notebooks except SUNDRY PHANSIES came to Mr. Owen D. Young from someone other than Miss Garrard, someone to whom Kipling sent them after having filled them with longhand excerpts from his published verse and prose. Apart from offending a biographer's natural unwillingness to postulate unknown correspondents, this hypothesis would require us to conclude that Kipling gave or sent to a third party a gift inscribed with the name of a person who had once played an important part in his life. Kipling's natural delicacy and very strong sense of privacy would seem to make such a gesture most unlikely; it is hard to imagine his giving to anyone but Florence Garrard herself a book she had once inscribed and given to him. Thus, although the Notebooks cannot all be traced to Miss Garrard with absolute certainty, it seems reasonable to accept the view that she received the Notebooks from Kipling, kept them until about 1926, then sold them through Rivière and Wells to Mr. Owen D. Young, who added them to his great collection.

The Notebooks have not been closely examined by Kipling scholars. Professor Carrington looked into them in the course of his research, but he pointed out in a letter to the *Kipling Journal* (Number 140, page 29) that he had time to give them only superficial attention. Therefore, I have thought it worth while to provide here a brief description of the contents of the Notebooks, along with such conclusions as I have been able to draw concerning their dates.

I have used Kipling's titles, except in the case of the UNTITLED NOTEBOOK. Using the latest published item in each Notebook as a hypothetical *terminus ad quem*, I have arranged them in approximately the order in which they were presumably sent to

Florence. It may be helpful for the reader to recall that Kipling met Florence in 1880, considered himself more or less engaged to her until 1884, then met her by chance or design on his return to London, either in 1889 or 1890. What occurred between them at that time is obscure: it has been assumed that Kipling's old love revived and that Florence rejected him again; in any event, he completed *The Light That Failed* — working at terrific speed — by August 1890. In January 1892 he married Caroline Balestier.

1. SUNDRY PHANSIES. See the discussion of the poems in Chapter I, above. Some of the poems were published in *Schoolboy Lyrics* (1881), *Echoes* (1884), and *Quartette* (1885). The title-page is dated February 1882, but in certain of the later Notebooks, the date on the title-page clearly refers to the time when Kipling began to copy material into the book, rather than the date at which he completed it and sent it to Florence. He left England in October 1882: it is possible that, like some of the other Notebooks, SUNDRY PHANSIES was sent to Florence from India.

Hypothetical date: 1882–3.

2. MY OWN TRUE GHOST STORY. The one story is complete in itself, on separate pages not a full Notebook. The story first appeared on 25 February 1888, and its milieu — a dâk-bungalow — suggests that it was conceived during or shortly after Kipling's railway journeys of 1887. Like several of the items, this is decorated with grotesque drawings.

Hypothetical date: 1887–8.

3. BLACK JACK. Written on torn pages like No. 2, above. The story first appeared in *Soldiers Three* (December 1888), but the title-page has the words 'Rudyard Kipling, Lahore' worked into the design. Kipling moved from Lahore to Allahabad towards the end of 1887, so that this story may antedate its publication by several months. The manuscript may have been sent together with that of MY OWN TRUE GHOST STORY.

Hypothetical date: 1887–8.

4. ESSAYS AND STORIES. Contains 'Letters of Marque, Nos. 5–7', and four of the stories Kipling published in 1888, the latest being 'Baa Baa, Black Sheep' (December). All are illustrated with pen-and-ink sketches. The last few pages are laid in, and the final page bears the following note: 'So sorry this and

the end pages got forgotten. I send them along now — but don't bother, the whole of this, and more also, is now in the hands of the printer. You shall receive a copy neat, and complete, in due course. *PRINTED.*' This note probably refers to the four stories, all of which appeared in the Indian Railway Library series in December 1888.

Hypothetical date: Autumn 1888.

5. DEPARTMENTAL DITTIES. Contains thirty poems, seven of which were not included in *Departmental Ditties* until the fourth edition appeared in 1890. Six of the seven had appeared in Indian newspapers during 1888, too late for inclusion in the third edition (1888). Thus, it looks as though Kipling copied these poems into the Notebook about the time he was preparing the fourth edition for publication. Since that edition appeared in London as well as Calcutta (thus becoming the first English edition of *Departmental Ditties*), it seems likely that Kipling prepared the manuscript for the printers *after* his arrival in London (October 1889). This Notebook is to be associated with a presentation copy of *Departmental Ditties* (4th ed.), also in the Berg Collection, inscribed as follows: 'To Flo from Ruddy who is supposed to have written this book. May: 90.'

Hypothetical date: Winter 1889–90.

6. THE CITY OF DREADFUL NIGHT. Contains the whole series of travel sketches of Calcutta. The series ended on 9 April 1888, but a curious textual discrepancy throws the dating into a state of some uncertainty. The first few sentences of 'Deeper and Deeper Still' follow not the wording of the first authorized printing (1891) but the revised wording of the version that appeared in *From Sea to Sea* (1899). Thus, we have a rare instance of Kipling's sending a holograph manuscript to Florence of a work already in print. It is just possible that he revised the text long before the appearance of *From Sea to Sea*, but, if he made the revisions before 1891, why did he not include them in the version published in that year?

Hypothetical date: *c.* 1899?

7. UNTITLED NOTEBOOK. Contains ten poems and excerpts from poems — chiefly the latter — ranging in date of publication from 'The English Flag' (4 April 1891) to 'The Explorer'

(1903). Although 'The Explorer' did not appear until the publication of *The Five Nations* (1903), it is one of thirty-one poems that first appeared in that collection, many of which date from the Boer War period. Thus, it is likely that 'The Explorer' was written earlier than 1903. A more reliable *terminus* is provided by 'A Song of the White Men', which was written shortly after the beginning of the Boer War and first appeared in 1900. All the remaining poems were published between 1891 and 1898.

Hypothetical date: 1899–1901.

8. WORDS WISE AND OTHERWISE. The flyleaf is inscribed: 'To you my dear Boy with all good wishes for Xmas and New Year / Florence 1888.' But the Notebook contains material which appeared as late as 1903. Thirteen poems are included, several of which are reproduced from *Departmental Ditties* (various eds.) but were not among those copied into DEPARTMENTAL DITTIES. The two late poems, which supply a *terminus ad quem*, are 'The English Flag' (dated 1891 in the Notebook) and 'Rimmon' (Boer War period, *c.* 1900). The arrangement of contents suggests the method Kipling employed. A group of poems, ranging in date from 1884 to 1891 but reproduced out of chronological order, is followed by a number of blank pages. Next comes 'Rimmon', the latest of the poems, followed by a section of prose, headed as follows: 'Occasional articles written by me for the Civil and Military Gazette and the Pioneer between 1887 and 1889. The illustrations (?) did not appear.' The prose section contains only material from the first four 'Letters of Marque'. Thus, it appears that Kipling began the Notebook about 1889–90, for he included material that fills some of the gaps in DEPARTMENTAL DITTIES and ESSAYS AND STORIES. He evidently abandoned the Notebook, after having left room for a number of poems, then copied 'Rimmon' into it about 1900 and sent the whole to Florence.

Hypothetical dates: 1890; 1900.

9. WRITINGS AND SONGS. The title-page is dated 1882, but a grotesque figure is drawn pointing at the date, with the words: 'Please don't think "Writings" all date back to this.' At the bottom of the same page is written: 'But have patience, and you'll find some quite new reading. Besides this is a work of *Art*, and Art is long!' The range of dates of the forty-odd poems is

less significant than the fact that all the poems appeared in *Songs from Books* (1912): the Notebook seems to have been filled at one time, a time roughly corresponding to the period during which Kipling was preparing *Songs from Books* for the printer. Latest of the Poems are five from *Rewards and Fairies* (1910). They are scattered amongst the others, not grouped together at the end, so that Kipling evidently did not copy poems into the Notebook over a long period of time.

Hypothetical date: 1910–12.

As literary manuscripts the Garrard Notebooks have little significance: if we except SUNDRY PHANSIES, they are no more than fair copies of sketches, stories, and poems that are readily available elsewhere. I have not subjected the texts to a close scrutiny, but various random collations suggest that they contain no interesting textual variants. As biographical documents, the Notebooks may be of slightly greater value: if they were indeed sent to Miss Garrard, then we can derive from their dates and contents a few suggestions as to her role in Kipling's early life. Thus, the fact that several of the Notebooks cluster around the time of Kipling's return to London implies that he hoped to see Florence in England and sought her out after he arrived there. This runs counter to Professor Carrington's view that they met by accident (*Kipling Journal*, Number 125, page 10), but either interpretation would fit equally well with the assumption that Florence was the original of Maisie in *The Light That Failed.* One's inferences as to how Kipling felt about the encounter will depend, of course, upon the degree to which one reads *The Light* as autobiography.

At the same time, it seems quite clear from the contrast between SUNDRY PHANSIES and all the rest of the Notebooks that Florence and Kipling were never again as close to one another as they had been in their schooldays. The poems in SUNDRY PHANSIES are romantic, personal, and unpublished; everything in the later Notebooks was published by Kipling at one time or another over his own name or an acknowledged pseudonym. In short, the SUNDRY PHANSIES poems were in some sense written *for* Florence Garrard; verse and prose in the other Notebooks were not; nothing in either the content or arrangement of the books suggests that Florence had returned to the place within the charmed circle of Kipling's confidence that she had once occupied.

Of the last four Notebooks in the series, three seem to have been filled around 1899–1900, and the fourth, about ten years later. As Mrs. Bambridge has pointed out to me, it is unlikely that Kipling would have resumed communication with Miss Garrard after his marriage. If we assume, however, that the Notebooks did come to Mr. Young by way of Miss Garrard — and the inscribed book is among these four — then it can be argued that in 1899 or 1900, after his disastrous final trip to America, Josephine's death, his own narrow escape, the difficulties now experienced at Rottingdean that were to cause him to seek a new home, it can be argued that this would have been an appropriate time for Kipling to have tried to revive a friendship long dormant as a way, perhaps, of escaping from the dismal present into the mood of a happier past. We note that at this time Kipling had to return to his minor Indian writings in order to revise the texts for the 1899 edition of *From Sea to Sea*; he had never completed the Notebook called WORDS WISE AND OTHERWISE, but had stopped working on it about a decade earlier. Both circumstances — the presence of the half-finished Notebook and the return to work on the sort of material he had once sent to Florence — suggest a situation that could have led Kipling, in a mood of nostalgia, to have resumed the mechanical task of copying poems and prose into manuscript books and sending them to an old friend who had once been close to him and who, on her part, would certainly have recognized the potential monetary value of these mementoes. I have no comparable explanation for the isolated WRITINGS AND SONGS of 1910–12, but one could infer, I suppose, the return of some such impulse as motivated Kipling at the turn of the century. In any case, with WRITINGS AND SONGS, the series came to an end.

Appendix III

KIPLING'S UNCOLLECTED NEWSPAPER WRITINGS

ONE of the most serious of the difficulties that plague the student of Kipling's early career arises from the fact that his many uncollected newspaper writings have remained for the most part in the obscurity of old newspaper files. And, although files of the relevant journals have survived, they are scattered to the four winds: the Stewart Collection at Dalhousie University owns a run of the *Pioneer*; the *Week's News* may be read at Harvard's Houghton Library; the most important, the *Civil and Military Gazette*, is at the library of the Commonwealth Relations Office in London. But even if the texts were at hand, it would be far from easy to determine which of the pieces are by Kipling, for most of his contributions were published anonymously or pseudonymously; nor had he, before about 1886, developed the characteristic style that lends such distinctness to his later work. Thus, the authenticity of numerous uncollected pieces that have been attributed to Kipling remains a matter for speculation. In this appendix I shall try to indicate the present state of our information about the uncollected pieces, the reasons for further investigation, and, finally, some conclusions I have drawn as to which of them are, in fact, by Rudyard Kipling.

That the texts of Kipling's uncollected newspaper writings are available to the American scholar in any form is the result of the enthusiasm of a group of collectors and amateur bibliographers. It is not clear just what their dealings were with Kipling and with one another, but we can reconstruct a plausible sequence of events from the available facts. The story begins in 1922, when the English collector, Ernest W. Martindell, published the first attempt at a full-scale bibliography of Kipling's writings.[1] As it was based on his own holdings, which included little uncollected material, Martindell did not try to take any account of the uncollected Indian writings. Evidently the first edition brought Martindell to the attention of other Kipling specialists, for he published a 'New Edition' in 1923 which lists a large number of attributed Indian items and expresses in its preface his obligations to Mrs. Luther S. Livingston and Mr. Ellis Ames Ballard.[2] Flora V. Livingston was then at work on her own bibliography of Kipling, so that she must have been able to call Martindell's attention to gaps and errors in his work; Ballard, on the other hand, was a collector rather than a bibliographer — a wealthy Philadelphia lawyer who then had perhaps the finest Kipling library in the world — and his collaboration with Martindell took a rather different form. The two decided to undertake an unusual project: they would print, in private editions, a very few copies of all the uncollected material in the *Pioneer* and *Civil and Military* that could reasonably be ascribed to Kipling. And so, between 1923 and 1937, a total of 140 of the so-called 'Ballard–Martindell Unauthorized Printings' were brought into the world. Their sponsors' motives were not, from a collector's point of view, of the purest, as James McGregor Stewart points out.[3] But in fact, Ballard and Martindell did Kipling scholars a real service, for they unearthed hundreds of pieces that would otherwise have remained almost wholly inaccessible. Of particular value is a volume devoted to uncollected verse; in it can be found a large number of the many uncollected newspaper poems that may possibly have come from Kipling's pen. A copy of that rare volume is in the Livingston Kipling Collection at Harvard, where

---

[1] *A Bibliography of the Works of Rudyard Kipling (1881–1921)* (London, 1922).

[2] *A Bibliography of the Works of Rudyard Kipling (1881–1923)*, New Edition (London, 1923), p. vii. Martindell considered 'the most important feature' of the new edition to be 'the publication for the first time of particulars and dates of Kipling's Indian work, as I have at last been able to search the files of *The Civil and Military Gazette* (Lahore), *The Pioneer* and *The Pioneer Mail* (Allahabad)' (p. vii).

[3] *Rudyard Kipling: A Bibliographical Catalogue*, ed. A. W. Yeats (Toronto, 1959), pp. 495–6.

Flora V. Livingston continued her work on a new and definitive Kipling bibliography.

Mrs. Livingston published the first instalment of her project in 1927. She was better trained and more careful than Martindell, but her task was enormous: she had to publish a supplement to her first volume in 1938, bringing the length of the whole to more than eight hundred pages, and she continued to work at the project until her eyesight failed.[1] Fortunately, she was aided by two American Kipling enthusiasts, as well as by Martindell and Ballard — they were Mr. William M. Carpenter and Admiral Lloyd H. Chandler, whose fine collections are now in the Library of Congress. Carpenter planned to write a life of Kipling; he was especially interested in Kipling's American associations, and he had the good luck to obtain Kipling's letters to Mrs. Edmonia Hill and Dr. James Conland, Kipling's closest American friends.[2] Chandler, on the other hand, was not a wealthy man. Knowing he could never hope to rival the major Kipling collections, he undertook a curious project of his own: the assembly of a complete set of Kipling's works, a set that would include one copy of every scrap that Kipling ever wrote. This he called his 'Special Edition' of Kipling, and it is an extraordinary artifact. Whenever he could, Chandler obtained cuttings from the periodicals wherein a work first appeared; when he could not, he dismantled published volumes into their component parts; then he pasted these pages into more than two hundred loose-leaf notebooks. Furthermore, he obtained typed transcripts of the texts of hundreds of uncollected items culled from Indian newspapers, and these, too, he pasted into his 'Special Edition'. By the time he had finished, he had created a unique and valuable Kipling archive.

---

[1] *Bibliography of the Works of Rudyard Kipling* (New York, 1927); and *Supplement to Bibliography of the Works of Rudyard Kipling* (Cambridge, Mass., 1938).

[2] The letters to Mrs. Hill were returned to the Kipling family before the Carpenter Collection was opened to the public. A note in one of Mrs. Livingston's scrapbooks asserts that they were then destroyed, but she was clearly in error, for Professor Charles Carrington refers to them in his authorized biography of Kipling; see *Rudyard Kipling: His Life and Work* (London, 1955), p. 112. Many of the Conland letters remain in the Library of Congress, as well as a priceless assortment of rare books, manuscripts, and memorabilia.

Admiral Chandler had, like Mrs. Livingston, the dedication of a scholar, and the two co-operated: Mrs. Livingston assembled at Harvard a scrapbook collection of uncollected Kipling material filled with carbon copies of the transcripts Chandler had commissioned, and Chandler used Mrs. Livingston's *Bibliography* to guide him in the production of his own book, the privately printed *Summary of the Work of Rudyard Kipling*.[1] Chandler's *Summary* is a remarkable piece of amateur scholarship. Based on the scrapbooks of the Special Edition, it lists in alphabetical order every piece that Kipling may be supposed to have written, including date and place of first appearance, signature or pen name, if any, and a capsule summary of the piece itself. Moreover, Chandler maintains a high rate of accuracy, often correcting the errors of Martindell and Mrs. Livingston. And, unlike nearly every other scholar and collector who has worked in this area, he managed not to antagonize Rudyard Kipling. One of the rewards of delving into the Special Edition is the discovery of the correspondence of these two elderly men, who came to salute one another as 'Kipling Sahib' and 'Admiral-san' as they traded stories of their experiences in remote parts of the globe.

It is noteworthy that none of these Kipling enthusiasts — Martindell, Ballard, Livingston, Carpenter, and Chandler — made any serious effort to separate the false Kipling attributions from the true. Mrs. Livingston was the most cautious; Ballard and Martindell tended to accept everything as genuine unless it was proved otherwise; and Admiral Chandler refused to make any judgments at all, merely presenting the evidence as it stood. The first steps towards establishing a reliable canon were taken by James McGregor Stewart and his editor, Professor A. W. Yeats. Unlike Ballard, Martindell, and Carpenter, Stewart was reserved, even secretive, about his Kipling collection: it came as a surprise to Kipling enthusiasts to discover that the greatest collection in the

[1] *A Summary of the Work of Rudyard Kipling, Including Items Ascribed to Him* (New York, 1930). Ballard opened his collection to Chandler and contributed an introduction to the *Summary* (pp. xi–xx, xxii). Mrs. Livingston, Martindell, and Carpenter are thanked in the preface, as well as Dr. A. S. W. Rosenbach, the famous dealer in rare books, who gave Chandler access to the file of the *Pioneer* that he had purchased from the London office of that newspaper (pp. xxii–xxiii).

Western Hemisphere had been bequeathed to Dalhousie University. But Stewart and Yeats, who undertook what is substantially a new bibliography of Kipling's writings, were determined not to fall into the error of Ballard and Martindell. Instead, they assumed that it was more to Kipling's credit that doubtful pieces should be excluded than that the work of inferior writers should be ascribed to him, and so they set up quite rigid criteria for the inclusion of unsigned, uncollected material in their Kipling canon.[1]

Thus, the problem that now confronts the Kipling scholar is to find a mean between two extremes. On the one hand, Ballard, Martindell, and Chandler discovered and put forward an excessive number of supposed Kipling items: they have provided no more than the raw material for a canon. Stewart and Yeats, on the other hand, have depended upon too rigid a set of criteria for separating wheat from chaff. The reader who compares their list of authentic items with the texts of the items themselves comes away with the sense that much remains to be done. Certain well-substantiated pieces are missing from the *Catalogue*; others are included for reasons that will not stand up under analysis; a third group, attributable to Kipling only on the basis of style and subject matter, must be recognized as having claims to authenticity and ought not to be excluded from the area of debate. In order to further that debate, I have assembled the list of early Kipling items that follows.

As might be expected, the list grew directly out of my study of Kipling's growth and development. At an early stage in my research, two facts became clear. First, I found that I could make no progress whatever without establishing a chronological list of works, works of whose authenticity I at least could be satisfied. Second, I was soon forced to realize that the wide scattering of the relevant newspaper files would make it impossible for me to complete the project in a reasonable time unless I could rely where necessary on the typed transcripts commissioned by Admiral Chandler. Accordingly, I can claim to have read and studied every one of the pieces discussed below; but I cannot in every case vouch for the absolute accuracy of the texts. It is my opinion that for my purposes the texts in question are sufficiently close to what appeared in the Indian newspapers: only the grossest of

[1] The criteria are set forth in the *Bibliographical Catalogue*, pp. 534–7.

clerical errors would affect my arguments as to authenticity. But I hope that, as Kipling studies develop beyond their present state, we shall be given sound and reliable texts of his less accessible writings. In any event, each of the items here discussed has been the subject of separate and careful consideration: in some cases, I have been able to satisfy myself that an item is or is not authentic; in many others, I have only been able to raise a question.

As there is no altogether satisfactory way to present the material that follows, I have made several arbitrary compromises. That the list takes the form of a series of disputes with the Stewart–Yeats *Catalogue*, necessarily results from the fact that they are the only bibliographers who have committed themselves to a canon; it can be assumed that items not mentioned here are adequately dealt with in their work. Since items tend to fall into groups, I have rejected a piece-by-piece listing as being intolerably repetitive. I have identified the items by title and date only, following the procedure I employ elsewhere in this study. The grouping I have chosen makes strict chronological or alphabetical listing impossible; the items occur in rough chronological order. Finally, I must echo the wise words of Stewart and Yeats: 'It will never be possible to make the list both complete and accurate.'[1]

1. *The Pseudonym 'Nick'*: Three prose articles signed 'Nick' appeared in the *Pioneer*: 'Jottings from Jeypore' (8 February 1883), 'Jack Sprat' (27 February 1883), and 'On Certain Uncut Pages' (23 August 1884). The pseudonym has been widely accepted as Kipling's on the basis of some very early pieces he wrote over the signature 'Nickson'; but there are good reasons for rejecting the three 'Nick' articles. In the first place, Kipling did not send copies of them to Mr. Crofts at the United Services College; in so far as Crofts did receive copies of some very much shorter newspaper pieces from his former pupil, it seems most unlikely that Kipling would not have sent him these three substantial articles. In the second place, Kipling wrote in a letter of 1885 to the effect that the *Pioneer* was only then beginning to accept material from him.[2] Finally, neither the matter nor the style accords with other pieces we can identify as being by Kipling and of that time. It is possible that the three articles were written

[1] Ibid., p. 534.

[2] Quoted in Carrington, *Rudyard Kipling*, p. 66.

by Lockwood Kipling, who contributed irregularly to the *Pioneer*. The first displays a thorough knowledge of Indian architecture, which would be in keeping with Lockwood's profession; and if Lockwood were 'Nick', then it would be natural for Rudyard to sign himself 'Nickson'.

2. *Journalistic Scraps from 1883:* The *Catalogue* fails to list 'Lord Truro and Indian Crime' (9 August), 'The Dasera Festival' (2 October), 'The Volcanic Explosion in Java' (2 October), and 'William Morris's Poem "The Day Is Coming"' (7 November) as uncollected pieces. All four items are attested by the Crofts Collection, and none has been collected.

3. *'Twenty Years After' (9 January 1885) and 'What Came of It' (17 September 1886):* Attribution of these two pieces depends on a combination of internal evidence with the testimony of the *Kipling Birthday Book.*[1] The latter is a compilation of lines and phrases from Kipling's writings, including several uncollected pieces. As Kipling authorized its publication, the inclusion of any uncollected material in the *Birthday Book* is strong evidence for Kipling's authorship. The narrator of one piece so included, a poem called 'Exchange' (18 December 1885), is named Orion Golightly, as is the speaker of the poem 'From the Hills' in *Quartette* (Christmas, 1885). Both 'Twenty Years After' and 'What Came of It' involve Orion Golightly, are in a style like Kipling's, and treat the same subject as does 'Exchange' — that is, the effects to be expected from the decline in the exchange value of the rupee. The evidence for their authenticity appears conclusive.

4. *The Pseudonym 'Humphrey Clinker':* Several bibliographers have attributed pieces entitled 'Self-Sacrifice', 'A Moral Duty', and 'Exchange Quotations' to Kipling. The ascription has been based on the *Birthday Book*, as the result of a confusion of 'Exchange Quotations' with 'Exchange' (see §3 above). In fact, 'Exchange Quotations' does not appear in the *Birthday Book*, and 'Humphrey Clinker's' style is nothing like Kipling's. The pieces can be rejected with confidence.

---

[1] Joseph Finn, comp., *The Kipling Birthday Book* (London, 1896).

5. *'A Lost Leader' (31 August 1885):* Attested by the *Birthday Book.*

6. *'Trial by Judge' (16 September 1885):* This item is attested by Kipling's manuscript diary for 1885, now in the Houghton Library. 'Trial' is the first of several poems, both signed and unsigned, written in a style that parodies the libretti of the Savoy Operas. Its authenticity strongly supports the claims of two other unsigned, uncollected poems written in this libretto style: 'The Indian Delegates' (21 November 1885) and 'Parturiunt Montes' (26 April 1886).

7. *'The Installation at Jummu' (13 and 14 May 1886):* Attested by the Crofts Collection.

8. *The Pseudonym 'K.':* One poem and nine prose sketches appear over this pseudonym between 3 June 1886 and 9 October 1890. Only one of the ten, in my opinion, is unquestionably by Kipling: the poem 'At the Bar' (9 October 1886).[1] Of the nine prose pieces, one can only say that Kipling may possibly have written some of them, but that others are certainly not from his pen. As we need only undermine the authenticity of one in order to call the others in doubt, I should single out 'Transport Shortcomings' (2 March 1887). This is a verbose and highly technical critique of the conduct of a minor military campaign that occurred in 1885; a glance at its characteristic style should dispel any doubt as to its spuriousness.[2] Three pieces published after Kipling's departure from India show no affinity to his style and subject matter and were almost certainly written by a different 'K.',

---

[1] Kipling transferred the first stanza of 'At the Bar' to the poem '"Cleared"', leaving it virtually unchanged. The first line of 'At the Bar' runs: 'Help for a Councillor distressed — a spotless spirit hurt!' And '"Cleared"' begins: 'Help for a patriot distressed, a spotless spirit hurt.' The parallel continues through the next five lines of both poems.

[2] I reproduce a typical sentence: 'And though we may temper the severity of his criticisms with the reflection that every zealous officer has a high standard for measuring the efficiency of his own branch, and that it is impossible in the stress of sudden preparation for a great campaign that everything can come up to the required ideal: yet the shortcomings of the past are the lessons for the future, and in this light there is much to be learnt from this interesting report.'

perhaps an imitator trying to capitalize on Kipling's growing reputation: 'Tripati' (24 August 1889), 'The Two Cousins (Tales from East Bengal No. 1)' (29 December 1889), and 'The Pitch We Come To' (9 October 1889). The other five are more doubtful, but in none of them does the style or subject matter point unequivocally to Kipling; in my opinion, he did not write any of them. It is more plausible to assume that the pseudonym 'K.' was either in the public domain, so to speak, or the property of someone else; and that Kipling did not discover this fact until after he had signed 'At the Bar'. For the record, the five doubtful items are: 'The Burns Manuscripts' (3 June 1886), 'Honorary Magistrates (Sketches by Native Writers No. 1)' (6 August 1888), '"In the Days of Alexander"' (26 May 1888), 'Reflections on the National Congress' (26 August 1888), and '"The Joker"' (1 January 1889).

9. *'King Solomon's Horses' (July 1886):* This uncollected poem does not appear in Stewart's list of uncollected pieces, but is ascribed to Kipling elsewhere in the *Catalogue*; I mention it only to correct the oversight.

10. *'"From Olympus to Hades"' (12 August 1886):* Closely resembles Kipling's style and subject matter; no other evidence.

11. *'"Les Misérables"' (28 August 1886) and 'Le Roi en Exil' (15 November 1886):* Recalling his years as a journalist, Kipling later wrote: 'At that time . . . the French Press was not nationally enamoured of England. I answered some of their criticisms by what I then conceived to be parodies of Victor Hugo's more extravagant prose.'[1] The earliest of these parodies to have been identified is 'The History of a Crime' (5 February 1886), which is attested by the Crofts Collection. Other pieces in the same style are '"Les Misérables"' (Crofts Collection), 'Le Roi en Exil', and 'An Interesting Condition' (20 December 1888). All four are certainly by Kipling.

12. *Uncollected 'Plain Tales':* The problem of ascription is made complicated by the fact that we know Trix Kipling contributed some pieces to the 'Plain Tales' series: one of them, 'A

[1] *Souvenirs of France* (London, 1933), p. 11. See also Chapter IV, above.

Pinchbeck Goddess' (10 December 1886), she later expanded into a full-length novel with the same title (New York, 1897). As the members of the Kipling family often collaborated, stylistic evidence is very uncertain. The story 'Love: A "Miss"' (26 November 1886), however, refers to Lahore as 'Maidanpore'; this euphemism appears in another of Alice's novels, *The Heart of a Maid* (New York, 1891), but nowhere in Rudyard Kipling's known work. As for Rudyard's contributions, I think that 'How It Happened' (11 November 1886) is in Kipling's characteristic style, though there is no firm way to prove its authenticity; perhaps Alice shared its authorship with her brother. Finally, the first of the 'Plain Tales', 'Love-in-a-Mist' (2 November 1886), is, I think, by Kipling himself. The style resembles his; and, more important, the story describes a newly married couple on a honeymoon trip, in the pouring rain, to the Himalayas behind Simla. We know from Kipling's manuscript diary of 1885 that he accompanied such a couple on such a trip at the end of the summer of 1885. In view of Kipling's habit of using his friend's experiences in his fiction, it seems likely that he himself initiated the series that has since become so famous.

13. '*New Year Resolutions*' (*1 January 1887*): Attested by the *Birthday Book*.

14. '*An Excellent Reason*' (*23 May 1887*): This is a dubious item, though the *Catalogue* accepts it. The ascription is based wholly on stylistic evidence, but the style of this poem — a parody of Chaucerian English — is not especially characteristic of Kipling at this time.

15. '*In Gilded Halls*' (*18 May 1888*): This piece has been wrongly identified with 'The World Without', an episode in *The Story of the Gadsbys*. Both are set in a men's club and are in dialogue form, but that is the only connection between them.

16. '*To the Address of W.W.H.*' (*1 June 1888*): Attested by the *Birthday Book*.

17. '*The Fountain of Honour*' (*4 June 1888*): Closely resembles Kipling's style and attitudes; no other evidence.

18. '*Special Correspondence: Simla*' (*July 1888*): These Simla letters appeared in the *Pioneer Mail* from 9 May to 10

October 1888. Not all of them are by Rudyard Kipling; miscellaneous bits of evidence suggest their true authorship. In the first place, Kipling could not have spent the entire hot season away from his increasingly important editorial responsibilities in Allahabad. In the second place, there is a marked change in the style of the letters, beginning and ending in July. Finally, Mrs. Livingston asserts in a manuscript note that all the letters were written by Mrs. Kipling.[1] What evidently happened is that Mrs. Kipling, who would have gone up early to the Hills, wrote the first few letters — accounts of parties and theatricals; Rudyard came up in July and wrote the letters for that month, using them as a sounding-board for his own opinions and not troubling to disguise his characteristic prose style; when he went down again to Allahabad at the end of his month's leave, his mother resumed the series.

19. '*His Natural Destiny*' (*10 July 1888*)*:* The style and the criticism of W. W. Hunter, whom Kipling chided constantly at this time, mark this piece as unquestionably by Kipling.

20. '*A Horrible Scandal*' (*24 June 1888*)*:* The style is Kipling's; and the subject, the pretentiousness of Bombay, is one of his favourites at this time.

21. '*A Job Lot*' (*1 September 1888*)*:* Admitted by Kipling in *Something of Myself*.

22. '*Hans Breitmann as an Administrator*' (*15 September 1888*)*:* Although Kipling often borrowed C. G. Leland's German-American character Hans Breitmann, this piece is not necessarily authentic: one parody of Leland would sound much like another. Attribution remains highly probable but not certain.

23. '*The Supplication of Kerr Cross, Missionary*' (*29 September 1888*)*:* Signed 'R. K.'

24. '"*A Free Hand*"' (*10 November 1888*)*:* Closely resembles Kipling's style; no other evidence.

---

[1] This statement appears without further comment in 'Scrapbook No. VII' of the Kipling Collection in the Houghton Library. This is one of several large scrapbooks assembled by Mrs. Livingston in the course of preparing her bibliography.

25. *The Garth Album or Scrapbook:* This collection of clippings, made by one of Kipling's Anglo-Indian contemporaries, has long been considered definite evidence for Kipling's authorship of certain unsigned items. Recently Mr. R. E. Harbord of the Kipling Society has questioned the wisdom of accepting Garth's opinions as *prima facie* evidence, and I find myself in complete agreement with him.[1] Towards the end of 1888, in particular, Garth clipped a number of pieces that are not at all in Kipling's usual style. As there is no evidence to support Garth's opinion, I see no reason to accept as authentic 'The Dignity of It' (6 October 1888), 'To Save Trouble' (18 October), 'Addison and Ginwalla' (22 November), 'The Question of Givens' (18 January 1889), and 'The Rhyme of Lord Lansdowne' (24 January 1889).

[1] R. E. H[arbord], 'Two Queries', *Kipling Journal*, xxix (1962), no. 143, p. 30.

List of Works Consulted

THIS list includes all works cited in the notes and some others that I found helpful but had no opportunity to cite directly. It is in no sense intended as an exhaustive bibliography of the subject. A number of interesting critical treatments of Kipling do not appear — for example, important studies by Professor Dobrée and Mr. Stewart, and Mr. Frank O'Connor's fascinating rejection of Kipling as a story-writer. But due consideration of the nimbus of critical opinion that surrounds Kipling's reputation would be a formidable task: I can make no apology for having evaded so heavy a responsibility in this sketch of the writer's early years.

UNPUBLISHED MATERIAL

Kipling letters and manuscripts in the Henry W. and Albert A. Berg Collection, New York Public Library.

Kipling letters and manuscripts in the Pierpont Morgan Library.

Kipling's holograph diary and Mrs. Flora V. Livingston's working scrapbooks in the Houghton Library, Harvard University.

Kipling letters and Admiral Lloyd H. Chandler's 'Special Edition' of Kipling's works in the Rare Book Department, Library of Congress.

PUBLISHED MATERIAL

Aberigh-Mackay, George. *Twenty-One Days in India: Being the Tour of Sir Ali Baba, K.C.B.* 2nd ed. London: W. H. Allen, 1880.

'A'iph Cheem' [pseud. of Walter Yeldham]. *Lays of Ind.* 6th ed. Calcutta: Thacker, Spink, 1879.

Ames, Charles L. 'Lalun, the Baragun', *Kipling Journal*, xxii, no. 114 (July 1955), 6–8.

Annan, Noel. 'Kipling's Place in the History of Ideas', *Victorian Studies*, iii (1960), 323–48.

Anon. *Catalogue of Nineteenth-Century and Modern First Editions, Presentation Copies, Autograph Letters and Literary Manuscripts* (30 November, 1 December 1964). London: Sotheby & Co., 1964.

— *Catalogue of the Works of Rudyard Kipling Exhibited at the Grolier Club from February 21 to March 30, 1929.* New York: Grolier Club, 1930.

— 'Child-Life by the Ganges', *Atlantic Monthly*, I (1857–8), 625–33.

— Review of *Echoes*, *Calcutta Review*, lxxx (Jan. 1885), iv–vii.

— *Sale Catalogue of the G. M. Williamson Collection.* New York: Anderson Auction Company, 1915.

— 'Some Anglo-Indian Poets', *The University Magazine* (Dublin), v (May 1880), 513–24.

Arnold, William Delafield. *Oakfield: or, Fellowship in the East.* Boston: Ticknor & Fields, 1855.

Auden, Wystan Hugh. 'The Poet of the Encirclement', *New Republic*, cix (1943), 579–81.

Baker, Ernest A. *The History of the English Novel.* 10 vols. London: Witherby, 1924–39.

Baldwin, Arthur Windham. *The Macdonald Sisters.* London: Davies, 1960.

Ballard, Ellis Ames. *Catalogue Intimate and Descriptive of My Kipling Collection.* Philadelphia: Privately printed, 1935.

Bamford, Alfred J. *Turbans and Tails: Or, Sketches in the Unromantic East.* London: Sampson, Low, 1888.

Barns, Margarita. *The Indian Press: A History of the Growth of Public Opinion in India.* London: Allen & Unwin, 1940.

Beresford, George C. *Schooldays with Kipling.* London: Gollancz, 1936.

Birkenhead, [Frederick] Earl of. 'The Young Rudyard Kipling', *Essays by Diverse Hands*, N.S., xxvii. London: Oxford University Press, 1955.

Blunt, Wilfrid Scawen. *Ideas about India.* London: Kegan Paul, 1885.

Bodelsen, C. A. *Aspects of Kipling's Art.* Manchester: Manchester University Press, 1964.

Booth, Wayne C. *The Rhetoric of Fiction.* Chicago: University of Chicago Press, 1961.

Brown, Hilton. *Rudyard Kipling.* New York: Harper, 1945.

Brown, Hilton (ed.). *The Sahibs: The Life and Ways of the British in India as Recorded by Themselves.* London: Hodge, 1948.

Browning, Robert. *The Poetical Works of Robert Browning.* Ed. Augustine Birrell. 2 vols. New York: Macmillan, 1900.

Buck, Edward John. *Simla, Past and Present.* 2nd ed. Bombay: The Times Press, 1925.

Buckland, C. E. *Dictionary of Indian Biography.* London: Swan Sonnenschein, 1906.

Buckland, C. T. *Sketches of Social Life in India.* London: W. H. Allen, 1884.

Burke, Kenneth. *Counter-Statement.* 2nd ed. Chicago: University of Chicago, Phoenix, 1957.

Bushnell, Nelson S. 'Kipling's Ken of India', *University of Toronto Quarterly*, xxvii (1957), 62–78.

Canby, Henry Seidel. *The Short Story in English.* New York: Holt, 1909.

Carnac, John Harry Rivett. *Many Memories of Life in India, at Home and Abroad.* Edinburgh: Blackwood, 1910.

Carpenter, William M. '"Kipling about" in London for a Week: By a Hustling American', *Kipling Journal*, no. 7 (Oct. 1928), 9–16.

— *Kipling's College.* Evanston: Privately printed, 1929.

Carrington, Charles. *Rudyard Kipling: His Life and Work.* London: Macmillan, 1955.

Cazamian, Madeleine L. *Le Roman et les idées en Angleterre: 1860–1914.* Publications de la Faculté des Lettres de l'Université de Strasbourg. 4 vols. Paris [various imprints], 1923–[ ].

Chandler, Lloyd Horwitz. *A Summary of the Work of Rudyard Kipling, Including Items Ascribed to Him.* New York: Grolier Club, 1930.

Chatterjee, Sir Atul Chandra. *British Contributions to Indian Studies.* London: Longmans, 1943.

Chevalley, Abel. *Le Roman anglais de notre temps.* London: Milford, 1921.

Chirol, Sir Valentine. *India.* London: Benn, 1926.

— *India Old and New.* London: Macmillan, 1921.

— *Indian Unrest.* London: Macmillan, 1910.

Collins, J. P. 'Rudyard Kipling at Lahore', *The Nineteenth Century and After*, cxxi (1937), 80–90.

Colvin, Ian. 'The Old Shekarry', *National Review*, cx (1938), 362–5.

— 'This Bore Fruit Afterwards: Kipling's Childhood Reading', *National Review*, cx (1938), 215–21.

Cunningham, Henry Stewart. *Chronicles of Dustypore: A Tale of Modern Anglo-Indian Society*. New ed. London: Smith, Elder, 1877.

— *The Cœruleans: A Vacation Idyll.* 2 vols. London: Macmillan, 1887.

Dunlap, Joseph R. 'Beetle's Browning', *Kipling Journal*, no. 120 (Dec. 1956), 7–8; no. 121 (Apr. 1957), 7–8.

Dunsterville, Lionel C. *Stalky's Reminiscences*. London: Cape, 1928.

Durand, Sir Mortimer. *Life of the Right Hon. Sir Alfred Comyn Lyall*. Edinburgh: Blackwood, 1913.

'Eha' [pseud. of Edward Hamilton Aitken]. *Behind the Bungalow*. 2nd ed. Calcutta: Thacker, Spink, 1889.

Eliot, Thomas Stearns (ed.). *A Choice of Kipling's Verse*. London: Faber & Faber, 1941.

Ferguson, J. De Lancey. 'The Education of Rudyard Kipling', *Education*, xlv (Nov. 1924), 171–82.

— 'The Pen Took Charge', *New Colophon*, i (Oct. 1948), 335–48.

— 'Rudyard Kipling's Revisions of His Published Work', *JEGP*, xxii (Jan. 1923), 114–24.

Fleming, Alice Macdonald [Kipling]. 'More Childhood Memories of Rudyard Kipling', *Chambers's Journal*, 8th ser., viii (July 1939), 506–11.

— 'My Brother, Rudyard Kipling', *Kipling Journal*, no. 84 (Dec. 1947), 3–5; no. 85 (Apr. 1948), 7–8.

— *A Pinchbeck Goddess*. New York: D. Appleton, 1897.

— 'Some Childhood Memories of Rudyard Kipling', *Chambers's Journal*, 8th ser., viii (Mar. 1939), 168–73.

— 'Some Reminiscences of My Brother', *Kipling Journal*, no. 44 (Dec. 1937), 116–21.

Ford, Boris. 'A Case for Kipling?', *Scrutiny*, xi (1942–3), 23–33.

'Four Anglo-Indian Writers' [pseud. of J. L. Kipling family]. *Quartette: The Christmas Annual of the Civil and Military Gazette*. Lahore: The Civil and Military Gazette Press, 1885.

Frierson, William Coleman. *The English Novel in Transition: 1885–1940*. Norman: University of Oklahoma Press, 1942.

Frierson, William Coleman. *L'Influence du naturalisme français sur les romanciers anglais de 1885 à 1900.* Paris: Giard, 1925.

Fussell, Paul, Jr. 'Irony, Freemasonry, and Humane Ethics in Kipling's "The Man Who Would Be King"', *ELH*, xxv (1958), 216–33.

'G. B.-J.' [Georgiana Burne-Jones]. *Memorials of Edward Burne-Jones.* 2 vols. New York: Macmillan, 1904.

Gerber, Helmut E., and Edward Lauterbach (eds.). 'Rudyard Kipling: An Annotated Bibliography of Writings about Him', *English Fiction in Transition*, iii (1960), nos. 3–5.

Gohdes, Clarence. *American Literature in Nineteenth-Century England.* New York: Columbia University Press, 1944.

Gopal, Sarvepalli. *The Viceroyalty of Lord Ripon, 1880–1884.* London: Oxford University Press, 1953.

Hart, Walter Morris. *Kipling the Story-Writer.* Berkeley: University of California Press, 1918.

Harte, Bret. 'Stories Three: By R–dy–d K–pl–g.' In *Condensed Novels: Second Series.* Boston: Houghton Mifflin, 1902.

Hill, Edmonia. 'The Young Kipling: Personal Recollections', *Atlantic Monthly*, clvii (1936), 406–15.

Hopkins, R. Thurston. *Rudyard Kipling: The Story of a Genius.* London: Palmer, 1930.

Hough, Graham. *The Last Romantics.* London: Duckworth, 1947.

Howe [Nobbe], Susanne. *Novels of Empire.* New York: Columbia University Press, 1949.

Hunter, Sir William Wilson. *England's Work in India.* London: Smith, Elder, 1881.

Jarrell, Randall (ed.). *In the Vernacular: The English in India: Short Stories by Rudyard Kipling.* New York: Doubleday Anchor, 1963.

Kincaid, Dennis. *British Social Life in India, 1608–1937.* London: Routledge, 1939.

[Kipling, Alice M., and Alice M. Fleming.] *Hand in Hand: Verses by a Mother and Daughter.* London: Elkin Mathews, 1902.

'Kipling, Beatrice' [pseud. of Alice M. Fleming]. *The Heart of a Maid.* New York: J. W. Lovell, 1891.

Kipling Birthday Book. Compiled by Joseph Finn. London: Macmillan, 1896.

Kipling, John Lockwood. *Beast and Man in India.* London: Macmillan, 1891.

Kipling Journal. 1927–62.

Kipling, Rudyard. *Abaft the Funnel.* Authorized edition. New York: Doubleday, 1909.

— *The City of Dreadful Night and Other Places.* London: Sampson Low [1891].

— *Departmental Ditties and Other Verses.* Lahore: The Civil and Military Gazette Press [1886].

— 'Departmental Ditties.' In *My First Book*, ed. Jerome K. Jerome. London: Chatto & Windus, 1894.

— *The Phantom 'Rickshaw and Other Tales.* Allahabad: A. H. Wheeler [1888].

— *Schoolboy Lyrics.* Lahore: The Civil and Military Gazette Press, 1881.

— *Souvenirs of France.* London: Macmillan, 1933.

— *Verse.* 'Definitive Edition.' London: Hodder & Stoughton, 1940.

— *Works.* 'Library Edition.' London: Macmillan, 1949–59.

— *The Writings in Prose and Verse of Rudyard Kipling.* 'Outward Bound Edition.' 36 vols. New York: Scribner's, 1897–1937.

Léaud, Francis. *La Poétique de Rudyard Kipling: essai d'interprétation générale de son œuvre.* Paris: Didier, 1958.

Lewis, Clive Staples. *They Asked for a Paper.* London: Bles, 1962.

Leyden, John. *The Poetical Works of John Leyden.* Edinburgh: Nimmo, 1875.

Livingston, Flora V. *Bibliography of the Works of Rudyard Kipling.* New York: Edgar H. Wells, 1927.

— *Supplement to Bibliography of the Works of Rudyard Kipling.* Cambridge: Harvard University Press, 1938.

'Loti, Pierre' [pseud. of Julien Viaud]. *India.* Trans. George A. F. Inman; ed. Robert H. Sherard. New York: Stokes, n.d.

Lyall, Sir Alfred Comyn. *The Rise and Expansion of the British Dominion in India.* 5th ed. London: Murray, 1910.

— *Studies in Literature and History.* London: Murray, 1915.

— *Verses Written in India.* London: Kegan Paul, 1889.

Macdonald, Florence. 'The Father and Mother of Rudyard Kipling', *Kipling Journal*, no. 39 (Sept. 1936), 99–101.

Macdonald, Florence. 'In Memoriam: Mrs. Alice Macdonald Fleming', *Kipling Journal*, no. 89 (Apr. 1949), 7–8.

— 'Some Memories of My Cousin', *Kipling Journal*, no. 46 (July 1938), 45–50.

Macdonald, Frederic William. *As a Tale That Is Told*. London: Cassell, 1919.

Mack, Edward C. *Public Schools and British Opinion since 1860*. New York: Columbia University Press, 1941.

MacMunn, Sir George. 'Kipling and Alfred Lyall', *Kipling Journal*, no. 65 (Apr. 1943), 4–6.

— 'The Rough Ashlar: Some Kipling Affinities', *Kipling Journal*, no. 61 (Apr. 1942), 5–6.

— *Rudyard Kipling: Craftsman*. Revised ed. London: Hale, 1938.

Martindell, Ernest W. *A Bibliography of the Works of Rudyard Kipling (1881–1921)*. London: The Bookman's Journal, 1922.

— *A Bibliography of the Works of Rudyard Kipling (1881–1923)*. New ed. London: John Lane, 1923.

Maugham, W. Somerset (ed.). *Maugham's Choice of Kipling's Best*. Garden City: Doubleday, 1953.

Moreland, William H., and Atul Chandra Chatterjee. *A Short History of India*. London: Longmans, 1936.

Oaten, Edward Farley. 'Anglo-Indian Literature.' In *Cambridge History of English Literature*, xiv. 366–79.

— *A Sketch of Anglo-Indian Literature*. London: Kegan Paul, 1908.

O'Faolain, Sean. *The Short Story*. New York: Devin-Adair, 1951.

'An Old Punjaubee' [pseud. of H. W. H. Coxe]. *The Punjaub and North-West Frontier of India*. London: Kegan Paul, 1878.

Oman, John Campbell. *Indian Life: Religious and Social*. Philadelphia: Gebbie, 1889.

Pain, Barry. *The Short Story*. New York: George H. Doran, n.d.

Pearson, R. *Eastern Interlude: A Social History of the European Community in Calcutta*. Calcutta: Thacker, Spink, 1954.

Penzoldt, Peter. *The Supernatural in Fiction*. London: Nevill, 1952.

'R. E. H.' [R. E. Harbord]. 'Two Queries', *Kipling Journal*, xxix (1962), no. 143, 30.

Rimington, J. C. 'Westward Ho Reminiscences', *Kipling Journal*, no. 59 (Oct. 1941), 11–13.

Robinson, Edward Kay. 'Kipling in India: Reminiscences by the Editor of the Newspaper on Which Kipling Served at Lahore', *McClure's Magazine*, vii (1896), 99–109.

— 'Rudyard Kipling as Journalist', *Literature* (London), iv (18 March 1899), 284–6.

Rutherford, Andrew, ed. *Kipling's Mind and Art*. London: Oliver & Boyd, 1964.

'Sencourt, Robert' [pseud. of Robert E. G. George]. *India in English Literature*. London: Simpkin, Marshall, 1925.

Shanks, Edward. *Rudyard Kipling: A Study in Literature and Political Ideas*. London: Macmillan, 1940.

Singh, Bhupal. *A Survey of Anglo-Indian Fiction*. London: Oxford University Press, 1934.

Skrine, Francis Henry. *Life of Sir William Wilson Hunter*. London: Longmans, 1901.

Spear, T. G. Percival. *India: A Modern History*. Ann Arbor: University of Michigan Press, 1961.

— *The Nabobs: A Study of the Social Life of the English in Eighteenth Century India*. London: Oxford University Press, 1932.

Stevenson, Lionel. *The English Novel: A Panorama*. Boston: Houghton Mifflin, 1960.

Stewart, James McGregor. *Rudyard Kipling: A Bibliographical Catalogue*. Ed. A. W. Yeats. Halifax: Dalhousie University Press, 1959.

Temple, Sir Richard. *India in 1880*. 3rd ed. London: John Murray, 1881.

Thirkell, Angela. *Three Houses*. London: Oxford University Press, 1931.

Thornton, Archibald P. *The Imperial Idea and Its Enemies: A Study in British Power*. London: Macmillan, 1959.

Tompkins, Joyce M. S. *The Art of Rudyard Kipling*. London: Methuen, 1959.

Trevelyan, George Otto. *The Competition Wallah*. London: Macmillan, 1864.

Trilling, Lionel. *The Liberal Imagination*. Garden City: Doubleday Anchor, 1957.

— 'Mr. Eliot's Kipling', *Nation*, clvii (1943), 436–42.

'Two Writers' [pseud. of Rudyard and Alice Kipling]. *Echoes.* Lahore: The Civil and Military Gazette Press [1884].

Vogüé, Eugène Marie Melchior, Vicomte de. *Pages d'histoire.* Paris: Colin, 1902.

Week's News (Allahabad). 1888–91.

Weygandt, Ann M. *Kipling's Reading and Its Influence on His Poetry.* Philadelphia: University of Pennsylvania Press, 1939.

Wheeler, Stephen. 'Home-Rule for India', *Macmillan's Magazine*, lix (1888–9), 291–6.

Wilkins, W. J. *Daily Life and Work in India.* London: Unwin, 1887.

Wilson, Edmund. *The Wound and the Bow.* Boston: Houghton Mifflin, 1941.

Wolf, Lucien. *Life of the First Marquess of Ripon.* 2 vols. London: Murray, 1921.

Wolfe, Humbert. *Dialogues and Monologues.* New York: Knopf, 1929.

Woodruff, Philip. *The Men Who Ruled India.* 2 vols. London: Jonathan Cape, 1953.

Worth, George J. 'The English "Maupassant" School of the 1890's: Some Reservations', *MLN*, lxxii (1957), 337–40.

Wright, Arnold. *Baboo English as 'Tis Writ: Being Curiosities of Indian Journalism.* London: Unwin, 1891.

General Index

Index of Kipling's Characters and Works

SOMETHING OF MYSELF *is not indexed, on account of frequency of citation. Title entries which refer to pages 169–84 list occurrences of titles in Appendix I: 'A Chronological List of Kipling's Writings from October 1882 to March 1889'.*

PRINTED BY R. & R. CLARK, LTD., EDINBURGH